Religion in America

ADVISORY EDITOR

Edwin S. Gaustad

SERMONS

SEVEN SERMONS

A DISCOURSE, CONCERNING THE UNLIMITED SUBMISSION
AND NON-RESISTANCE TO THE HIGHER POWERS

THE SNARE BROKEN

Jonathan Mayhew

Library
Southwestern State College
Weatherford, Oklahoma

ARNO PRESS & THE NEW YORK TIMES
New York 1969

Reprint edition 1969 by Arno Press, Inc.

*

Library of Congress Catalog Card No. 76-83429

*

Seven Sermons and *The Snare Broken* are reprinted
from copies in The New York State Library

*A Discourse, Concerning Unlimited Submission and
Non-Resistance to the Higher Powers*
is reprinted from a copy in the
State Historical Society of Wisconsin Library

*

Manufactured in the United States of America

252
M45a

SEVEN
SERMONS
Upon the following
SUBJECTS

158566

SEVEN
SERMONS

Upon the following

SUBJECTS;

VIZ.

I. The Difference betwixt Truth and Falſhood, Right and Wrong.

II. The natural Abilities of Men for diſcerning theſe Differences.

III. The Right and Duty of private Judgment.

IV. Objections conſidered.

V. The Love of God.

VI. The Love of our Neighbour.

VII. The firſt and great Commandment, &c.

Preached at a

LECTURE

IN THE

Weſt Meeting-Houſe in BOSTON,

Begun the firſt *Thurſday* in *June*, and ended the laſt *Thurſday* in *Auguſt*, 1748.

BY

JONATHAN MAYHEW, D. D.

Paſtor of the Weſt Church in *Boſton*.

Firſt Printed at BOSTON in *New-England*.

LONDON Reprinted,

For JOHN NOON, at the *White-Hart* in the *Poultry*, near *Mercers-Chapel, Cheapſide*.

MDCCL.

TO THE

Chriſtian Society,

Uſually Worſhiping in the *Weſt Meeting-Houſe* in *Boſton.*

THESE SERMONS, at firſt preached, and now publiſhed, at their Requeſt, are humbly inſcribed, in Acknowledgment of their Kindneſs and Generoſity to

The AUTHOR.

THE

CONTENTS.

SERMON

SERMON I.

The Difference betwixt Truth and Falfhood, Right and Wrong.

LUKE XII. 54——57.

And he said also to the people, When ye see a
cloud rise out of the west, straightway ye say,
There cometh a shower; and so it is.
And when ye see the south-wind blow, ye say,
There will be heat; and it cometh to pass.
Ye hypocrites, ye can discern the face of the
sky, and of the earth: but how is it, that ye
do not discern this time?
Yea, and why even of yourselves judge ye not
what is right?

THESE are the words of our Lord Jesus
Christ: and the occasion of them seems
to have been as follows—He had been
preaching the gospel in *Jerusalem*, and
the neighbouring cities of the *Jews*; and had, by
the purity of his doctrine, and the holiness of life,
together with the nature and number of his mira-
racles, convinced many persons, that he was the
Messiah that was to come, and that they were not
to *look for another*. However the chief of the
Scribes and *Pharisees* rejected him as an impostor,
attributing his miraculous works to the power of
magic, or his supposed familiarity with *evil spirits*.

Now it is easy to see what an influence this conduct of the *Scribes* and *Pharisees* in vilifying our

B   blessed

blessed Saviour, must unavoidably have upon the generality of the people. For they were in the highest esteem amongst the *Jews*, both because they were supposed to have the deepest insight into things of a religious nature, and, at the same time, to be men of extraordinary piety. This favourable opinion concerning them, was indeed ill-grounded. But they had the talent of imposing upon the people, in great perfection; and, in fact, managed matters with so much craft and subtilty, that they were thought almost the only faints in the world, and the great oracles to be consulted upon all occasions. The people placed an implicit faith in their dogma's and decisions. Nothing was thought to bear the genuine stamp of truth, unless they had had the coining of it : And their censure of any particular person, or doctrine, was sufficient to make either of them odious to the multitude.

When, therefore, these infallible guides stigmatized our Lord as an ill man ; when they reproached him as one, who, without any reason or authority, was attempting to discredit certain opinions which they had *received to have and to hold from their fore-fathers*; when they accused him of making innovations in the old established religion, to the great hazard of the souls of men ; I say, when they talked and railed in this *pious strain*, it gave a general alarm to the people, especially to the *superstitious vulgar*; and exposed our Lord to their contempt and hatred and insults. They gave themselves no farther trouble to inquire into the grounds of his pretensions to the *Messiahship* ; concluding that *he* must needs be a deceiver, who was condemned by such a learned and holy body of men, as that of the *Scribes* and *Pharisees*.

Few of them condescended so far as to come and hear him preach (this being represented to them as dangerous) that so they might know what
he

he had to fay for himfelf: and thofe that did, came rather as fpies, that they might find occafion to cavil, and to accufe him to the *Priefts* and *Phari-fees*, than with fuch an unprejudiced and candid difpofition as became inquirers after the truth.

But although the generality of the *Jews* were fuch abject flaves to the dictates of their fpiritual inftructors, never daring to hefitate concerning the truth of what they had afferted upon religious fub-jects, but receiving every thing, how abfurd foe-ver, with all the humility of implicit faith ; yet it feems, that in their *temporal* and *worldly* concerns, they were cautious enough. Here they were not fond of taking up fatisfied with any man's word ; but were forward to think, inquire, and judge for themfelves.

This is a fhort character of the people to whom our Lord fpeaks in the text. And this being kept in view, his addrefs will appear very natural and feafonable.—*And he faid alfo to the people, When ye fee a cloud rife out of the weft, ftraightway ye fay, There cometh a fhower ; and fo it is. And when ye fee the fouth-wind blow, ye fay, There will be heat ; and it cometh to pafs. Ye hypocrites, ye can difcern the face of the fky, and of the earth : but how is it, that ye do not difcern this time? Yea, and why even of yourfelves judge ye not what is right?*

Thefe Words feem to be very plain of them-felves: but the fenfe of them may be expreffed more at large in the following paraphrafe.—

" And after thefe things, *Jefus* addreffed him-
" felf to the *Jews*, who were generally prejudiced
" againft him, through their blind attachment to
" their fpiritual guides; and faid—Ye that fuffer
" yourfelves to be led blindfold by others, with
" regard to me and my doctrine, and things of a
" religious concern in general, are neverthelefs fa-
" gacious enough in matters of equal difficulty,

B 2 " and

" and much leſs importance—Ye are apt and ſkil-
" ful enough at diſtinguiſhing the ſigns and tokens
" of things that are to come to paſs in the natural
" world, in which your preſent intereſt is concern-
" ed. * Ye can (for example) by obſerving the co-
" lour of the ſky, and the blowing of the wind,
" form a true judgment concerning the future
" change of the weather.   How comes it to paſs,
" then, ye deluded hypocrites, that amidſt all
" your ſagacity in things that relate to the preſent
" world, ye are ſtill blind and undiſcerning in
" things of a religious nature ? why do not ye that
" can preſage various changes from the appear-
" ance of the earth and heavens, diſcern alſo the
" periods and revolutions of things ; the various
" diſpenſations of providence in the moral world ?
" In particular, how comes it to paſs that ye do
" not diſtinguiſh the preſent ſeaſon, in which God
" is erecting a new diſpenſation, to ſucceed that
" of *Moſes ?* There are ſigns and tokens enough
" to convince you that ſuch a revolution is now
" taking place, if ye would but examine them
" attentively.   Why, then, will ye ſuffer your-
" ſelves to be blinded by the authority of the
" *Prieſts* and *Phariſees*, when God has given you
" ſufficient abilities to gain the knowledge of the
" truth ? Why will ye not exert your own facul-
" ties, and judge for yourſelves what is true and
" right in this matter, as ye do in things of a
" worldly nature ?"

Thus I have endeavoured to give a true idea of
the original ſcope and meaning of the words which
I have choſen for the ſubject of my preſent diſcourſe. I ſhall now wave every thing in them peculiar to the time and circumſtances wherein they
were ſpoken ; and obſerve from them ſeveral uni-

---

* *See Dr.* Clarke's *paraphraſe.*

verſal

verfal truths which concern all times and perfons
and places alike. As,

I. That there is a natural difference betwixt
truth and falfhood, right and wrong.

II. That men are naturally endowed with faculties proper for the difcerning of thefe differences.

III. *And laftly,* That men are under obligation
to exert thefe faculties ; and to judge for themfelves
in things of a religious concern.

I. Then there is a natural difference betwixt
truth and falfhood, right and wrong.—*Why even
of yourfelves judge ye not what is* right?

By *what is right,* it is probable that our Saviour
here more immediately intends, what is *true* ; for
his difcourfe in this place turns upon *examining,
judging,* and *inferring* one thing from another.
But whether by this term we underftand, what is
true in theory, or what is *right in practice,* it will
come to much the fame thing at laft ; for there is
an infeparable connexion betwixt them. If certain
things are *true* in fpeculation, there muft be fome
correfpondent *fitnefs* of actions refulting therefrom.
And, on the other hand, if any thing be allowed
fit in a practical fenfe, that *fitnefs* or *rightnefs* muft
be founded in certain *truths* and *relations* before
fubfifting. I fhall, therefore, take it for granted,
that the text fuppofes, That there is in nature both
a *True,* as diftinguifhed from fpeculative *Error* ;
and a *Right,* as diftinguifhed from *Wrong* in *Conduct.* And the remainder of this difcourfe will be
taken up with thefe important diftinctions.

Indeed the fpending of time to prove that there
are really fuch differences as thofe mentioned,
may appear to fome to be rather childifh imperti-
nence, or formal trifling, than a proper employ-

ment

ment for reaſonable Creatures, it being ſuch a
plain and obvious truth. However it is to be remembered, that no notion is too abſurd to deſerve
to be refuted, while ſome are abſurd enough to
propagate, and others to believe, it: eſpecially if
it be ſuch an one as ſtrikes at the root of all religion, and every thing wherein the happineſs of mankind conſiſts.

And ſuch is the notion of an abſolute indifference in nature with relation to truth and falſhood,
right and wrong. For this being allowed, it follows that we have no invariable rule of life and
conduct. No man upon this ſuppoſition is under
a poſſibility either of judging or acting *amiſs* ; or
of the contrary. Each man *thinks* as juſtly as another, how contrary ſoever his ſentiments are :
And ſo alſo each one *acts* as rightly as any other,
let him act how he will. This is to make ſhort
work with all queſtions and debates concerning
truth, religion, and the rule of human conduct :
it ſuperſedes all inquiries about them by preſuppo-
ſing that they have no exiſtence but in the idea of
certain doting men who have employed themſelves
in inventing arbitrary diſtinctions.

There ſeem to have been two *ſpecies* of *Scepticks*
in the World : one of which exploded the whole
notion of truth and right, as oppoſed to falſhood
and wrong conduct : and another which ſeeming-
ly allowed ſuch differences to have an exiſtence in
nature ; but held it impoſſible for *us* to *diſcern*
them. It is only the firſt of theſe opinions that
we are concerned with at preſent ; the latter will
be conſidered in our next diſcourſe.

To begin with *truth*—Notwithſtanding what
ſome are pleaſed to pronounce with their lips concerning the indifference of truth and falſhood, it
is hardly poſſible but that their hearts ſhould be
at variance with their mouths, and give them the
lye,

lye, even while they are denying there is any such thing as *falshood.* For if there be any thing *existing* (which surely no body was ever so absurd as to deny) there must necessarily be such a thing as truth; truth, as abstracted from mind or intelligence, being nothing distinct from the real nature and properties of things existing. Whatever exists, has a real existence; and if so, it cannot be true that it has no existence. Whatever has a being, must also exist in *some certain, determinate manner*; with such and such properties, affections, and attributes; with such and such proportions, aspects, and relations. And we can as little alter *these* by our opinions, as we can cause the things themselves to exist and not exist, alternately, as our thoughts vary concerning them. Thus truth is somewhat determinate in itself; it exists independently of our notions concerning it: And the precise boundaries betwixt *that*, and *falshood*, are also determined by the real nature and properties of things, whether they are perceptible to us, or not.

Truth, as it exists in the *mind*, is nothing but the perception or knowledge of that independent truth now mentioned; or a knowledge of things as they really exist. And as it relates to *words* and *propositions*, it is nothing but the *right* use of certain arbitrary signs, having a meaning annexed to them by common consent; *i. e.* the using them in such a manner that they shall be conformable to, and expressive of, the real nature and properties of the thing treated of.

To return—Can any man think it equally true that he does, and that he does not, exist? I instance in this, because it is familiar; but the same question may be asked concerning every thing else. This is an universal dilemma, applicable to every thing that comes under consideration—" It " is, or it is not." No middle way can be taken.

This

This is indeed no new diſcovery: it is ſelf-evident, and a firſt principle.

Thus, that we either do, or do not, converſe with ſenſible objects, ſo that one may be truly affirmed, and the other denied, is as plain as it is, that we either do, or do not exiſt. We may proceed in the ſame manner to conſider things, which, if they exiſt at all, lie beyond the reach of our animal ſenſes. It is as certain in itſelf, that there are, or that there are not, ſpiritual and inviſible agents, as it is that there are, or are not, ſenſible objects. And with relation to the being of a GOD, it is as plain, that there is, or that there is not, ſuch a *Being*, as that there are, or are not, inviſible agents in general.

We may deſcend in the ſame way to all the particular queſtions that have ariſen concerning the particular nature of his *Being*, upon ſuppoſition he exiſts—concerning the nature of his government —concerning the reality of a revelation from him —concerning the immortality of our ſouls, *&c.* There muſt neceſſarily be a *true* and a *falſe*, with relation to every queſtion that can be propoſed, or come into our minds. We cannot ſo much as doubt of the truth of any particular propoſition, without ſuppoſing that truth lies on one ſide or the other.

It will be obſerved that I have not attempted to determine any of the above-mentioned queſtions. This was beyond my preſent deſign. All I aim at, is to ſhew, that there is, and muſt be, a natural diſtinction betwixt truth and error, in *general*; a diſtinction which does not depend upon the precarious humours and opinions of men: Whatever judgment we may form in any particular caſe, it no ways affects the truth of it. Truth ſtill remains the ſame ſimple, uniform, conſiſtent thing, amidſt all

all the various and contrary opinions of mankind concerning it.

The natural diftinction betwixt truth and falfe-hood being exploded, fuch paradoxes as thefe muft follow—That no man's opinions are either *right* or *wrong*—That however contrary the fentiments of different men are to one another, they are both e-qually conformable to the nature and reality of the things they judge upon—That there are neither any knowing nor any foolifh men in the world—That what we ufually call wifdom and folly, are the fame—And, what is ftranger than all, That thefe paradoxes are neither true nor falfe—

If there be any fuch thing as wifdom, as oppofed to ignorance and folly, it confifts in knowing the truth ; and a man is wife in the fame degree that he does fo. There is no knowledge, but of fome truth or fact : Or, in other words, knowledge pre-fuppofes the being of truth, or fomething to be known. Now if there be no fuch thing as truth, there is nothing to be known ; and, confequently, every man, yea, every being whatever, muft be intirely ignorant and deftitute of knowledge ; as deftitute of it, not only as *the horfe and mule which hath no underftanding*, but as any part of fenfelefs in-animate matter. So that notwithftanding all the noife there has been in the world about wifdom and folly ; notwithftanding the univerfal applaufe that has been beftowed on fome perfons, as glorioufly diftinguifhed from the reft of mankind by a happy *genius* and peculiar *fagacity* ; yet in reality all this is at bottom nothing but empty words without any meaning at all. *Socrates* and *Plato*, *Locke* and *Newton*, were not fuperior, in point of wifdom, to the moft illiterate hufband-man. Nay ; upon this fuppofition, even *Pyrrho* and *Arcefilaus* themfelves, the great leaders of the *fceptic* tribe, knew no more than thofe whom they upbraided with their igno-rance.

rance. This, indeed, is a conſequence which the *Pyrrhoniſts* will hardly be perſuaded to own. For there are none more apt than they, to value themſelves upon their ſuperior wiſdom and penetration. And they pleaſe themſelves in particular with the thought of their being the diſcoverers of this mighty *arcanum*, that there is no ſuch thing as truth, as diſtinguiſhed from error. But if there be no ſuch thing as truth, why will they pleaſe themſelves for their ſagacity in making this diſcovery? Or why will they endeavour to bring others over to their opinion, when by their firſt, and, I might add, their only, principle, thoſe *others* are no more in an error than themſelves. Such is the perplexity, the endleſs labyrinth, that a man brings himſelf into, by aſſerting for truth, that there is no ſuch thing as truth.

We are, indeed, left intirely in the dark, with reſpect to many things; our knowledge is, at beſt, but of ſmall extent ; and the opinions of men are various. It is this that has given ſome men occaſion to confound truth and error, as though there were in nature no difference betwixt them. But I hope it is needleſs to ſay any thing more in oppoſition to an opinion ſo directly contrary to common ſenſe.

I proceed now to the other diſtinction mentioned above ; the diſtinction betwixt *right* and *wrong* in *conduct*. And, as it was before obſerved, ſuch a diſtinction muſt neceſſarily take place in conſequence of the former. There are, perhaps, ſome things ſo indifferent as no ways to affect practice, whether they are true or falſe. But there are other principles which, being allowed true, immediately induce upon us an obligation to act in a *particular, determinate manner* ; ſo that to act thus ſhall be *right* and *reaſonable* ; and to do the contrary *unfit* and *wrong*.

Thus, for example, it being ſuppoſed, That there is ſome particular courſe or method of acting,

ing, which tends to promote our happinefs upon the whole ; and that a contrary conduct tends to our mifery, (which by the way are not bare fuppofitions, but plain facts) a fitnefs of the former courfe of action, in oppofition to the latter, neceffarily follows. For happinefs being in itfelf a *good*, and mifery an *evil*, it is in itfelf right and reafonable to purfue the former, and to avoid the latter. If to this we add (which experience fhews to be fact alfo) that the fame courfe of action which tends to *private* happinefs, tends to *publick* alfo, this lays us under a twofold obligation to take that courfe. For it is in itfelf right to do good to others, as well as to ourfelves, happinefs being as valuable to them as it is to us. From this general principle our obligation to what is ufually called moral and focial virtue ; to fidelity, juftice, charity ; to humility and temperance, may be eafily inferred. For it is apparent, from experience, that by the fteady, uniform practice of thefe virtues, both the good of individuals, and of the publick, is promoted. Indeed, it feems impoffible but that fuch a practice as tends to the good of the one, fhould tend to the good of the other alfo. For publick happinefs is nothing but the happinefs of a *number* of *individuals* united in fociety : So that if the individuals of which the fociety confifts, be happy, the community muft neceffarily be happy alfo. And, on the other hand, the *community* is rendered miferable in the fame degree that *individuals* are fo. Virtue, then, is what we are under obligation to practife, without the confideration of the being of a God, or of a future ftate, barely from its apparent tendency to make mankind happy at prefent.

Again, let us fuppofe (what is at leaft fuppofeable) That there is a God ; a being who created, and who governs the world, in infinite wifdom and

and goodneſs, *i. e.* in ſuch a manner as to commu-
nicate the greateſt poſſible happineſs to his creatures conſidered collectively.—This being is plainly the object of eſteem, gratitude, love, reverence,
truſt, *&c.* to all his rational creatures. His character is in itſelf amiable and perfect. To treat
him with contempt, or diſregard, is to treat him
as being what he *is not* ; which certainly cannot be
right. *Piety,* therefore, is what we are under obligation to, upon ſuppoſition there is any ſuch being
as this, exiſting.

But farther—If there be ſuch a being, he is *perfect* in all moral excellence, and therefore we, and
all other intelligent beings, are under obligation to
copy after, and imitate, him, according to the
condition and capacity of our natures, without the
conſideration of his enjoining it upon us by any expreſs and poſitive law. For ſo far as we fall ſhort
of him, we fall ſhort of perfection, according to
the ſuppoſition, he being the rule and ſtandard of
perfection. And ſo, on the other hand, we are
perfect, in proportion as we reſemble him in the
temper of our minds; and imitate him in the conduct of our lives. And this brings us, in another
way, to the former concluſion, *viz.* That we are
under obligation to practiſe what is uſually called
moral virtue ; for by this we imitate God : and fall
in with his benevolent deſign in creating and governing the world.

Again—It follows upon the ſuppoſition of ſuch
a being, That his declared will ought to be univerſally the rule of our actions, in whatever manner it
is made known to us, whether by natural *reaſon,*
or ſupernatural *revelation* ; and whether we are able
to ſee the reaſon and grounds of his injunctions, or
not. For, properly ſpeaking, our obligation to
obey the commands of ſuch a being as knows and
wills always what is beſt, does not ariſe in any degree

gree from the particular *manner* in which we come
to the knowledge of his commands ; or from our
feeing the grounds of them : but folely from our
knowing that they are *in fact* his commands : Thus,
if this being has commanded us, befides practifing
fuch moral virtues as thofe mentioned above, to
do certain things not dictated by the light of nature ; if he has commanded us to fubmit ourfelves
to *Jefus* of *Nazareth* as *his* Son and Delegate, and
our Lord and Mafter ; we ought to comply immediately with his will, affoon as it is made known
to us. For it is apparently wrong and unreafonable to thwart the will and authority of him who is
infinitely wife and good, although he had no power
to chaftize us for it. It will not fo much as bear a
difpute, whether it is wrong or not, to act counter
to the injunctions of that being in *any* cafe, who in
every cafe injoins that, and that only, which is reafonable for him to injoin.—If he command with
wifdom and goodnefs, we cannot difobey without
folly and wickednefs.

But, after all, there is really no neceffity of going fo far to find our obligation to what is ufually
called *moral virtue*, as to confider its tendency to
happinefs ; its rendering us like to God, the ftandard of perfection ; or to enquire whether the practice of it be enjoined upon us by the pofitive will
and command of God. We may find the grounds
of this obligation nearer home, even in our own
breafts. There is fuch a *law written in our hearts* ;
fuch an internal confcioufnefs of the moral excellency of virtue, and of the odioufnefs of its contrary, as really leaves us no room to doubt of our
obligation to it ; and fo, in a great meafure, fu-
perfedes all other arguments. For we cannot ordinarily violate the rules of juftice, *&c.* without violating our own minds at the fame time ; and turning our own accufers.

The

The principal objection that can be urged againſt the moral difference of actions, is taken from the difficulty there is, in ſome caſes, to determine the boundaries betwixt right and wrong; the variety of opinions that have prevailed in the world concerning queſtions of right, eſpecially in political affairs; and the different, yea, contrary laws, enacted by wiſe men in different ages and countries, and all equally under the notion of their being right and equitable. " But (to uſe the words of a learn-
" ed writer *) as in painting, two very different
" colours, by diluting each other very ſlowly and
" gradually, may, from the higheſt intenſeneſs in
" either extreme, terminate in the midſt inſenſi-
" bly; and ſo run one into the other, that it ſhall
" not be poſſible even for a ſkilful eye to determine
" exactly where the one ends and the other be-
" gins; and yet the colours differ as much as can
" be, not in *degree* only, but entirely in *kind*, as
" *red* and *blue*, or *white* and *black :* So though,
" perhaps, it may be very difficult in ſome nice
" and perplexed caſes (which yet are very far
" from occurring frequently) to define exactly the
" bounds of right and wrong, juſt and unjuſt, and
" there may be ſome latitude in the judgment of
" different men, and the laws of divers nations;
" yet right and wrong are neverthelefs totally and
" eſſentially different; even altogether as much as
" white and black, light and darkneſs."
The admirable writer whoſe words I have here quoted, ſeems very charitably to attribute men's intirely confounding right and wrong, to the difficulty which they find in ſome caſes, to determine what is right and equitable, and what wrong and injurious; or to diſcern the terminating line be-

---

* Dr. S. Clarke.

twixt them. And this difficulty is doubtlefs what gives men an opportunity to oppofe the notion of fuch a moral difference in actions, under fome little colour of argument. However, an internal perception of the moral difference of things in general, is fo interwoven with our very nature, that it is hardly credible that any man fhould really think all actions to be indifferent in their own nature. Or, if any actually entertain fuch an opinion, it is not *natural.* It does not proceed fo much from men's originally wanting clear ideas of the difference in general betwixt right and wrong, as from their having *made* thefe things indifferent, as far as their own *practice* could effect it. Men have naturally as clear a conception of the general difference betwixt moral good and evil, antecedent to all confideration of human laws and compacts, yea, to the confideration of the will of God himfelf, as they have of the difference betwixt light and darknefs. But as the organs of fight may be abufed and weakened to fuch a degree, that a man fhall at laft perceive no difference betwixt the night and the day: And as moft of our other animal fenfes may be perverted and debauched, fo as to be incapable of anfwering their original defign ; fo alfo men's natural confcience of good and evil may, by frequent violations, lofe its quicknefs ; and the mind itfelf become blind, callous, and infenfible. Our natural fenfe of the moral difference in actions and characters, may be rendered dull and ufelefs. And thus the law written in the hearts of men by the finger of God himfelf, may be repealed, and erafed by the powerful influence of vice : Whereupon they deny that there was ever any fuch law engraved on their minds. This is juft as if *Mofes*, when his *anger waxed hot*, and he caft the two *tables of the law* out of his hands, and brake them beneath the mount, fhould have immediately denied

nied that God had ever written them, or given them to him to preserve. It is natural for men of corrupt minds and morals, to endeavour to get rid of all uneafy reflections upon what is paft, and terrible prefages of what may be future, by intirely throwing afide the diftinction betwixt moral good and evil, as if thefe were but empty names without any meaning, invented by civil and ecclefiaftical *tyrants* to keep the world in awe.

However, although the vices of men may go far towards darkening their underftandings, it is not to be fuppofed that the moft degenerate of them ever arrive at fuch a ftate of blindnefs as to have no real fenfe of the difference betwixt right and wrong, whatever they may pretend. For fuch a fenfe, in fome degree of it, feems infeparable from a rational nature : and cannot be totally extinguifhed, but with reafon itfelf. And it is worth obferving, That with how good a confcience foever the greateft mafters of *fcepticifm* pretend they commit the moft flagrant immoralities, under the notion of all things being indifferent in their own nature ; yet they cannot help betraying themfelves, and fhewing their natural fenfe of right and wrong, upon certain occafions. For who are more averfe than *they,* to take the character of *knave* to themfelves, though they generally take no care not to *deferve* it ? They chufe to be efteemed as men of honefty and integrity, and when it comes to their own turn to be injured, they are as ready as any of their neighbours to accufe the aggreffor of wrong and injuftice. If their moral fenfe were before afleep, fuffering injuries awakens it in a moment. And if they are not right down *atheifts,* they are ready to think ftrange that God fhould let his thunder fleep while fuch villainies are perpetrated.—Thus hard is it for men to difguife the inward fentiments of their hearts in this cafe :
the

the mask will drop off, and nature peep out in some unguarded hour—

If men would go no farther than to assert, That there are some questions of right, so intricate and complicated, that it is difficult, or even impossible, to determine them, none would contradict them but such arrogant and conceited persons as imagine their knowledge has no limits. But when, not content with this, they boldly strike at the foundation of every thing that is good and praise-worthy, by denying the moral difference of actions in general ; and yet upon every turn are complaining of injuries and abuses, done, or offered to themselves ; it is hard to say whether they are more proper objects of pity or contempt ; of indignation or ridicule : For they have doubtless a good title to all.

There can be no danger of being too severe in censuring men of this stamp. For what they say concerning the absolute indifference of actions is either false or true. If it be false, nothing is too bad to be said of them for thus setting aside the moral difference of actions; for putting the most excellent virtues and the most odious vices upon the same footing; for making it as innocent for a child to murther his aged parents, as to kill a viper ; and to blaspheme his Maker, as it is to deride a sot, and, in this way, dissolving all the ties and obligations both of private and of social virtue. But, on the other hand, if what they assert be true, there is not even a bare possibility of injuring them ; for there can be no such thing as wrong or injury, if all actions are absolutely indifferent in their own nature.

I hope it in some measure appears from what has been said, That as *truth* has a real existence in nature, so the distinction betwixt *right* and *wrong* necessarily takes place in consequence thereof. And thus I have done with the *first* thing proposed.

C

The

The next thing propofed was to fhew, That men are naturally endowed with faculties proper for the difcerning of thofe differences, of which we have been fpeaking. But this muft be left for the fubject of another difcourfe.

I fhall conclude for the prefent with an obvious inference from what has been faid ; *viz.* That fince *truth* and *right* have a real exiftence in nature, independent on the *fentiments* and *practices* of men, they do not neceffarily follow the multitude, or major part : nor ought we to make *number* the *criterion* of the true religion. Men are fickle and various and contradictory in their opinions and practices : but truth and moral rectitude are things fixed, ftable and uniform, having their foundation in the nature of things. They will not change their nature out of complaifance to the moft numerous and powerful body of men in the world. We may *conform* to them ; but they will not *condefcend* to us. Were number the mark of truth and right, religion itfelf would be a perfect *Proteus*, fometimes one thing, and fometimes another, according to the opinion that happens to prevail in the world. But if one man may err, why not two ? And if two, why not two thoufand ? And then, why not all mankind ? If truth and right are fomewhat fixed, and men fickle and various, men may err both with refpect to principle and practice. But upon the other hand, if truth and right have no exiftence but in the opinions of men, then indeed they might depend upon number and multitude. But then it may be reafonably afked how many votes are neceffary to change a great lye into a glorious truth ? how many, to change a flagrant crime into a meritorious virtue ? and a finner into a faint ? The church of *Rome* has been trying a great while to bring about thefe wonderful changes and revolutions : and has

has indeed effected it to the fatisfaction of many. But neverthelefs thefe are but fome of the *lying wonders of him, whofe coming is after the working of fatan, with all deceivablenefs of unrighteoufnefs.* It is ftill falfe that bread is flefh ; or wine, blood. Murther remains a vice ftill : nor is breach of faith and perjury any virtue at all.

The *multitude* may *do evil,* and the *many, judge falfly. Iniquity* may be *eftablifhed by a law* ; it may have all the power and wealth of the world engaged on its fide to fupport it, while truth and right may be left folitary and friendlefs. *Noah* was left alone ; fingular indeed, but ftill *a preacher of righteoufnefs.* He was a *perfect and upright man in his generation* ; and, for that reafon, was preferved in the ark, the multitude being firft drowned in a flood of vice, and then deluged in a flood of water. Thus alfo was *Lot* fingularly righteous, while the multitude in *Sodom* and *Gomorrah* firft *burned* with impure lufts, and were then devoured with *flames* from heaven, *being fet forth for an example, fuffering the vengeance of eternal fire.* And how few were there that adhered to our bleffed Saviour while he was in this world ? He was *defpifed and rejected of Men,* as well as *a man of forrows and acquainted with grief.* It was the *body of the people* that was againft him. They did not *difcern the time,* nor *judge what was right.* Even to this day, how fmall is the number of thofe who *worfhip the Father in fpirit and in truth,* according to the fimplicity of the gofpel, compared to thofe that are immerfed in grofs ignorance, fuperftition, and all kinds of immorality ? The whole collective body of *chriftians* makes but a fmall company, compared to the reft of mankind. The *Roman Catholicks* again are much more numerous than the *Proteftants* : and they have long ago voted *Us, Hereticks.* However there is no man in his fenfes that will allow

him-

himſelf to be in an error, becauſe he cannot get ſo many hands held up in favour of his tenets, as another. Infallibility cannot be the reſult of a great *number* of *fallibles:* nor perfection be found in a large body of ſuch as are each of them, conſidered ſingly, *imperfect.* But nevertheleſs we daily ſee that the principal argument with which ſome endeavour to propagate their opinions, is, that they are generally received, *i. e.* in that particular place or country : and if they can but add, that they were the doctrines embraced by their pious fore-fathers, this they reckon ſuch demonſtration as no man in his ſenſes can reſiſt. Such idle, ſuperficial cant may gull the thoughtleſs multitude ; but will be deſpiſed by all others.

If we muſt needs be governed by number in the choice of our religion, it is certainly reaſonable to be governed by the *greateſt* number. And if ſo, we muſt be neither *Calviniſts* nor *Arminians ; Trinitarians* nor *Unitarians ; Quakers* nor *Anabaptiſts ; Churchmen* nor *Preſbyterians ; Papiſts* nor *Proteſtants ;* nor *Jews,* nor *Mahometants ;* but we muſt even turn *Heathens* at once, *Paganiſm* being the moſt univerſal *Orthodoxy* in the world.

It will be obſerved, that I have ſaid nothing for, or againſt, any of the different parties here enumerated : All I propoſe, is to ſhew the unreaſonableneſs of chuſing our religion by vote. This, conſidering the fickleneſs and capriciouſneſs of mankind, amounts to much the ſame thing with chuſing it by *lot.* For whether the major or minor part ſhall have truth and right of their ſide, is intirely precarious : To-day it may be ſo : To-morrow, otherwiſe.

Nor is it needleſs for us to be upon our guard in this matter, conſidering how natural it is to the generality of mankind, eſpecially to ſuch as are of an indolent, incurious make, to follow the moſt numerous and powerful party, both in principle
and

and practice, without troubling themselves about the merits of the cause. Many would almost shudder at the thoughts of an unfashionable vice, or an unpopular doctrine, who would nevertheless readily embrace the same vice and the same doctrine, when unattended with the disadvantage of being contrary to the *mode.* What we abhor when out of date and fashion, we are apt to admire upon a change of times, when it comes to be reputable. It is most agreeable to us to herd with the multitude; to believe and act as they do, right or wrong. This gratifies our innate propensity towards *society:* and many advantages naturally attend him that has the majority on his side. He procures the good-will of all about him, by falling in with their favourite opinions and practices, while the *dissenter* is either ridiculed or railed at, and labours under innumerable inconveniencies. Hence it often comes to pass, that we are insensibly attached to such corrupt opinions and practices as we should have abhorred, had they not been reputable and popular. For the sake of being with *the many,* we daily see some not only renounce their reason and understanding; but break through all the ties of honour, friendship, humanity, charity and piety, making intire shipwreck of a good conscience. Afterwards they imagine that number is the principal criterion of truth; and flatter themselves that they are always secure of being in the right, while they adhere to that side that can carry the vote. This *conforming* humour is too prevalent in the world at present; and always was. Particularly it was so amongst the *Israelites* in the time of *Moses.* For which reason that great *Jewish* Lawgiver gave them the prohibition with which I shall close the present discourse———*Thou shalt not follow a multitude to do evil: neither shalt thou speak in a cause to decline after many to wrest judgment.*

C 3 SERMON

SERMON II.

Men, endowed with Faculties proper
for difcerning the Difference be‑
twixt Truth and Falſhood, &c.

LUKE XII. 54——57.

*And he ſaid alſo to the people, When ye ſee a
cloud riſe out of the weſt, ſtraightway ye ſay,
There cometh a ſhower ; and ſo it is.
And when ye ſee the ſouth-wind blow, ye ſay,
There will be heat ; and it cometh to paſs.
Ye hypocrites, ye can diſcern the face of the ſky,
and of the earth : but how is it, that ye do
not diſcern this time ?
Yea, and why even of yourſelves judge ye not
what is right ?*

THE *ſecond* thing propoſed, was to ſhew,

II. That as there is a natural difference be‑
twixt truth and falſhood, right and wrong ; ſo
men are naturally endowed with faculties proper
for the diſcerning of theſe differences.

This is evidently implied in my text——*How
is it that ye do not diſcern this time ? Yea, and
why even of yourſelves judge ye not what is right?*

IT muſt be acknowledged that the *Pyrrhoniſts,*
who demand great encomiums for teaching men
(not to *know* any thing, but) to *doubt* of every
thing,

thing, have not generally carried their *Scepticifm* any farther than to deny all certainty in a relative fenfe, or with *refpect to us.* To the moft of them it appears too grofs to affirm that there is no difference in things themfelves ; and fo no fuch thing as right abfolutely, in oppofition to error and wrong conduct. What they principally infift upon is, that all things are totally incomprehenfible by us ; that there is no *criterion* of truth and right ; by which they may be diftinguifhed from error and wrong action : So that although there be, in nature, a difference betwixt them, yet *we* have no faculties for difcovering it.

Now upon this ftate of the cafe, it is evident that the Queftions in the text would be altogether impertinent——as impertinent as they would have been upon the former fuppofition, That there is no real difference in things ; but all propofitions, equally true ; and all actions, equally right. When it was afked—*How is it that ye do not difcern this time ? Yea, and why even of yourfelves judge ye not what is right ?* it would have been eafy and natural to anfwer—" Becaufe we have no faculties to dif-
" tinguifh betwixt truth and error, right and wrong.
" Thefe things are left fo uncertain and precari-
" ous with refpect to us, that after all our re-
" fearches, we are as diftant from them as ever.
" It is not poffible for the moft critical inquirer to
" find the truth in any inftance, this being like
" a bird that conftantly flies from us with a
" fpeed proportioned to that with which we pur-
" fue it. All we can do, is firft to fatigue our-
" felves in queft of truth, and then to delude our-
" felves by fancying we have found her."

Such is the dark and unhappy condition in which the *fceptical* doctrine fuppofes mankind ! doomed to total ignorance, and wandering from the right path : Or, if in any cafe, they think and act right, it

is

is by mere *chance* ; nor can they have the pleafure
of knowing it, if they happen to be in the right.
But it is to be hoped that the Author of our being
has not been fo fparing of his favours to us, as to
leave us at fuch uncertainties about every thing,
efpecially about what concerns our own welfare. However, were this really our cafe, one
would think that thofe who are fenfible it is fo,
inftead of deriding the doctrine of a fupernatural
revelation, (as is the practice of modern *Scepticks*)
fhould accommodate the words of *David* to their
own cafe and circumftances—*Who will fhew us any
good? Lord, lift thou up the light of thy countenance
upon us!* The blinder we are naturally, the more
need we have of fupernatural light and inftruction.

The doctrine of our total *incapacity* to diftinguifh
betwixt truth and falfhood, right and wrong, has
much the fame afpect upon common life, civil fociety, philofophy and religion, with that of the abfolute indifference of all things *in their own nature:*
And the like abfurdities will follow from it. Thus
(for example) it follows that there is no difference
at all in men with refpect to wifdom and knowledge.
For in order to conftitute fuch a difference, it is
not only neceffary that there fhould be a natural
diftinction betwixt truth and falfhood ; but alfo
that fome at leaft fhould have faculties for difcovering it. Knowledge, if there be any fuch thing,
confifts in *feeing* or *perceiving* truth. But if no
men have a capacity for this, all men muft be intirely deftitute of knowledge ; as deftitute of it,
as if there were in nature no diftinction betwixt
truth and error.

The doctrine of our inability to *difcover* truth
and right, (as was faid above) has much the fame
afpect upon common life, civil fociety, philofophy
and religion, with that of the abfolute *indifference*
of all things in their own nature. It as effectually
preclude$

precludes all inquiries concerning truth and virtue, private and publick good; and every other fubject. For what does it fignify to us, that there is a true and a right in nature, while it is fuppofed, we have no faculties for difcovering them ? If they lie intirely beyond our reach, we have no more concern with them, than if they had no exiftence at all ; and it is folly for any one to bufy himfelf about them.   Nor can any man confiftently take fatisfaction in his own opinions and actions, as though the former were true, and the latter, right ; or blame another for error in principle or practice, while he afferts that there is equal evidence for the truth of all opinions, and for the regularity of all actions, *i. e.* no real evidence for the truth and regularity of any.   Upon this fuppofition, he that denies his own exiftence, and commits murther, adultery and robbery, has as much to fay in his own vindication, as he that afferts a circle is not a fquare, and faves his country from ruin.   And from hence it appears, that thofe who carry their *fcepticifm* no farther than to queftion the abilities of men to difcover truth and right in all cafes, are guilty of the fame inconfiftency with thofe who explode the whole notion of a real diftinction betwixt truth and right, and their contraries.   For why will they attempt to inveftigate truth ?   Or why will they plume themfelves upon their fuppofed difcovery of this notable truth, That men are unable to difcover truth ?   Why will they upbraid their antagonifts with ignorance ?   Why will they, in any cafe, attempt to vindicate their own conduct, under the notion of its being right ?   Or why will they cenfure that of others, and refent things under the notion of *injury* ?   This has ever been their practice ; which goes wholly upon the fuppofition, that truth and right are not only fomewhat real in nature ; but alfo, that they may be *diftinguifhed* from their contraries,

traries, at leaft by thefe fagacious men themfelves.
What *Ariadne's clue* can be found to extricate them
from this labyrinth of folly and contradiction ? If
there be no *criterion* of truth, let them not pretend to have found one themfelves; and then deride others for fuppofing that truth may be difcovered.   There are many dogmatifts about the
world, who allow themfelves only to be the proper judges of truth and right; which is arrogant
enough.   But no bigotted dogmatift is half fo abfurd and infolent as the *Sceptic*.   For he endeavours to make a monopoly of truth, and to engrofs
the whole of that facred treafure, to the beggar-
ing of the reft of mankind, even while the firft
(and I might add the only) article of his creed is,
That truth cannot be difcovered by any.   It it hard to
fay, whether this conduct has in it more of ftupi-
dity or of infolence.   But thus much is certain,
that a thorough-pac'd *Sceptic* is the moft filly, conceited and inconfiftent bigot in the world.

He that allows of no certainty in any cafe, cannot even be fure that he imagines there is no fuch
thing as certainty.   Perhaps he may be miftaken
in thinking he believes what he fays he believes.
To fay he is certain he believes what he thinks he
does, is to admit of certainty in general, which is
to give up the point in queftion.   But fuppofing
him certainly to know what his own fentiments are,
how comes he to know that any one contradicts
them; or differs from him in opinion ? He need
not make himfelf uneafy at the oppofition of any
fuppofed adverfaries : For, upon his own fcheme,
thefe adverfaries and their oppofition may not be
real, but wholly *imaginary*.   And if one fhould
call him hard names, perfecute him for his opinion,
and anfwer his arguments with a brick-bat inftead
of a fyllogifm, this may be *imaginary* alfo.   At
leaft, he has nothing to complain of, upon his own
principles ;

principles ; for such a conduct towards him, may possibly be as right and reasonable, as it is to feed the hungry, and clothe the naked.   And indeed such treatment might possibly be the most effectual way to bring him to his senses. †

But to come more directly to the point — Some things are in themselves so evidently true, that no *criterion* is necessary in order to our knowing them with *certainty*.   Thus, for example, that we exist, is what we have an immediate and intuitive certainty of.   And the same may be said concerning the *reality* of all our own *ideas* and *perceptions*.   That we experience pleasure and pain ; that we converse with various objects which affect us in a different manner ; that colour is one thing, and sound another ; and that smelling is not tasting ; these things are self-evident, and no *medium* can make them plainer.   But it will perhaps be said, that all this is only phansy and imagination, there being no archetypes existing *without* us, of which these perceptions are the *images* or *representations*.   Be it so : still the perceptions and ideas themselves are *real* : this we are *certain* of, whether there be any thing *external*, of which they are the antitypes, or not.   So that certainty may be had in some respects at least.   And this is sufficient to our present purpose ; for we are not speaking concerning the *extent*, but the *certainty*, of human knowledge.

Of the truth of other things we may be certain in a different manner, *viz.* by reason, deducing them from other truths of which we have an intuitive

† *Epictetus* used to say, " Were I a servant to those *Pyrrho-*
" *nists,* I should take a pleasure in tiezing them.   If they should
" bid me pour oil into the bathing tub, I would throw brine
" upon their head.   If they should ask me to give them ptisan,
" I would bring them vinegar.   And if they offered to complain,
" I would tell they were mistaken ; or persuade them that the vi-
" negar was ptisan: or else make them renounce their notions."
Bayle's Hist. and *Crit. Dict.* Art. *Pyrrho,* Note K.

knowledge,

knowledge. Thus it is that a thousand mathematical truths are demonstrated ; and that with a certainty little or nothing inferior to those first principles from which they are deduced, the connection in every step through the whole process being so apparent, that to suppose the contrary would be a plain contradiction, and amount to the denying a thing to be what it-is acknowledged to be. And in the same way many moral and religious truths may be demonstrated also—As the being of a God ; his power, wisdom, goodness and providence : and our obligation to obey him.

For the truth of many other things we can, indeed, have no more than *probable* evidence ; but which is, in many cases, almost as satisfactory to the mind as *intuitive* and *demonstrative* certainty. Thus who doubts but that the sun will set in a few hours ?—that the sea will ebb and flow to-morrow, as usual ?—that autumn will succeed to summer ; winter, to autumn ; and spring, to winter, as in times past ? But of these things there is no certainty. For God has power to put a stop to the usual course of nature : and we cannot be certain that he will not do it the next moment. Thus also probable evidence is all we can have for the truth of facts recorded in ancient history. Men may possibly deceive us. But whoever has been in such a doubting humour, as to question whether there have been such men as *Alexander the great*, and *Julius Cæsar* ; whether they fought and triumphed, &c ? Indeed we can have no more than probable evidence that food and sleep will refresh us for the future, as heretofore. Our whole institution of life, as it relates to the present world, is grounded upon evidence of this sort, and not upon intuitive or demonstrative certainty. Such evidence is easy to be had ; and is sufficient to the purposes of life, as daily experience shews us, We may, if we please,

perplex

perplex ourfelves about the nature of *time, place* and *motion*: But men who are no philofophers, find the way *home* at *one o'clock* without any difficulty. We may puzzle ourfelves about the *effences* of things, and the *manner* in which one operates upon another: But experience teaches the hufbandman how to manure his fields, fo as to make them fruitful: We all know that drink allays our thirft, and food, our hunger; nor do we ever hefitate whether we fhall make ufe of *them*, or of fomething elfe, to remove thofe natural uneafineffes. But ftill there is no infallible and neceffary connection betwixt thofe caufes and the effects that are ufually produced by them.

Nor is there more room for *fcepticifm* in relation to morals and religion, than in common life; nor indeed fo much, with regard to the principal branches of our *duty*. But however it comes to pafs, men take more pains to doubt in one cafe than in the other. We have ftronger evidence for the proof of the chief articles of religion, than we have for moft other things, of which we are fully fatisfied. The being and perfections of God may be known without much difficulty; and thefe being known, it is as eafy to know how we ought to conduct ourfelves towards him in general, as it is for a fervant to know how to pleafe a mafter whofe temper and character he is acquainted with. And it is at leaft as plain that the Sovereign of the world will make a diftinction betwixt the righteous and the wicked, as that a wife and good prince will make a diftinction betwixt dutiful fubjects and rebels.

Thus it appears, in general, that men are able to diftinguifh betwixt truth and falfhood, right and wrong. But I fhall now make feveral obfervations upon this propofition, in order to farther explain the real intention of it, to obviate fome objections againft it, and to guard it againft thofe abufes to which it may appear liable. And

1. It

1. It is not intended in this affertion, that all men have *equal abilities* for judging what is true and right. The whole creation is diverfified, and men in particular. There is a great variety in their intellectual faculties. That which principally diftinguifhes fome men from the beafts of the field, is the different formation of their bodies. Their bodies are *human*, but they are in a manner *brute* all befide. Whether the difference that there is in the natural powers of men, proceeds from the original make of their minds, or from fome difference in thofe bodily organs upon which the *exercife* of the rational faculties may be fuppofed to depend ; it is apparent that there is, in fact, fuch a difference. And therefore when it is faid that men are able to judge what is true and right, it muft be underftood in fuch a fenfe as is confiftent with this fact. Thofe of the lower clafs can go but a little way with their inquiries into the natural and moral conftitution of the world. But even thefe may have the power of judging in *fome degree.* However, upon fuppofition that fome were wholly ignorant of their own exiftence, it does not follow that all muft be fo, any more than that all bodies muft be round, becaufe fome are of that particular figure. From the moft dull and ftupid of the human fpecies, there is a continual rife or gradation, there being as great a variety in the intellectual powers of men, as in their bodily and active powers. And fo it may be true of fome in an higher and more proper fenfe than of others, that they may *even of themfelves judge what is right.* Many things are obvious, and, in a manner, firft principles to *them*, which to others are myfterious and incomprehenfible.

2. As a farther limitation of this affertion, I would obferve, that it does not imply, that the *fame perfons* are equally adequate judges of truth and right, in all conditions and circumftances. There is a
great

great difference in the powers of different men: But no one differs more from another than he does from himself, considered in childhood and mature life, before and after his mind is cultivated by study and exercise. The *man* knows what the *child* was ignorant of. We come into the world ignorant of every thing. But he that, in his natural, rude and uncultivated state is unqualified to judge what is true and right, unless it be in a few obvious cases, is capable of considerable improvements by study and experience. Our intellectual faculties were given us to improve: they rust for want of use; but are brightened by exercise. Exercise strengthens and invigorates our mental faculties as well as our bodily. And the more a man habituates himself to intellectual employments, the greater will be his aptness and facility in discovering truth, and detecting error. Without some previous study and application, it is as impossible that men should be accurate judges of truth and right, as it is that they should be compleat artificers in any mechanical business, without spending time to learn the trade. They may *bungle* and *cobble*; but can do nothing that will bear the inspection of a *master-workman*. It is the unhappiness of a great part of mankind that they do not sufficiently consider this natural weakness, ineptitude and awkardness of human reason before cultivation; but sit down contented with their imaginary sagacity and promptness of understanding, without using the proper means to qualify them for judging of things that may come under their consideration. Hence it is that we have so many *quacks* and ignorant pretenders in all arts and sciences—— What need of study to come at an acquaintance with those subjects which we may understand at any time only by opening our eyes? Who will descend into the bowels of the earth to dig for gold, while it lies in plenty within his reach upon the surface of the ground?

ground? Who will dive for pearls, while he imagines they float upon the waves? Or what need has
that field of tillage, whose foil is so fertile, that, like
that of *Eden*, it produces spontaneously the richeft
fruits? When men imagine that the depths of science
may be fathomed by a single glance of thought, without any previous application to intellectual exercises,
it cannot be expected that they should be able to determine juftly upon any points but some of the moft
familiar and obvious. In this cafe, he that was
born like the wild affes-colt, muft needs continue to
be fo? or, at beft, come to maturity, and grow up
into an afs himfelf.

The alteration which time and ftudy make in the
abilities of men for judging concerning truth and
right, is fufficient to account for the diverfity of fentiments entertained by the *fame perfons* at different
periods of their life, without having recourfe to
fcepticifm, or fuppofing all our notions, from firft
to laft, to be mere fancy and illufion. A man may
err once without erring always. Nor can we argue
from the reveries of youth, and the abfurd conceits
of the illiterate, that all mankind are but a mighty
nation of fools and lunaticks, pleafing themfelves
with idle dreams and delufive appearances, inftead
of realities.

3. That men are able *even of themfelves to judge
what is right*, does not imply, that they can receive
no affiftance from books, and the converfation of
learned men ; Or that they may judge as well without thefe helps, as with them. Although all men are
capable of difcerning truth and right in fome degree,
by the bare exercife of their own natural faculties,
it does not follow that they can ftand in no need of
any foreign aid, in order to their judging in a more
perfect manner. The more knowing may be helpful to others in their purfuit of knowledge. And
the abilities of men for reafoning juftly, and judging

ing truly, may depend, in a great meafure, upon
the method of their education, the books they read,
and the genius and abilities of the perfons they con-
verfe with. Who will pretend that the natives of
Greenland, or the *Cape of Good Hope*, enjoy the fame,
or equal, means of knowledge, with thofe that are
born in the polite and learned nations of *Europe*?
Who imagines that one brought up at the plough
is as likely to form right notions of things, as if he
had been educated at a univerfity? Or that a man
who has converfed only with ordinary Mechanics,
has the fame advantages with thofe who have enjoyed the familiarity of the greateft proficients in
literature? To fuppofe thefe things, is to contradict daily experience. And, therefore, to decline
all affiftances from others in the fearch of knowledge,
under a notion, that we are able to *judge even of
ourfelves what is right*, is pride and vanity, and not
the part of an ingenuous inquirer after truth. This
may be allowed by the moft ftrenuous afferter of
mens natural abilities, and natural right, to judge
for themfelves, without any appearance of inconfiftency or contradiction. For it amounts to no
more than this, that fome men are fuperior to o-
thers, and may help them to the knowledge of
fome things which they would not have known
without their affiftance.

4. It is not implied in this doctrine, that mens
intellectual powers have *no bounds at all*; or that
they are equally able to determine upon *all points*, although they fhould improve all the helps to knowledge and cultivate their reafon in the beft manner
poffible. There are many cafes wherein the wifeft
of men are unable to form any judgment at all——
difficulties which they cannot folve——heights
which they cannot climb—depths which they cannot fathom—Some may, perhaps, think this a reflection upon human underftanding. And indeed it
is fo, if it be any reflection upon it to fay, that it is

not

not infinite like that of God; but not otherwife. To fay that human reafon is confined to a certain fphere, beyond which it cannot penetrate, is, in reality, no more than to affert that man is a finite, and not an infinite, being; a creature, and not the Creator. There are probably created intelligences much fuperior to man even *in his beft eftate:* But it is no derogation from their real dignity, to fay they are not omnifcient. Why then fhould man grafp at omnifcience? imagine he may know every thing becaufe he may know fome? and look upon it as a reproach, when it is faid that his reafon, and all his other faculties are circumfcribed?

We may know what is proper to be known by beings of our rank, fo as to fill our place, and anfwer the defign of our creation, without being able to comprehend all things. We may know that *this earth* is inhabited by creatures, the law of whofe nature is virtue, and its end happinefs; although we cannot certainly tell whether the *planets* are inhabited, or not; or, if they are, by what kind of beings; and what their condition and circumftances. We may know, in general, what tends to health and felicity in this world, although the real effences of things fhould be beyond our reach. We may know that whatever *came into exiftence*, (as it is demonftrable that every thing did which we behold) muft have fome *invifible* caufe adequate to it, although we were not able to form a clear idea of creative power, or the manner of its exertion. We may know that beauty, order, harmony and defign, in the works of nature, prefuppofe a *defigner*, or, intelligent artificer; although we cannot comprehend the fyftem of the univerfe. We may know that a conftitution of things, actually tending to happinefs, muft be the product of goodnefs, although we are not able exactly to define, beforehand, that fyftem the correfpondent parts of which
                                                        fhall

shall be so adjusted as to effect the greatest possible good. We may know in general that the Author of the world must be a wise and good being, although the final causes of some things which we see in it, are beyond our sight. In fine we may know that *God is, and that he is a rewarder of them that diligently seek him*; although we cannot *by searching find out the almighty unto perfection*; or comprehend his nature; or see through the whole scheme of his works, government and providence.

The wisest of men was not ashamed to own this imperfection of human reason, even under its greatest improvements, and carried to its most exalted pitch. *When I applied mine heart to know wisdom,* says Solomon, *then I beheld all the work of God, that a man cannot find out all the work that is done under the sun; because though a man seek it out, yet shall he not find it; yea farther, though a wise man think to know it, yet shall he not be able to find it.* However *Solomon* was no *Sceptic.* In the same book we find him saying, *that wisdom excelleth folly, as much as light excelleth darkness:* And with him the conclusion of the whole matter is,—*Fear God, and keep his commandments; for this is the whole of man.* Whatever he might be in doubt about, he was satisfied of this, That there was a God who governed the world, that his will and commandments might be known, and the business and happiness of man, consists in obeying them. Again,

5. When it is said we are able *even of ourselves to judge what is right*, this is not designed to suggest that our intellectual faculties are so capacious as to render a *supernatural revelation* of *no use* or *importance* to us. Certainly we cannot suppose this to be the intention of him that uttered the words of our text, since one of the titles which he took upon himself, was that of a *Prophet*, or a *Teacher sent from God.* And indeed it necessarily follows from the supposition of

our rational faculties being *limited*, that there is *room* for our being inftructed by revelation. If one man may inftruct another, much more may we fuppofe it poffible for *him that is perfect in knowledge* to fupply the natural defects of human reafon by a fupernatural communication of light and knowledge. When, and how far, it is expedient for him to do this, He only knows. However upon fuppofition of fuch a revelation, we muft be fuppofed to be able to fee the evidence of its being fuch. It is the proper office of reafon to determine whether what is propofed to us under the notion of a revelation from God, be attended with fuitable atteftations and credentials, or not. So that even in this cafe, we may *of ourfelves judge what is right.* If there be no rational evidence of its coming from God, no rational man can receive it as fuch : And, on the other hand, if it be accompanied with rational evidence, no reafonable man can reject it. Indeed what Jefus Chrift, particularly blames the *Jews* for in the text, is their not exercifing their reafon in this way. He had fufficiently proved his divine miffion ; but they would not *difcern the time*, nor *judge what was right*, being under the influence of prejudice, and not of reafon.

Moreover, it is the proper office of reafon to determine the meaning of the particular parts of a revelation, after the divine authority of it in general is eftablifhed and allowed. And this mens natural faculties qualify them for, much in the fame manner that they qualify them for interpreting other writings. If God gives men a revelation, he gives it to be underftood by men : And if he gives it to be underftood by men, he muft give it in human language, and accommodate it to human capacity. For otherwife, a fecond revelation would be neceffary to explain the firft : And then, why not a third to explain the fecond ; and fo on *in infinitum* ?

And

And fo nothing would be really *revealed* after all.

I fhall juft add in the

6th, And *laft place*, as a farther limitation of the propofition before us, That it does not intend that we are able to determine, with an *equal degree of certainty*, all points which we are capable, in fome fenfe, of coming to a conclufion about.   Although truth does not admit of *degrees*, yet the evidence of truth does.   So that of various propofitions equally true in themfelves, fome may be known with greater certainty than others.   Probable evidence is indeed all that can be had in moft cafes, as was obferved before.   It i by virtue of this, that that the intercourfe of man with man, and all the bufinefs and commerce of the world is carried on. Experience fhews that fuch evidence is fufficient in *fecular* affairs : And it may be fufficient in *religious* affairs alfo, in thofe cafes where abfolute certainty cannot be had.

I fhall now conclude this head concerning the certainty and fufficiency of human knowledge, with the words of Mr. *Locke*. " If any one," fays he, " will be fo fceptical as to diftruft his fenfes, and " to affirm that all we fee and hear, feel and tafte, " think and do, during our whole being, is but " the feries and deluding appearances of a long " dream, whereof there is no reality ; and there- " fore will queftion the exiftence of all things, or " our knowledge of any thing : I muft defire " him to confider, that if all be a dream, then he " doth but dream that he makes the queftion ; " and fo it is not much matter, that a waking man " fhould anfwer him.   But yet, if he pleafes, he " may dream that I make him this anfwer, that " the certainty of things exifting *in rerum natura*, " when we have the teftimony of our fenfes for " it, is not only as great as our frame can attain " to, but as our condition needs.   For our fa--

" culties

" culties being suited not to the full extent of be-
" ing, nor to a perfect, clear and comprehensive.
" knowledge of things, free from all doubt and
" scruple ; but to the preservation of us in whom
" they are ; and accommodated to the use of life;
" they serve our purpose well enough, if they will
" but give us certain notice of those things which
" are convenient, or inconvenient to us. For he
" that sees a candle burning, and hath experi-
" mented the force of its flame, by putting his
" finger in it, will little doubt that this is some-
" thing existing,—which does him harm, and puts
" him to great pain : which is assurance enough,
" when no man requires greater certainty to go-
" vern his actions by, than what is as certain as
" his actions themselves.   And if our dreamer
" pleases to try, whether the glowing heat of a
" glass furnace, be barely a wandering imagina-
" tion, in a drowsy man's fancy ; by putting his
" hand into it, he may perhaps be wakened into
" a certainty, that it is something more than bare
" imagination.   So that this evidence is as great as
" we can desire, being as certain to us as our plea-
" sure or pain, *i. e.* happiness or misery ; beyond
" which we have no concernment, either of know-
" ing or being." †

Thus it appears that men are naturally endowed
with faculties proper for distinguishing betwixt
truth and error, right and wrong.   And hence it
follows, that the doctrine of a total ignorance, and
incapacity to judge of moral and religious truths,
brought upon mankind by the apostacy of our
First Parents, is without foundation.   How much
brighter and more vigorous our intellectual faculties were in *Adam*, six thousand years before we
had any existence, I leave others to determine.   It

---

† Mr. *Locke's* works, edit. 4th, Vol. I. *p.* 312.

is fufficient for my purpofe to confider mankind as
they are at prefent, without inquiring what they
were before they had any being. And it appears that they have now a natural power to judge
what is true and right, with the reftrictions mentioned above. But it is, neverthelefs, the manner of
vain *Enthufiafts,* when the abfurdity of their doctrines is laid open, to fall a railing, telling their op-
pofers that they are in a *carnal ftate, blind,* and unable to judge : but that themfelves are *fpiritually
illuminated.* Thus they endeavour to palm the
groffeft abfurdities upon their neighbours, under
the notion of their being divine truths and holy
myfteries ; fo that thefe enlightened Ideots make
infpiration, and the Spirit of truth and wifdom, the
vehicle of nonfenfe and contradictions. Whatever
is reafonable, is, with them, carnal : and nothing
is worthy of belief, but what is impoffible and abfurd in the eye of human reafon.

We fee that our Bleffed Saviour did not fuppofe
that the minds of men had fuffered any fuch total
eclipfe, or were wholly overfpread with darknefs.
He addreffes the unbelieving *Jews* as if they had
proper faculties for judging of religious truths ;
and blames them for not exerting them—*why even
of yourfelves judge ye not what is right ?*——The
candle of the Lord which was lighted up in man at
firft, when *the infpiration of the almighty gave him
underftanding,* was not extinguifhed by the original
apoftacy, but has kept burning ever fince. The
divine flame has catcht from father to fon ; and
has been propagated quite down to the prefent generation : Nor will it be put out 'till the *fun himfelf fhall be darkened, and the moon fhall not give her
light.*

Let us retain a fuitable fenfe of the dignity of
our nature in this refpect. It is by our reafon that
we are exalted above the beafts of the field. It is

D 4   by

by this that we are allied to angels, and all the glorious intelligences of the heavenly world : yea, by this we refemble God himfelf. It is principally on account of our reafon, that we are faid to have been *created in the image of God.* So that how weak foever our intellectual faculties are, yet to fpeak reproachfully of reafon in general, is nothing lefs than blafphemy againft God. Let us, therefore, inftead of contemning this ineftimable gift, in which confifts the glory of our nature, employ it to the ends for which it was defigned, in the fervice of the great Father of our fpirits.

But we have had occafion, in this difcourfe, to fpeak of the imperfection, as well as of the ftrength, of human reafon. He that is not fenfible of this imperfection, is fo far from being the wifeft of men, that he *knoweth nothing yet as he ought to know it. Profeffing himfelf to be wife, he becomes a fool* ; the knowledge of ourfelves being the firft, laft, point, the *alpha* and *omega* of human wifdom. The knowledge of our own ignorance, is the moft important and beneficial of all fciences. This will naturally lead us to humility, and excite us to improve, with gratitude and diligence, all the means of knowledge which we are favoured with ; efpecially that revelation which God has given us by his Son, whom he has fent from heaven to be *a light unto the Gentiles* as well as *the glory of his people Ifrael.* A Senfe of our ignorance would alfo teach us modefty in criticifing the works of nature and providence. The fcheme of God's government is vaft ; our underftandings are narrow, and not proportion'd to it. We are at prefent, as it were, but rational beings in *embrio*, unborn to light and knowledge. At beft we are mere *babes* in fpeculation ; we *fpeak as children* ; we *think as children* ; we *underftand as children* : But perhaps we may e're long *become men, and put*

away

away childifh things. 'Till we arrive at that maturity of life and knowledge, towards which we
are in progrefs during our abode in the prefent
world, we ought not to think ftrange that our
underftandings are baffled ; or that many things
remain myfterious and unaccountable to us, both
in the natural and moral government of God.
And inftead of boldly cenfuring the author of the
univerfe, as taking wrong meafures in any refpect, it becomes us to ufe that humble language,
not only of a great man, but an infpired *apoftle*
—*O! the depths of the riches both of the wifdom
and knowledge of God! How unfearchable are his
judgments ; and his ways paft finding out!——Now
to the King eternal, immortal, invifible, the only wife
God, be honour and glory for ever, through Jefus
Chrift our Lord.* Amen.

SERMON

SERMON III.

The Right and Duty of private Judgment asserted.

LUKE XII. 54——57.

And he said also to the people, When ye see a cloud rise out of the west, straightway ye say, There cometh a shower ; and so it is.

And when ye see the south-wind blow, ye say, There will be heat ; and it cometh to pass.

Ye hypocrites, ye can discern the face of the sky, and of the earth : but how is it, that ye do not discern this time?

Yea, and why even of yourselves judge ye not what is right?

HAVING attempted to shew, in two former discourses upon these words, That there is a natural difference betwixt truth and falshood, right and wrong: And, That men are naturally endowed with faculties proper for the discerning of these differences: I proceed now to shew in the

IIId. *And last place,* That men are under obligation to exert these faculties ; and to judge for themselves in things of a religious concern. It cannot be doubted but that this is fairly implied in my text. For the words evidently carry in them a severe censure and reproof of the persons to whom they were originally addressed, on account of their

neglect-

neglecting to judge for themselves concerning our bleffed Saviour, and his doctrine. He makes this neglect, an argument of their hypocrify, one of the bafeft vices—*Ye hypocrites, ye can difcern the face of the fky—and why even of yourfelves judge ye not what is right* ?

The fubject before us being the duty of private judgment, I fhall briefly explain what I intend by perfons judging for themfelves ; or by freedom of thought and inquiry in religious matters : And then fhew, that this is what we are all obliged to.

Now what I intend by a man's judging for himfelf with freedom, and exerting his own faculties in the fearch of truth and right, may be comprifed under the following particulars—

That he fufpends his judgment intirely concerning the truth or falfhood of all doctrines; and the fitnefs or unfitnefs of all actions ; 'till fuch time as he fees fome reafon to determine his judgment one way rather than the other. He that defires to come to the knowledge of the truth, puts himfelf in a ftate of *indifferency* with regard to the point to be judged of ; that fo his mind being as it were, in *æquilibrio*, his judgment may be determined folely by reafon and argument. He does not bring his old prejudices and prepoffeffions to determine the point ; but comes prepared, by an unbiaffed mind, to receive the impreffions of reafon, and of reafon only. All propofitions are the proper fubject of inquiry and examination, except *firft principles*, which are few in number, and which do not extend to any doctrines either of *natural* or *revealed* religion, how nearly foever they may be connected with fome of *both*. And, therefore, in order to our judging with true freedom, we ought to confider all fuch doctrines with an eye of indifferency, neither fancying them to be true or falfe ; nor even *wifhing* them to be fo, till we fee they are connected

nected with, or contrary to, some of those first principles of human knowledge, which, being self-evident, are not the subject of examination. Thus,
for example, we ought not to believe that there is,
or that there is not a God ; that the Christian religion is from God, or an imposture ; that any particular doctrine fathered upon it, is really contained in it, or not ; or that any particular sect of christians, is in the right, or in the wrong ; till we
have impartially examined the matter, and see evidence on one side or the other. For to determine any
point without reason or proof, cannot be to judge
freely, unless it be in a bad sense of the word. So
that suspense or indifferency, is the first thing implied in free inquiry : Or, to speak more properly, it is a pre-requisite, and preparatory to it.

Again : The next step towards freedom of examination and judgment, is the exerting of our own
reason in weighing arguments and evidences that
offer themselves to us, or that are offered by o-
thers. He that inquires freely after truth, is not
content with barely suspending his judgment till
such time as evidence forces itself upon his mind.
In this way, a man may, perhaps, avoid error ;
but will not gain much knowledge ; for truth is
coy, and must be courted. To gain any considerable degree of knowledge, it is necessary that we
are active and vigorous in the pursuit of it ; that
we make use of all the means and helps to knowledge that are within our reach ; that we inquire
into facts ; that we view things in different lights,
not taking up satisfied with first appearances ; that
we weigh the arguments that are brought to support any doctrine or practice ; that we balance
them with contrary arguments ; and the like.

Another thing implied in the freedom of judgment is, that a man honestly *embraces* for truth,
whatever there appears evidence for, without endeavouring

deavouring to evade it, to shift it off, or stifle the conviction of his own mind. To inquire into evidence, is to no purpose, unless we follow it wherever it leads, and chearfully receive the truth wherever it is to be found ; whatever notions it may contradict ; whatever censures it may expose us to. It is an idle and inconsistent thing to examine, if we are determined before-hand to retain our former sentiments ; to believe as our forefathers did, or as any particular body of men does at present. A man does not really inquire after truth and right at all, unless he determines from the very first, to have no superstitious veneration for *great names* ; but to yield himself up to evidence wherever it appears ; and how much soever it might have contributed to his present interest and reputation to have embraced other tenets.

Lastly : Judging with freedom and impartiality, implies, that in giving our assent to any proposition, we give it in proportion to the degree of evidence that appears to support it. All truths are not equally clear and incontestable : Innumerable lie quite beyond our sight ; some just dawn upon our minds ; others appear in a strong and convinceing light, though not so strong as to exclude all doubt ; while others glare upon us with all the force of demonstration. Now as there are innumerable degrees of evidence betwixt the lowest probability, and that intuitive certainty which we have of first principles ; so a man ought not to give the same degree of assent to every thing he receives for truth ; but to proportion his assent to the nature and degree of the apparent evidence, whether it be greater or less. Not to assent to what is, in the lowest degree, probable, upon the whole, discovers a backwardness to entertain the truth. And, on the other hand, to give an assent to any truth, over and beyond what the nature of its evidence naturally

naturally demands and calls forth, is much the fame thing with believing without any evidence at all. For all that redundancy of affent, if I may fo exprefs it, is mere credulity and rafhnefs: And this is as unbecoming a reafonable creature as obftinacy and perverfenefs.

Having thus briefly explained what I intend by judging for ourfelves, with freedom, I proceed now to fhew, That this is what every man is under obligation to do. This I propofe to prove *directly* by reafon and revelation; and then to anfwer the principal *objections* that are urged againft it.

Each individual has an intereft of *his own* depending. We find, by experience, that we are all capable of being happy or miferable to a great degree. Pain and pleafure, at leaft, are private and perfonal things. And even they that arrogate to themfelves the right of *judging for us*, do not pretend to *feel for us* alfo. Now if it be of any importance to us to be happy for ourfelves, it is of importance to judge for ourfelves alfo; for this is abfolutely neceffary, in order to our finding the path that leads to happinefs. Indeed, if others can afford us any affiftance in finding this path, it is reafonable to make ufe of it; but not to give ourfelves up entirely to their direction. It is the greateft folly imaginable, to give ourfelves no concern about our own welfare, unlefs we were certain it is fecured to us already, fo that we cannot poffibly mifs of it, which is a fuppofition contrary to daily experience. We find that our happinefs depends, at leaft in fome degree, upon our conduct; and that we often take fome wrong ftep, through ignorance; which ought to be a warning to us to look about us, and take heed to our ways.—Without knowing

ing which is the right path, we can never take it,
unlefs it be by *chance* ; and though we fhould be
fo fortunate as to get into it, we cannot have the
fatisfaction of knowing it.

In our prefent imperfect ftate, fuch inquiries as
the following, become every man that has not yet
refolved them in his own mind—" What is my
" chief good ? Where is the road that will convey
" me to my happinefs ? Where fhall I find this
" ineftimable jewel ? this *pearl of great price?* In
" what mountain fhall I dig for it ? In what ocean
" fhall I dive ? Amidft the various opinions, and
" contrary purfuits of mankind, what road fhall I
" myfelf travel ? What courfe fhall I fteer ?
" Shall I find my felicity in retirement and foli-
" tude ? Or in the noife and buftle of the world ?
" Is it to be found in the humble and quiet cot-
" tage ? Or in proud and envious courts ? Is it to
" be found in peace at home ? Or in war abroad ?
" Does it confift in indulging to my animal nature
" without controul ? Or in improving my mind
" in what fome men call *wifdom* and *virtue ?*
" Shall I feek it in my own country ? Or explore
" fome diftant region in hopes to find it ? Shall I
" fearch it upon the feas, or upon the dry land ?
" In the earth beneath, or in the heavens above ?
" In this world, or in *fome other ?* Is my fpirit
" immortal ? Am I to furvive the diffolution of
" my body, and to live for ever in fome other
" ftate ? Or fhall this vital fpark that thinks, per-
" ceives, and wills, and is anxious about futurity,
" be wholly extinguifhed in a few days, when my
" body falls to duft ? Is there any being who cre-
" ated, and who governs the world ? Or is this
" beautiful and ftupendous fabrick of the univerfe,
" the offspring of chance ? And without any *guide,*
" *overfeer* or *ruler ?*—a fatherlefs World, which the
" next

" next moment may fall into ruins, or into no-
" thing? If there be a God, what is his character?
" Is he powerful, wife, righteous, and good ; or
" is he not? Does my happiness depend upon
" pleasing and obeying him, and conforming my-
" felf to his will? If it does, what is his will?
" What are his laws? What does he expect of
" me? What kind of government is it I am un-
" der? What is the particular and certain way,
" in which I may obtain the good-will of this great
" Parent of the world, *in whose favour is life, and*
" *whose loving-kindness is better than life.*

Thefe, methinks, are fuch inquiries as every
man fhould endeavour to get fome fatisfaction a-
bout in his own mind—fatisfaction of quite another kind than any that can be had barely from
the decifions of others concerning them. The
queftions are too interefting and important to be
fubmitted to the determination of a fecond perfon.

But were we difpofed to leave matters of this
confequence to reference, who fhall be the judges?
There are almoft as many opinions in the world,
as there are men. The *Talapoins* of *Siam* have one
fyftem of religion : The *Mufti* at *Conftantinople*,
another : And *Chriftians*, *a* third ; and fo on.
And almoft all alledge divine revelation in their
own favour. There are even fome *fools* who *fay
in their heart, there is no God* ; and not only in
their *heart*, but repeat it with their *lips* alfo. Now
fhall we fubmit to the *Theifts*, or to the *Atheifts?*
How fhall we know on which fide the truth lies,
without examination? But, fuppofe we embrace
Theifm, what fect of the *Theifts* fhall we fall in
with? With thofe who deny, or thofe who maintain, a revelation from God? Is it reafonable to
give in to either party, before we enquire which
has the beft of the argument? But fuppofe we fall
in

in with the *latter*, there are several sects of them, the principal of which are *Jews, Mahometans*, and *Christians*. It cannot be a *reasonable* part to fall in with one, in opposition to the other two, *without reason*. But suppose we are convinced that the *Christian* religion is true, do not *Christians* differ very widely in their sentiments? Do they not differ so much in explaining the doctrines of their common revelation, as to agree in hardly any thing besides the name of *Christian?* Are they not divided into many sects, the most of which strenuously maintain, that not only truth, but salvation also, is confined to themselves? Do they not deal out their curses mutually with a liberal hand? Are they not continually *throwing fire-brands, arrows, and death* (not, indeed, in *sport*, like other *fools*, but) in sober earnest?

Now amidst these differences and altercations, what is the part of a reasonable man, but to sit down, and exercise, as well as he can, his own intellectual powers; and so to *judge even of himself what is right?* What system of doctrine—what mode of worship—what form of church-government and discipline, is most agreeable to scripture and reason—what sect of *Christians* he shall unite with—and whether with any one, in all its minute and distinguishing tenets and usages—? " A man " must join himself to the *true, primitive*, and *ca-* " *tholick* church.". What church is that? all churches lay claim to that title: And the question to be decided is, which of them supports its claim the best? which cannot be decided without previous inquiry. " But there is a *living infallible guide* " upon earth, to whom it is easy to repair; and " then we may be sure of being in the right without " out any farther trouble." Where is he? Many deny there is any such unerring guide, and infallible umpire, as confidently as others affirm it. But

E   even

even thofe who agree that there is fuch a fovereign
judge of religious controverfy, are not yet fully a-
greed who he is ; or whether infallibility be to be
found in one fingle perfon or more. The heads of
all fects ufually decide difputable matters with full
as much affurance and lordlinefs as it would become infallibility itfelf to do it, although they do
not all, in fo many words, pretend to be exempted from a poffibility of erring. Thofe who claim
infallibility, often decide and order as if they were
fallible : And thofe who do not claim it, are often full as pofitive, and given to domineering as
much, as if it unqueftionably belonged to them.

We know the *King* of *Great-Britain* (or the
Queen in a female reign) is the *Supreme Head* of the
church of *England*, as by law eftablifhed ; which
church claims *power to decree rites or ceremonies, and
authority in controverfies of faith.*

But his *Holinefs* at *Rome* thinks this a bold in-
fringement of his prerogative, and univerfal jurifdiction in ecclefiaftical matters. Whofe word, then,
is to be taken ? How fhall we act a rational part
without *judging even of ourfelves which is in the right ?*
Or whether either of them be fo. Indeed there is
no doubt but his *Holinefs* is really the *Supreme Head*
of the church of *Rome* ; and, as fuch, has authority *therein* in matters of faith, worfhip, and difcipline. Thus alfo the *King* or *Queen* of *Great-Britain*, is doubtlefs the *Supreme Head* of the truly *primitive, apoftolical* church of *England*, as *lately eftablifhed* by *human laws.* But neverthelefs, it may
perhaps admit of fome difpute, whether *Jefus Chrift*
is not the *Supreme Head* of *his own* church ? and
confequently, whether thefe are not three different
churches, they having each of them a different *Supreme Head ?* It is of fome importance to us to be
fettled with regard to thefe points ; and they are
fuch as cannot be well determined without fome

exa-

examination, though perhaps a very little may suffice.

Thus it appears that a regard to our own interest ought to put us upon examining and judging for ourselves in religious concerns. The same thing might be argued from the faculty of reason itself, which is *common* to all. If we suppose an intelligent author of our nature, who had some *design* in giving us our present constitution, it is plain that his end in endowing us with faculties proper for the investigating of truth and right, was, that we should exercise them in this way. Each of our bodily organs, and animal faculties, has an apparent *final cause*. Our eyes are for seeing; our ears, for hearing; our hands, for handling; our feet, for walking, &c. Nor is it less apparent that our understandings were given us to be employed in the search of truth, and in embracing it. Truth is the natural object of reason, as much as any thing else is the proper object of that particular faculty or passion, to which God and nature have adapted it. Our obligation, therefore, to inquire after truth, and to judge what is right, may be found within us, in our own frame and constitution. This obligation is as universal as reason itself; for every one that is endowed with this faculty, is, by the very nature of it, obliged to exercise it in the pursuit of knowledge; especially of moral and religious knowledge. All men are not obliged to study the *mathematicks*, *law*, and *physick*. But all are obliged to acquaint themselves with their *duty* —what they owe to God, to their neighbour and themselves. If one man is to think and judge for all the rest of the species, why was reason given to all? why was it not confined to him alone who has a right to use it? In short, we may say with as much propriety, that we are to see only with another's

E 2 eyes,

eyes, hear with another's ears, fpeak with another's tongue, and walk with another's feet, and neglect our own ; as, that we are to think, and judge, and believe, with another's underftanding.

It appears, then, that reafon is no enemy to free inquiry, and private judgment, in religious matters. And I fhall now endeavour to fhew that the *Chriftian religion* is no enemy to it ; but, on the contrary, enjoins it upon us as a duty.

Our Lord Jefus Chrift, *the author and finifher of our faith*, conftantly appealed to the fenfes, and to the reafon of mankind, as the proper judges of his miracles, divine miffion and doctrine. He did not demand of men an implicit and blind belief in himfelf, without offering matter of conviction to their underftandings ; but put them upon examining in a fober rational way, whether he was authorized from heaven, or were an impoftor ; and fo, whether his doctrine were *of God, or whether he fpake of himfelf.* He reafons with the *Jews* in my text : he blames them for their blind attachment to the *Scribes* and *Pharifees*, their *fpiritual guides* ; and for not judging for themfelves in religious matters. Our Lord, pretended (at leaft) to prove his divine miffion to the unprejudiced reafon of mankind, in a fober, argumentative way. In difputing with the *Jews*, he appealed to their ancient writings whofe divine authority they acknowledged ; and to the miracles which he wrought, in order to convince them that he was the *Meffiah*. This is evident from almoft every page of the evangelical hiftory, notwithftanding what the difingenuous author of *Chriftianity not founded upon argument*, has confidently afferted upon this fubject, taking advantage of what fome weak Chriftians have advanced concerning the nature and grounds of *faith*. Whether

ther the arguments which our Lord uſed for the
conviction of the *Jews*, were concluſive or not, is
a queſtion, which I am not now concerned with.
But it is plain that he conſidered them as being ſo,
requiring people to examine them, and to judge
whether they were concluſive or not. Barely propoſing arguments to the conſideration of another,
is a diſclaiming of *authority* properly ſo called:
for it implies, that the arguments are to be judged
of by the reaſon of him to whom they are propoſed. I might bring many paſſages from the *Evan-*
geliſts, to ſhew that the method which our Lord
took to gain proſelytes, was to *reaſon* them into
faith. But I muſt content myſelf with quoting one
paſſage only to this purpoſe, for the preſent—
John v. 31. and onward, *If I bear witneſs of myſelf,*
my witneſs is not true [*i. e.* my teſtimony in my own
favour—my declaring myſelf to be the *Meſſiah*,
ought not to be depended upon as true, without
farther evidence.] *There is another that beareth*
witneſs of me—Ye ſent unto John, *and he bare wit-*
neſs unto the truth—But I have greater witneſs than
that of John ; *for the works that the Father hath given*
me to finiſh, the ſame works that I do, bear witneſs of
me, that the Father hath ſent me—Search the ſcrip-
tures, for in them ye think ye have eternal life ; *and*
they are they which teſtify of me—There is one that
accuſeth you, even Moſes, *in whom ye truſt. For*
had ye believed Moſes, *ye would have believed me.*
But if ye believe not his writings, how ſhall ye be-
lieve my words ? There cannot be a more explicit
appeal than this, to the reaſon and underſtandings
of men, or a fairer invitation given them to examine and judge for themſelves. And this alſo
ſhews that our Lord aimed at bringing men to believe in him, only by dint of argument. And as
our Lord performed his mighty works with a deſign to beget in thoſe that beheld them a rational

belief,

belief, a belief refulting from proper evidence ; fo the *Evangelifts* committed thofe facts to writing, that they might have a like effect upon thofe that had not been eye-witnefles of them—*Thefe things are written that ye might believe that Jefus is the Chrift the Son of God* ; *and that believing, ye might have life through his name.* John xx. 31.

The apoftles alfo conftantly incouraged free inquiry, as it is natural for honeft undefigning men to do. It is for the intereft of fome to difcourage it, and to keep people muffled up in darknefs and ignorance, that fo they may fubmit to their dictates with the more readinefs and humility. Their *craft is in danger* of being detected, and their doctrine, of being exploded, as foon as people have fo much prefumption as to open their eyes. Free inquiry bodes ill to the defign which they are engaged in ; for they are fenfible it will not be fafe for themfelves to be *knaves* any longer than others are *fools*. But he that has nothing in view but the intereft of truth and virtue, defires nothing more, than that perfons would give themfelves the trouble of a free and impartial examination. Now the apoftles knowing the goodnefs of their caufe, and following the example of their divine Mafter, made it their practice to incourage liberty and freedom of thought ; never intimating, as moft of their *pretended fuccefjors* have done, that this is hazardous to men's fouls.

In the apoftolic age there were many impoftors and enthufiafts ; falfe pretenders to infpiration, as there are at prefent, and as there have been in almoft every age of the chriftian church. And for this reafon the apoftles directed chriftians to examine the pretenfions of all, that fo they might diftinguifh betwixt really infpired perfons and deceivers—Thus 1 *John* iv. 1. *Beloved, believe not every fpirit* ; *but try the fpirits, whether they are of God* ;

*God ; for many falſe ſpirits are gonè out into the
world.* No one, ſurely, will be ſo abſurd as to
ſuppoſe this was a direction to *try deceivers only* ;
and not *true* prophets and apoſtles. For this would
ſuppoſe that they might be known one from the
other, without *trying* them at all : and then no examination of either of them would be neceſſary.
" Determine firſt, and then examine ;" is the *plea-
ſant* advice of ſome *grave divines :* But the apoſtles
exhort us to examine all things, before we believe
any thing. The *Jews* at *Berea* are celebrated,
Acts xvii. 10. and onwards, for not believing the
apoſtles themſelves without critically examining
their doctrine, and comparing it with the writings
of *Moſes* and the prophets : and in the ſame paſſage, an implicit cenſure at leaſt, is paſſed upon
the *Theſſalonians,* as being indolent, credulous, and
too eaſy of belief. The words of the hiſtorian are
theſe, *And the brethren——ſent away* Paul *and* Silas——
unto Berea ; *who coming there, went into the ſyna-
gogue of the* Jews. *Theſe were more noble than thoſe
of* Theſſalonica ; *for they received the word with all
readineſs of mind : and ſearched the ſcriptures daily
whether thoſe things were ſo.* By their *receiving the
word with all readineſs of mind,* nothing more is
here intended, than that they gave a ready and
candid attention to what *Paul* and *Silas* had to ſay :
Afterwards, like prudent and rational men, they
examined into the truth of it. And it follows immediately in the next verſe——*Therefore many of
them believed*——A natural conſequence of a free and
impartial inquiry into the grounds of the *chriſtian*
religion. I obſerved above, that the *Theſſalonians*
are cenſured in this paſſage, for their credulity,
and not uſing ſuitable precaution in receiving chriſtianity. And it is probable that the apoſtle *Paul*
had a view at this incurious and over credulous
humour of theirs, in his 1ſt Epiſtle to them, *Chap.* v.

ver. 21.   *Prove* (or examine) *all things,* fays he ;
hold faſt that which is good.   This advice was, indeed, proper for all ; but peculiarly fo for thofe
who were backward to examine, and forward to
believe, thefe being in the greateſt danger of being
feduced.

Again, What befides free inquiry after truth
and knowledge, does the apoſtle intend, *Phil.* xix.
10 ?   *And this I pray, that your love may abound yet
more and more in knowledge and in all judgment, that
ye may approve things that are excellent*—(Or as fome
underſtand thefe laſt words, *that ye may try things
that differ, and are controverted.*)   To the fame
purpoſe are the Words of this apoſtle, *Eph.* vi.
14, 15.   *That we be henceforth no more children, tof-
fed to and fro, and carried about with every wind of
doctrine, by the ſleight of men, and cunning crafti-
nefs whereby they lie in wait to deceive : but ſpeaking
the truth in love,* &c.   So St. *John* cautions the
elect lady and her children, againſt feducers and deceivers—*Many deceivers are entered into the world*—
Look to yourſelves—2 John 7, 8.   The apoſtle here
alludes to thofe deceivers *who confeſſed not that Jefus Chriſt was come in the fleſh.*   And in his *firſt*
Epiſtle he cautions thofe to whom he wrote, againſt
another kind of deceivers, whofe doctrine is equally fatal, *viz.* thofe who taught that faith without
works, denominates a man righteous—*Little children, let no man deceive you : He that doth righteoufnefs is righteous—He that committeth ſin is of the
devil*—1 John iii. 7, 8.   Thus alfo the apoſtle *Paul,*
Eph. v. 5, 6.—*Ye know that no whore-monger,* &c.
*hath any inheritance in the kingdom of Chriſt, and of
God.   Let no man deceive you with vain words : for
becaufe of thefe things cometh the wrath of God upon
the children of diſobedience.*   Do not all thefe exhortations given to chriſtians, to take care that *no
man deceive* them, imply that they are to examine

mine and judge for themfelves; and not to fubmit
implicitly to the dictates of any, even though they
pretend to a commiffion from heaven? Unlefs it
be their right and duty to do thus, nothing can
be more impertinent than exhortations of this
kind.

Although the apoftle *Paul* were an infpired writer, yet he is far from puttir.g on thofe dogmatical airs which are now too common amongft thofe
who do not pretend to infpiration. He often con-
defcends to make an appeal to the reafon and judgment of thofe to whom he writes, and invites them
to examine what he fays. Thus 1 *Cor.* x. 15. *I
fpeak as to wife men ; judge ye what I fay.* And
fo, *Chap.* i. *ver.* 12. *Judge in yourfelves, is it come-
ly,* &c.

In a controverfy betwixt the *Jewifh* and *Gentile* converts at *Rome,* the apoftle gave his own
fenfe concerning the point in debate ; he exhorted
them to mutual love and forbearance : and then,
like a reafonable, catholic man, and a friend to the
rights of private judgment, he concludes—*Let
every man be fully perfuaded in his own mind.*
Rom. xvi. 5.

When the *Jewifh* converts in *Galatia* (being ftill
zealoufly attached to the law of *Mofes*) were for
impofing certain opinions and practices upon the
Gentiles, the fame apoftle took the part of the *latter* ; and even enjoined it upon them to vindicate
their religious and chriftian rights againft all fuch
encroachments.—*Stand faft,* fays he, *in the liberty,
wherewith Chrift has made you free : (i. e.* affert
your freedom from the *Mofaic law,* and all the old
*Jewifh inftitutions) and be not again intangled with any
yoke of bondage.** *(i. e.* ftand up in defence of your
chriftian liberty, not only againft thefe your judai-

---

* *Gal.* v. 1.

zing

zing brethren ; but alſo againſt all others who ſhall
attempt to exerciſe any kind of ſpiritual tyranny
over you.) So that it is not left to the option of
chriſtians whether they will relinquiſh their natural
liberty in religious matters, or not ; they are commanded to aſſert it. God has given us abilities to
judge even of ourſelves what is right : and requires
us to improve them. He forbids us to *call any
man maſter upon earth.* And as he has forbidden us
to ſubmit implicitly to the dictates of any man ;
ſo he has alſo expreſly forbid all chriſtians to aſ-
ſume or uſurp any authority over their brethren.
Ye know, ſays our bleſſed Saviour, *that the Princes
of the* Gentiles *exerciſe dominion over them, and they
that are great, exerciſe authority upon them : But it
ſhall not be ſo among you. But whoſoever—will be
chief among you, let him be your ſervant, even as
the ſon of man came not to be miniſtered unto, but to
miniſter.* How does our Lord upbraid the *Scribes*
and *Phariſees,* who *ſat in* Moſes's *ſeat,* for aſſuming an unreaſonable authority, and affecting more
honour and ſubmiſſion than was due to them ? *The*
Scribes *and* Phariſees—*love the uppermoſt 'rooms at
feaſts, and the chief ſeats in the ſynagogues, and
greetings in the markets, and to be called of men,* Rabbi, Rabbi. *But be not ye called* Rabbi, *for one is
your maſter even Chriſt ; and all ye are brethren.*†
The firſt propagators of Chriſtianity carefully obſerved this prohibition. They were meek, humble, and charitable. They claimed no *dominion o-
ver the faith* of Chriſtians, but were content with
being *helpers of their joy.* 2 Cor. i. 24. They
*preached not themſelves to be the Lord or Lords, but
Chriſt Jeſus ; and themſelves the ſervants of Chriſtians for Jeſus ſake.* 2 Cor. iv. 5. This was the manner in which the holy apoſtles demeaned them-

---

* *Matt.* xx. † *Matt.* xxiii.

ſelves

felves in their office. But fince their day Ecclefiafticks have been for lefs humility and more
power. The ftyle of *fervants* is below their dignity: And they muft *be called of men Lords, Reverend* and *Right Reverend Fathers in God*, &c.
Their fellow chriftians and brethren muft approach
them upon the bended knee: Sovereign princes
muft think themfelves honoured in having the liberty to kifs the toe of an old *Monk*, who calls
himfelf Chrift's *Vicar*: And thus it is that the *Pope*
imitates him who was *meek* and *lowly in heart*; and
who condefcended to *wafh his difciples feet*.

I hope it appears from what has been faid, that
both reafon and fcripture oppofe the claims of
thofe arrogant men who love to *lord it over God's
heritage*; and had rather *have dominion over our
faith*, than be *helpers of our joy*: And that it is the
duty of chriftians to affert their right of private
judgment in religious matters, in oppofition to all
that are for ufurping authority over them. I pro-
mifed, in the next place, to confider the principal
objections againft this doctrine. But I believe I
need make no apology for deferring this to another
opportunity.

I fhall, however, beg leave, from what has been
faid already, to look upon the point as proved;
and fo to clofe with a few reflections fuitable to the
fubject.

It appears, then, that all who any ways difcourage freedom of inquiry and judgment in religious
matters, are, fo far forth as they are guilty of this,
incroachers upon the natural rights of mankind;
that they fet up their own authority in oppofition
to that of almighty God: and that they are enemies
to truth, and the gofpel of Jefus Chrift.—They
are incroachers upon the natural rights of mankind,
becaufe it is the natural right and privilege of
every man to make the beft ufe he can of his own
in-

intellectual faculties—They set up their own authority in opposition to that of almighty God, because God has not only given us liberty to examine and judge for ourselves ; but exprefly required us to do it—They are enemies to truth, and the gospel of Jesus Chrift ; because free examination is the way to truth, and the gospel in particular, gains ground the faster, the more its doctrines and evidences are examined.—While other tyrants enflave the bodies of men, these throw their chains and fetters upon the mind, which (as the *Jews* faid of themselves) was *born free*; and which ought not to be *in bondage to any man :* but only to the *Father of Spirits*. If it be asked who these spiritual invaders are, it may be answered, All in general who set themselves up to judge for their neighbours ; All who are for imposing their own opinions upon others : All who any ways diftrefs and afflict fuch as differ from them in their religious fentiments : All who make ufe of any other weapons befides thofe of reafon and argument, in order to demolifh error, and propagate truth. If a man has a right to judge for himfelf, certainly no other has a right to judge for him : And to attempt it, is to ftrike at the moft valuable intereft of a man confidered as a reafonable creature.

Thofe that are guilty of this crime in the higheft degree, are fuch as inflict capital punifhments upon thofe that embrace opinions contrary to their own. The heathens fometimes practifed this barbarity among themfelves before chriftianity made its appearance in the world. Afterwards they united their force againft the doctrine of Chrift, as the moft dangerous *herefy* that had ever been heard of : and butchered millions. Scarce had they laid down the practice, when Chriftians, filled with more than pagan Cruelty, took it up, and perfecuted one another ; Nor is it quite laid afide to this
day,

day, in some parts of Christendom. *The mother
of harlots,* who has long *made herself drunk with the
blood of the martyrs of Jesus,* has still her *inquisition*;
and is frequently adding to the number of those
whom St. *John* saw in his vision, *under the altar,*
while they *cried with a loud voice, saying—How long,
O Lord, holy and true! dost thou not judge, and a-
venge our blood on them that dwell on the earth!*

In a somewhat lower degree are they chargeable
with the same crime, who punish *dissenters* and
nonsubscribers, by fines and imprisonments, and by
depriving them of those civil privileges, emolu-
ments and honours, which, as good subjects and
friends, to the state, they might justly expect. It
is well known in what church this inhuman practice has been carried to a prodigious length : and
in which it is not yet wholly laid aside. It is well
that, not *Jesus Christ,* but *another Person,* is said
to be the *supreme Head* of this church. For it
would be absurd to suppose, that He who said his
kingdom was not of this world, should allow of any
such practice among the members of that body of
which He is the *Head.*

Again : Another practice akin to those mentioned above, and which has an apparent tendency
to hinder men from judging for themselves, is that of
Creed-making; setting up human tests of *orthodoxy,*
instead of the infallible word of God ; and making
other terms of christian communion than those
explicitly pointed out in the gospel. For any
man, or any set of men whatever, to do thus, is
plainly to arrogate to themselves the right of judging for their neighbours ; and to deter people, as
far as they are able, from seeing with their own
eyes, and *judging even of themselves what is right.*
Indeed this practice is not so criminal as that of
persecuting and murthering men for their religious
sentiments : for any reasonable man had rather be
the

the object of a thousand *anathema*'s than have his
life, or even his temporal subſtance taken from
him. But ſtill, if theſe *faith-makers* I am ſpeaking of are ſo compaſſionate as *only to give their
brethren to the devil*, for not ſubmitting to their
doctrines and decrees, even this has ſome tendency
to intimidate them ; eſpecially ſuch as are naturally
of a weak and puſillanimous make. For when a
creed is begun, or eked out with ſeveral reverend,
eccleſiaſtical curſes ; and when it is confidently affirmed, that *unleſs a man believe faithfully* every article contained in it, *he ſhall without doubt periſh
everlaſtingly* ; it cannot be ſuppoſed, that the generality of people ſhould ever have the courage to
heſitate in the leaſt concerning the truth of it, although it may be really an affront to common ſenſe,
a medly of nonſenſe and contradiction. Nor are
there wanting innumerable inſtances of perſons,
who have, in this way, been firſt frighted out of
their ſenſes, and then into the belief of the groſſeſt
abſurdities ; and paying a ſacred regard to them
under the notion of their being orthodox, ſoul-ſav-
ing truths and divine myſteries—ſuch as are not to
be examined *with reaſon*, but to be believed and
adored *without it*.

It is indeed pretended that all theſe different methods of keeping men from exerciſing their own rational faculties, are entered upon with a very pious and
godly deſign ; with an holy zeal to keep hereſies out
of the church ; to reclaim thoſe that are unſound
in the faith ; and to preſerve the chriſtian verity
pure and undefiled. But the proud, domineering,
unchriſtian ſpirit that has been betrayed by theſe holy
murtherers, robbers and faith-impoſers, leaves us
but little room to think that they were actuated by
a real concern for the intereſts of chriſtianity, and
the ſalvation of men's ſouls. However, to let
alone their views and intentions which we have little

tle or nothing to do with, thefe practices themfelves are unjuftifiable ; they are imperious
and tyrannical : and contrary to the fpirit and
doctrines of the gofpel. They are an infringe-
ment upon thofe rights of confcience, which ought
to be facred ; they have an apparent tendency to
prevent all improvements in religious knowledge,
and to entail ignorance, error, and fuperftition upon
future generations. What improvements can we
fuppofe would have been made in the feveral arts
and fciences comparable to the prefent, had the
ftudy of them been incumbered with fuch reftraints,
and almoft infuperable difficulties ?

Let us fuppofe, for example, that fome great
Monarch a few centuries ago, together with the
Philofophers of that age, had interpofed with their
authority in the *fciences :* Let us fuppofe that an
oath of fupremacy to the *King,* or *Queen,* had been
required ; and devifed in fuch terms as thefe
—*That the King or Queen for the time being, is the
fupreme head of the fociety* [or *church*] *of* Philofophers——*Vefted with all power to exercife all manner
of* philofophical *difcipline : And other* philofophical
perfons have no manner of jurifdiction philofophical,
*but by and under the King's or Queen's moft Excellent
Majefty* ; *who hath full power and authority to hear
and determine all manner of caufes* philofophical,
and to reform and correct all philofophical *errors,
herefies, enormities and abufes whatfoever, within his,
or her realm.* Let us fuppofe farther, that *philofophical creeds and articles of faith* had been compofed, and authoritatively iffued out with certain *mi-
natory* and *damnatory* claufes ; and that they had
been regiftered among the *other laws of the land.* Let
us fuppofe farther, that *philofophical courts* had been
erected, where *hereticks in philofophy,* and all *non-
fubfcribers to the philofophy by law eftablifhed,* were
to be arraigned, harraffed, fined, whipped, hang-
ed

ed or burnt. I say, if such measures as these had been entered upon a few centuries ago, must we not suppose that they would have been very absurd and injurious? Must we not suppose, that they would have damped the greatest and most enterprizing *Genius*'s ; and so have been a means of keeping the world in ignorance? Would not this have prevented those valuable improvements in natural knowledge, which the world is blest with at present? Had such methods been taken seasonably, might it not have been *Heresy* still, to think this earth a *globe?* to deny that the sun *revolves* about us once every twenty-four hours ? or to question the *equality* of the sun and moon ? And might not the *orthodox* philosophy at this day, have possibly been that concerning the *great cow* and *tortoise*, &c ? In short we cannot think of supporting and propagating the sciences, by dint of *authority*, without smiling. And it is equally ridiculous to attempt to propagate religious knowledge and the doctrines of the gospel, by *authority*. And every one that pleases may easily see what attempts of this nature have usually issued in ; and what must necessarily be the effect of them, *viz. ignorance* and *hypocrisy*. Error, as well as *iniquity*, may be *established by a law*. And when it is so, a man must either subscribe to it, contrary to his sentiments ; or seriously embrace it for truth : A sad dilemma ! when a man is thus forced to be a knave or a fool ! Mankind in general seem to be quite indolent enough, backward enough to examine into moral and religious subjects, without those unnatural restraints which are put upon them by the setting up of authority in matters of faith. There are indeed some foolish and conceited men who take a pleasure in being singular in their opinions ; and who never suppose they *think freely enough*, till they are run *wild* and *mad* ; and have rejected every thing that others

have

have believed before. But thefe inftances are not
frequent. Men are generally too prone to follow
the multitude, to embrace implicitly the tenets
of their *fpiritual inftructors*, their *fore-fathers*, their
good mothers and nurfes ; and to fall in with the
opinions of the rich and powerful, which is the
road to wealth and prefer ment. And there is really much more need of incouraging freedom of
thought, and an inquifitive turn of mind, by
handfome gratuities ; than there is of keeping people in the old beaten track by the terror of penal
laws, gibbets, inquifitions, *fpiritual* courts, and
carnal curfes. Whatever is pretended, thefe com-
pulfive methods were not thofe by which *the truth
as it is in Jefus*, was at firft propagated and defended : neither can they be of any fervice to the caufe
of truth and religion at prefent. A pecuniary
mulct may impoverifh a man in this world ; but
it cannot make him *rich in faith*, and an *heir of the
Kingdom*——The rack may torture his limbs ; but
it cannot draw out the fting from a guilty confcience.——A dark and filthy dungeon may throw us
into a mortal diftemper ; but it cannot bring light
and health into our minds, and make our *fouls profper*——A burning faggot may fet our bodies in a
light blaze ; but it has no tendency to illuminate
the underftanding. To attempt to *dragoon* men
into found orthodox *Chriftians*, is as unnatural
and fruitlefs as to attempt to *dragoon* them into
good *poets*, *phyficians* or *mathematicians*. A blow
with a club may fracture a man's fkull ; but I fuppofe he will not think and reafon the more clearly
for that ; though he may poffibly believe the more
orthodoxly, according to the opinions of fome.
And upon this account it muft be confeffed that
thofe who make ufe of thefe methods to propagate
their fentiments, act very prudently : for their doctrines are generally fuch as are much more readily
F   embraced

embraced by a man after his brains are knocked
out, than while he continues in his fenfes, and of
a found mind.

I fhall conclude with the words of the apoftle
Paul to *Timothy*, in which he points out the method of defending and propagating the doctrines of
the gofpel——*The fervant of the Lord fays he, muft
not ftrive ; but be gentle unto all men ; apt to teach ;
patient ; in meeknefs, inftructing thofe that oppofe
themfelves, if God peradventure will give them repentance to the acknowledging of the truth.*

SERMON

SERMON IV.

Objections confidered.

LUKE XII. 54——57.

*And he faid alfo to the people, When ye fee a
cloud rife out of the weft, ftraightway ye fay,
There cometh a fhower; and fo it is.*

*And when ye fee the fouth-wind blow, ye fay,
There will be heat; and it cometh to pafs.*

*Ye hypocrites, ye can difcern the face of the
fky, and of the earth: but how is it, that ye
do not difcern this time?*

*Yea, and why even of yourfelves judge ye not
what is right?*

HAVING, in the preceeding difcourfe, proved the right and duty of free inquiry and
private judgment in matters of religion, by direct
and plain arguments both from reafon and revelation, there was, perhaps, no occafion for my exercifing your patience any further, by entering upon a
confideration of the *objections* that have been raifed
againft this Doctrine. For no objections can fignify
any thing againft a doctrine once proved true in fact:
However, fince fome men may think themfelves ill
ufed, unlefs their arguments are diftinctly confidered, I fhall devote the following hour to examine the
principal objections againft the doctrine of the fore-
going difcourfe, fetting them in the ftrongeft point
of light I am able. The fpiritual tyrants and lord-
ly bigots of the earth have indeed *triumphed glori-*
oufly

oufly, as though they had gained a mighty victory over freedom of thought, *their old and mortal enemy*; and laid her *bleeding* and *gasping* at their feet. But whether thefe are the triumphs of *real heroes*, or only the vain *gasconades* and *Te Deums* of *imaginary conquerors*, will, perhaps, be eafy to determine, when we come to take a view of their *weapons*, and to fee the manner in which they have employed them.

I fhall not have much regard to order and method in propofing the objections now to be confidered; but mention them juft as they prefent themfelves to my mind. And, in the *firft* place, it may be objected,

1. " That God himfelf, under the *mofaic difpen-*
" *fation*, required that *idolaters*, and *diffenters from*
" *the eftablished church*, fhould be punifhed with
" death." From hence it may be argued, " That
" uncontrouled liberty in religious matters ought
" not to be allowed of; but the *true church* is ob-
" liged in duty to reftrain and correct infidels and
" fchifmaticks; and all in general that fhe judges
" unfound in the faith." To this it may be anfwered,

1ft. That we cannot argue from what was lawful under the *jewish* œconomy, to what is lawful fince that is abolished, and fuperfeded by another fo different from it as the *christian.* There might be, and doubtlefs were, fome peculiar reafons for authorizing and enjoining fuch a *difcipline* then, which do not take place at prefent. This might be as peculiar to *Judaifm* as *circumcifion*, or the *facrificing* of beafts, *&c.* And in reality it does not any more follow from the *Jews* being commanded to extirpate idolaters, that chriftians may deftroy heathens and hereticks, than it does from *Abraham*'s being commanded to facrifice his *fon*, that all *parents* may and ought to facrifice their *children* now.

It is to be remembered, that *Judaifm* was at leaft as much a *political* as a *religious* inftitution. The
Jews

Jews had God for their immediate *king* and *lawgiver*, both in *church* and *ſtate*. Their *civil* and *ecclefiaſtical* polity were blended together ; and being derived from the ſame ſource, every violation of the law of *Mofes* might be confidered and puniſhed as an offence againſt the ſtate, in a greater or leſs degree: And *idolatry* being in theſe circumſtances equivalent to *high treaſon*, it is not ſtrange that a capital puniſhment ſhould be annexed to it. But the caſe is much altered ſince the promulgation of the chriſtian religion. Chriſt's kingdom is not at all *a kingdom of this world.* It is wholly a religious inſtitution. The laws, the penalties, the rewards of it, are wholly of a ſpiritual nature: And men are to be won over to it, and kept in it, only by ſpiritual and moral means.

But 2*dly*, If the *true church* ought to puniſh ſuch as ſhe looks upon to be erroneous, heretical or ſchifmatical, then a war muſt immediately commence in *Chriſtendom*; and continue 'till all are deſtroyed, but one party: For each ſect thinks itſelf in the right; and that all the reſt are tinctured with hereſy : This muſt certainly be the conſequence of this maxim, that the right of uſing violence and perſecution is the prerogative of the true church; which one would think ſufficient to convince any reaſonable man, that the maxim is falſe. Beſides, from whence comes this doctrine, that true orthodox chriſtians have a right to perſecute hereticks and unbelievers? (*i. e.* to be *more wicked* and *immoral* than hereticks and unbelievers ?) The ſcripture, indeed, (and experience very often) teaches us, that *thoſe who will live godly in Chriſt Jeſus, muſt* ſuffer perſecution ; but not that they muſt *perſecute others.*

But perhaps it will be objected in the *ſecond* place,

2. " That our Lord himſelf required his apoſ-
" tles to uſe external force, in order to bring men
" over to the true faith, if gentler methods failed

F 3 " of

" of fuccefs." The objection will be taken from the *parable of the fupper*, Luke xiv. When the guefts that were bidden, refufed the invitation, the mafter of the feaft is reprefented as faying to his fervant, *ver.* 23. *Go out into the highways and hedges, and* compel *them to come in, that my houfe may be filled.* " Now as the fervant was commanded " to *compel* the guefts to come to the fupper, fo " the apoftles were injoined to ufe external violence, " if neceffary, in order to bring men over to a be- " lief of the gofpel; from whence it follows that " men are not left to their freedom in religious " matters." The

1*ft* Thing I would obferve with relation to this objection is, that great caution is neceffary in the application of parables and allegories, left the fimilitude fhould be carried farther than was originally intended. Nor is it by any means fafe to build fuch a doctrine, (or rather fuch a practice) as that of compulfion in religious matters, but upon the moft plain and exprefs command.

2*dly*, This parable, at moft, only authorizes the compelling *infidels* to embrace the gofpel: And fo it has nothing to do with the controverfies amongft the different fects of chriftians.

3*dly*, Although it fhould be allowed, that this parable injoined the *infpired* apoftles to compel men, by external violence, to embrace chriftianity, it will not follow that *uninfpired* men fince, men who have no commiffion *immediately* from heaven, have a right to do the fame.

4*thly*, It is to be obferved, that, according to the parable, the perfons to be compelled are not the *fame* who had before obftinately rejected the kind invitation given to them; but fuch as had not yet been fent to. For when the mafter fends out his fervant a fecond time, to compel people to *come in,*

it

it follows—*For I say unto you that those men who were bidden, shall not taste of my supper.* So that even according to this parable, those who will not be perfuaded by gentle methods, are to be given over, and not to have any farther means ufed with them. From whence it follows,

5*thly*, That none at all are to be compelled by external violence : for we cannot fuppofe that force fhould be applied firft of all ; and before other methods prove ineffectual, if at all.

6*thly*, Either the apoftles did not underftand this as a command to ufe violence in propagating chriftianity, or they neglected to obey it ; neither of which can be fuppofed, had there really been fuch a command. They never attempted to ufe force ; but declared, on the contrary, that *the weapons of their warfare were not carnal, but mighty through God to the pulling down of ftrong holds*, &c. 2 Cor. x. 4.

7*thly*, That this cannot be the fenfe of the parable, appears from hence, that it is, in the nature of the thing, impoffible to *force* men really to believe the gofpel, and become good chriftians, though one had more *dragoons* to employ in this *pious work*, than *Louis* the XIVth fent to convert the *Huguenots.* Faith and repentance are the work of *reafon* and the *fpirit* of God ; and cannot be wrought in a man by a *cudgel*, a *fword*, or a *gallows*.

8*thly*, Were this in itfelf poffible, how could twelve *unarmed* apoftles, who were allowed to carry only a *ftaff* with them in their journies, convert the whole world by force of arms?

9*thly*, And *laftly* ; After all the flourifh that has been made with this paffage by *Roman-Catholicks* and *popifh Proteftants*, the word we render *compel*, as often fignifies a *moral*, as a *phyfical* compulfion. And the fubject here fpoken of, neceffarily determines it to fuch a fignification in this place. It is as if the *mafter of the feaft* had faid to his fervant,

F 4 " Since

" Since the perfons before invited to my fupper,
" [the *Jews*] refufe to come, go to others, [the
" *Gentile* nations] and give them the fame invitati-
" on : And ufe the greateft importunity with them ;
" reafon with them, exhort and perfuade them ;
" ufe all rational methods to convince them, 'and
" bring them in."

But I muft proceed to another objection : And perhaps one may be urged in fome fuch manner as this--

3. " If every man is allowed to think and judge
" for himfelf, the confequence will be that many
" will fall into erroneous and hurtful opinions. This
" doctrine opens a door for herefies to enter into
" the church : it gives men a liberty to trample up-
" on all our creeds and confeffions of faith ; to depart
" from the doctrines of their pious fore-fathers ; and
" to defpife their fpiritual guides. And what will
" this iffue in, but the overthrow of all religion ?"
To this objection I would anfwer,

1*ft*. That it does not follow from men's being at
liberty to judge for themfelves, and to chufe their
own religion, that they are at liberty to judge wrong,
and to reject the true religion, let it be what it will.
If they are obliged to judge and chufe for themfelves at all, they are obliged to judge truly and
juftly, and to reject only what is wrong. The right
of private judgment does not imply, that it is indifferent whether a man judges truly, or not, any
more than a man's right of difpofing of his own
property, implies that he may as innocently fquan-
der it away in rioting and drunkennefs, as pay his
debts with it, or appropriate it to charitable ufes.
As a man has not a right to do what is wrong
with his own fubftance, fo neither has he any, to
judge wrong with his own underftanding. He is
under a moral obligation to reject error, and to embrace truth, as far as he is able to detect the former,
and to difcern the latter.

2*dly*, As the right of private judgment, does not leave men at liberty to judge wrong, and to embrace a falfe religion; fo neither has the exercifing that right any tendency to miflead men, as the objection fuppofes. The tendency of it is directly the contrary way. Free examination, weighing arguments *for*, and *againft*, with impartiality, is the way to find the truth. Who imagines that free inquiry into philofophical fubjects, has any tendency to lead men into a wrong idea of the natural world? No one was ever fo infatuated as to affert this. And it is in all refpects as improbable, that free inquiry into religious fubjects fhould lead us into wrong notions concerning the moral world. One would think that a man who had received his religious principles upon mature and deliberate confideration, and fo had in his own mind rational arguments to fupport them, could not have the leaft apprehenfion of their fuffering any thing by being thoroughly fcanned and examined to the bottom. Error and impofture fly from the light, like the *owl* and *bat:* But truth and honefty, like the noble *eagle*, face to the fun. The caufe of error and fuperftition may fuffer by a critical examination; its fecurity is to lurk in the dark : But the true religion flourifhes the more, the more people exercife their right of private judgment. This is apparent: And therefore it is no uncharitablenefs to fuppofe, that all who are backward to have their doctrines called in queftion, and to ftand a fair trial at the bar of impartial reafon, have at leaft fome fecret fufpicion in their own minds, that they will not ftand the teft, and *come forth as gold when it is tried*, but be found no better than *drofs*. We pay but a bad compliment to our religion, when we cry out that it is in danger, if men are left to the free exercife of their own rational faculties in judging of it. A man that
is

is confcious his caufe at court is good, chufes it
fhould be tried by the moft fevere and critical eye.
But he that either knows, or fufpects, he has a dir-
ty one, had much rather that people would fpare
themfelves the trouble of examining into its merits,
and take his own word for the goodnefs of it. But

3*dly*, As to the lamentable havock which the objection fuppofes will be made amongft our *creeds*
and *formularies*, if the doctrine of free inquiry fhould
prevail; this is, doubtlefs, a very natural confequence : for this would probably prove fatal, at leaft
to many articles contained in them. For it is plain
that many of them are ftuffed with the moft ridiculous jargon, and are as contrary to fcripture, as they
are to common fenfe. But this inftead of being an
objection againft free inquiry, is one of the ftrongeft arguments for it. If thefe creeds and formularies were true, agreeable to reafon and revelation,
the more thoroughly they are examined the better;
for then their truth would appear : But if they are
falfe, it is ftill beft they fhould be examined, in order to their being exploded. It is no matter how
old, or how *new* they are. Truth does not die with
age, and then revive again, as is fabled of the *phæ-
nix :* it flourifhes in immortal youth. Error may
indeed become *venerable* and *gray-headed* with length
of time : but a falfhood of a thoufand years ftanding, remains as much a falfhood as ever, although
it may have been confecrated by the church, and
tranfmitted to pofterity in a creed. Whatever
truths it may have had to *keep it company* ; and
however it may have been preferved amidft the
ftorms that have beat upon the church, it is only
like one of *Noah's unclean beafts* preferved in the
ark, amongft thofe of a pure, and more ufeful nature. There is nothing more foolifh and fuperftitious than a veneration for *ancient* creeds and doctrines, *as fuch* ; and nothing more unworthy a reafonable

fonable creature, than to value *principles* by
their *age*, as fome do their *wines*. But indeed this
is as common as it is ridiculous. With many
people, " Antiquity! Antiquity!" is the cry:
And, " Who will be fo hardy as to difpute the
" truth of what was believed a thoufand years a-
" go?" Juft as if what was falfe formerly, were
not fo ftill; but might be ripened and refined by age
into a *doctrine of grace*. Moft things are, indeed,
changed by *time*. *Time* makes the child a man:
Time makes the ignorant wife: *Time* often turns a
friend into a foe, and foe into a friend: *The fafhion
of the world paffeth away* by *time*. And *time* fhall
change the whole face of nature. But truth, like
the *Father of lights*, is without *variablenefs*, or *fhadow of turning*. To proceed,

4*thly*, It is fuppofed in the laft mentioned objection, that freedom of inquiry will naturally bring
our *fpiritual guides* into contempt, and weaken their
authority. To this I reply, That it cannot poffibly
be of any difadvantage to the fober and rational part
of the *clergy*; but has a tendency to make them more
efteemed. But as to the vain and proud; the ignorant and affuming; the enthufiaftic and fuperftitious; it has doubtlefs a natural tendency to bring
thefe into contempt: And the fooner the better,
that fo they may not have fo much power to do
mifchief. Thefe are the perfons that are generally
the moft averfe to people's feeing and judging for
themfelves: And the reafon why they are fo, is
too apparent to need mentioning. But

5*thly*, And *laftly*, Upon fuppofition that the caufe
of truth and real religion, might fuffer in fome refpects, by perfons exercifing their right of private
judgment; yet this is no juft reafon for denying them
fuch a liberty. This right is given them by God
and nature, and the gofpel of Chrift: And no man
has

has a right to deprive another of it, under a notion that he will make an ill ufe of it, and fall into erroneous opinions. We may as well pick our neighbour's pocket, for fear he fhould fpend his money in debauchery, as take from him his right of judging for himfelf, and chufing his religion, for fear he fhould judge amifs and abufe his liberty.

But I muft haften to another objection, which is frequently urged with a great deal of confidence, and very little reafon. It is near akin to that laft mentioned ; and may be put into fome fuch form as this,

4. " If all are left at liberty to chufe their own
" religion, and to enjoy it unmolefted, we fhall
" have innumerable *fects* fpringing up amongft us ;
" which tends to *confufion*, and deftroys the *peace*
" and *unity of the church*. It is therefore expedient
" that the *governors of the church* fhould injoin up-
" on all the belief of certain articles of faith, and
" the obfervation of certain modes and rites of
" worfhip. Without fome common rule of faith,
" worfhip, and difcipline, beyond what the fcriptures
" contain, there can be no fufficient bond of union
" amongft chriftians. And fo the church muft in-
" evitably be crumbled to pieces; whereas there
" ought to be *no fchifm in that fpiritual body.*"

With relation to this objection I would obferve,

1*ft.* That if any rule of faith, worfhip, and difcipline, befides that which our Saviour and his apoftles have left us, be neceffary in order to the peace and good government of the church, then the church had no peace and was not well governed during the apoftolic age. For chriftians had then no common rule of faith, worfhip, and difcipline befides that which they received from our Lord himfelf, or his apoftles, who were under the extraordinary influence and direction of his fpirit. Which rule is tranfmitted to us in the writings of the new teftament;

teftament; and is fufficient *now*, for the regulation of the church, if it was *then*. That this was fuffici-ent then, is not denied ; and therefore it cannot be deficient at prefent. But

2*dly*, If any farther regulations had been necef-fary in order to preferve the peace and unity of the church, it is ftrange that neither our bleffed Savi-our, who *loved the church and gave himfelf for it*, nor the apoftles, who liv'd and dy'd in the fervice of the church, fhould have taken more care to provide for its peace and profperity. Can we fuppofe that they did their work to the halves, and left others to finifh and perfect it?

3*dly*, Who gave the governors of the church any authority in matters of faith, worfhip, and dif-cipline? Do we find one word of it in fcripture? No. The church of Chrift, as fuch, has no legif-lator befides Chrift himfelf, whom the Father *has made head over all things to the church*. And what-ever church that be, whofe rulers have any power of legiflation, fo far forth it is not the church of Chrift. For Chrift equally forbids all his difciples to affume authority over their brethren ; and to fub-mit to any who fhall arrogate to themfelves any au-thority in matters of a religious concern.

4*thly*, And *laftly*, As no order of men has any authority to enjoin the belief of any articles of faith ; or the ufe of any modes of worfhip, not exprefly and explicitly pointed out in the fcriptures ; fo nei-ther has the injoining any fuch a tendency to pre-ferve the peace and harmony of the church ; but directly the contrary. The confufion and diforder that have hitherto been in the church, have not a-rifen from chriftians exercifing their own judgment, and worfhipping God according to their confciences ; (though in a manner fomewhat different from others) but from the pride and infolence of thofe who deny

their

their chriftian brethren this liberty ; and who undertake to prefcribe authoritatively to others what
they fhall believe, and how they fhall worfhip.
Were it not for the turbulent, domineering fpirit
of fome Ecclefiafticks, who defire more power than
Chrift faw fit to intruft them with, there would be
but little of that wrangling and difcord which have
hitherto difturbed the peace of the church. The
divifions and contentions that have hitherto happen-
ned, and ftill fubfift in the chriftian church, are
all, in a manner, owing to the unchriftian temper
and conduct of thofe who could not content themfelves with *fcripture orthodoxy*, with the fimple and
fpiritual worfhip of the Father, enjoined by our Saviour, and with the *platform of church difcipline* contained in the new teftament ; but muft go to coining new articles of faith, new modes and rites of
worfhip, making new canons, and prefcribing new
rules for the regulation of the church. It is about
thefe comparatively novel inventions, that the governors and *fathers of the church*, (as fome affect to
call them) have generally been more warm and zealous, than about an holy and godly life. They
have ordinarily given pretty good quarter to the
moft vicious and debauched of men, provided their
own authority was acknowledged ; their own peculiar whimfies embraced ; and their *decent* (or rather
ridiculous) *forms* and *ceremonies* were religioufly obferved. But the moft peaceable, fober and virtuous perfons, who would not fubmit to their tyrannical yoke, have all along been created with contempt and inhumanity, as being hereticks, fchifmaticks, *&c*. And all this perhaps only for not
practifing fuch rites, as have no more relation to
chriftianity than *telling beads*, or *cracking the fingers* ;
and for not believing fuch doctrines as have no more
to do with the gofpel of Jefus Chrift, than the idle
ftories of *Bell and the dragon*, or *Tobit and his dog*.

Her

Here is the true fource of religious difcord. Had Ecclefiafticks, inftead of *lording it over God's heritage*, and fetting up their own authority in the room of Chrift's, put on *the meeknefs and gentlenefs of Chrift* ; and fet a better *example to the flock* ; had they endeavoured to remove all *ftumbling blocks* out of the way, inftead of infifting upon indifferent things as neceffary terms of chriftian communion ; had they taught and practifed *the weightier matters of law*, inftead of fpending their zeal upon trifles ; had they taught mutual forbearance and charity, inftead of fomenting a furious party fpirit, and exciting ignorant bigots to rail at fober peaceable chriftians ; had they done thus, the peace and harmony of the church might have been very well preferved, without *creeds* and *formularies*, or an exact uniformity in faith and worfhip. Our bleffed Saviour and his apoftles, it is plain, have left matters fo that there may be a confiderable latitude and difference in the fentiments of good chriftians, and in the manner of their worfhip. But *His* ambaffadors, and *their* fucceffors, it feems, have found out that this is a great defect. Accordingly they undertake to fupply it, under the notion of preferving the peace of the church. And this is what has hitherto been, and muft continue to be, the caufe of angry debates and endlefs contentions ; a means of dividing the church, inftead of uniting it ; and of infpiring chriftians with mutual rage, inftead of mutual love and brotherly affection.

It may be objected, in the *fifth* place.

5. " That the doctrine of private judgment is " inconfiftent with that of a ftanding miniftry in " the chriftian church, appointed by Chrift to " inftruct people in religious matters. An order " of men was divinely inftituted to do the office of " *inftructors*, or *teachers* in the church: Confe- " quently there muft be others whofe duty it is to
" *learn*

" *learn of them*, and not to pretend to a right of
" judging for themfelves. It is incumbent upon
" the *Laity* to go to their fpiritual guides; and
" to receive their inftructions with humility
" and reverence, without pretending to difpute the
" truth of what they affert in the name of the
Lord." This, we know, is the manner in which
many exprefs themfelves upon this fubject. And
the pofitive, dogmatical air with which moft of
our pulpit-difcourfes are delivered is a fufficient
proof, that thefe fentiments are adopted by the
generality of thofe that ftile themfelves the *ambaffadors of Jefus Chrift.* But to this objection it may
be anfwered in the *firft* place,

1ft. That, allowing there is, fomewhere in the
chriftian church, a fet of men whofe office it is to
teach authoritatively, and by divine right, ftill
people muft judge for themfelves *who thefe men are.*
Almoft all publick teachers of religion pretend a
divine right to be fo. But they do not all teach
the fame doctrines. How then fhall we know
whom to chufe for our fpiritual inftructor, without examining into, and judging upon, the claims
of thofe who demand our attention, and the direction of our underftandings and confciences?
But

2dly. Suppofing we have found who thefe perfons are, to whom this authority is given, it does
not follow that they are to be *implicitly* believed in
every thing they fay, or even in any thing. No
man is to be believed implicitly, unlefs he is infallible: but infallibility is not neceffarily connected with a divine right to teach. Although it
fhould be allowed, that kings reign by divine right,
in the higheft fenfe pleaded for by the advocates
for *paffive obedience* and *non-refiftence*, ftill it is poffible that they may make an ill ufe of their power;
command things exprefly forbidden by God, and
forbid

forbid what God has injoined. In either of thefe cafes, it will be allowed that they have no title to the active obedience of their fubjects. So alfo, he that has a divine right to inftruct others in religion may poffibly fpeak falfe, either ignorantly, or with defign : And if he does fo, no one will be fo extravagant as to fay, that he ought to be believed. God has given him a right to teach ; but it is only to teach truth ; if therefore he *teaches for doctrines the commandments of men*, and lyes, for the gofpel of Chrift, he exceeds his commiffion ; and has no more right to demand our affent, than any other lyar or deceiver, who is *unconfecrated*. So that let us carry our idea of the authority of chriftian teachers ever fo high, yet if we ftop fhort of infallibility, we are in reafon obliged to examine all that they fay, and either to receive or reject it, as evidence of its truth does, or does not appear. Even the apoftles themfelves, (who were divinely authorized teachers in a much higher and more proper fenfe than any fet of men can pretend to be at this day) never pretended to fuch a right of dictating to others what they fhould believe and do, as interfered with the right of private judgment. Chriftian teachers in after ages are (or at leaft ought to be) only *commentators* upon the fcriptures : and we cannot fuppofe their *commentaries* have greater weight and authority than the *text* itfelf.

A man of fuperior knowledge and integrity may be of great advantage in a chriftian fociety, by helping his brethren and neighbours to a right underftanding of the fcriptures, although he be not infallible, and although nothing he advances is to be received for truth without examination and proof. We have *authorized* profeffors and teachers of *law*, *phyfic*, *philofophy*, &c. who are doubtlefs helpful to fuch as devote themfelves to the ftudy of thefe fciences. But who ever imagined that the end of

G   their

their inftitution was authoritatively to dictate what
is true in their refpective provinces, in fuch a fenfe as
to preclude examination ; and to render it unneceffary for their pupils and auditors to enquire into the
foundation of what they affert ? This is fo far from
being the cafe, that 'tis confeffed their chief bufinefs
is to open and enlarge the minds of their fcholars ;
to propofe reafons and arguments to their underftandings, and to endeavour to make them apprehend their force; and in this way to bring them acquainted with the fciences to which they refpectively
apply themfelves. A *mathematician* would think his
pupil had made but a fmall proficiency, if he only
believed, upon *authority*, all the propofitions in
Euclid, and other books of the fame kind, without
feeing what principles they were grounded upon, or
being able to demonftrate them himfelf. And as
the bufinefs of an inftructor is not to inforce certain
dogma's purely by dint of authority ; fo the bufinefs of a learner is not to receive for truth whatever his inftructor, in any fcience, advances as fuch ;
but to exercife his own intellectual powers, and to
enter into the reafons and grounds of what is
taught, and to receive nothing without evidence.
No one imagines that a perfon's exercifing his own
underftanding in this manner, is inconfiftent with the
notion of his having fomebody to lead and inftruct
him in any branch of natural knowledge. And
the cafe is much the fame in morals and religion.
A man's being an authorized (if you pleafe, a *divinely*
authorized) inftructor in religious matters, is no
ways inconfiftent with the right of private judgment in others. Indeed if they reject the truth
when it is fufficiently proved, they do it *at their
peril* ; and that, let it be offered by whom it will.
But ftill all are left at as much liberty to examine
and judge for themfelves, as if there were no public teachers at all.

I pro-

I proceed now to the *fixth*, and laft objection I
fhall have time to confider. The objection I intend may be put in fome fuch form as this—

6. " Although men may be at liberty to judge
" for themfelves, and to chufe their own religion,
" when the *civil magiftrate* does not interpofe with
" his authority.; yet when articles of faith have
" once received a royal fanction ; and a particular
" religion is eftablifhed by the laws of the land ;
" then certainly we are bound to difmifs all our
" former fcruples of confcience, and to fubmit to
" the *religion of the ftate*. For the apoftle has told
" us exprefly, That *the powers that be, are ordained*
" *of God, that he that refifteth the power, refifteth*
" *the ordinance of God, and fhall receive to himfelf*
" *damnation*, &c.

With refpect to this objection, I would beg leave
to query in the *firft* place, whether chriftians are
bound in confcience to believe and conform to that
religion, *whatever it be*, which is eftablifhed by
law, in the countries where they refpectively live?
This is a plain queftion : and they either are, or
are not fo obliged. There is no medium. If they
are not fo obliged, but only in cafe they apprehend
the eftablifhed religion is agreeable to the word
and will of God, this fuppofes a right of private
judgment, and fo gives up the whole point in debate. But on the other hand, if they are bound
in confcience to conform in the manner before expreffed, from hence it follows, that he that lives in
Scotland is bound in confcience to be a *Prefbyterian* ;
he that lives in *England* to be an *Epifcopalian* ; he
that lives in *Italy, France, Spain* or *Portugal* to be
a *Roman Catholick* ; he that lives in *Conftantinople*
muft be a *Mahometan* ; and he that lives in a *Hea-*
then country, muft confcientioufly comply with
all the idolatrous rites that are injoined by the civil
authority ; and fo be an *Heathen* in order to obey

the *gospel-precept* concerning submission to lawful authority. Moreover, upon this supposition, it follows that a traveller who has occasion to pass through all those different countries, must change his religion with his climate. He must successively be a *Presbyterian, Episcopalian, Papist, Mussulman,* and a *Heathen;* and then be a good *orthodox* believer when he comes into *Christendom* again. These consequences are unavoidable upon supposition that the subject ought universally to embrace the religion of the supreme magistrate. And some men will not be shocked at these consequences; for nothing pleases them better than to change their religion as often as they can with conveniency and profit; oaths and subscriptions are, with them, of no signification; if they *swear to their own hurt,* it is but to *change.* They are governed by the fashion in their religion, as much as they are in the cut of their cloaths; they have none but a state conscience; and either rail or smile at those who are so whimsical and superstitious as to pretend to have any other. What they have to do in order to know the true religion, is not to inquire into the nature of things, and the infallible oracles of God, but to search the *Codes* and *Registers* and *Law-books* in the country where they live. However it is to be hoped that some others do not trifle with their Maker in this manner; but think it of some importance to know the will of God; and to obey it conscientiously, whatever may be the religion by law established. Is it not possible for the command of the civil magistrate to interfere and clash with the laws of God? No man will pretend to deny this. Whose authority then is to be regarded, that of the King, or that of the Monarch of the universe, the King of Kings and Lord of Lords? Will any man say it is not our business as men, and especially as christians, to judge whether the

in-

injunctions of the civil magistrate may be complied with consistently with our allegiance and loyalty to the supreme Majesty of heaven and earth? And if they cannot, will any one make it a serious question, *whether it is better to obey God or man?* But

2*dly.* I would humbly inquire how any civil magistrate came by any authority at all in religious matters ; and *who gave him this authority?* Has the supreme magistrate of every nation, as such, a right to make a religion for his subjects? No. For then a heathen magistrate, would have a right to enjoin idolatry and paganism ; and to punish all christians that came within his territories, if they would not conform. Does the gospel of Christ give the christian magistrate authority in matters of faith and worship? No. It says not a word about any such thing. But

3*dly.* And *lastly* here, It is evident beyond all dispute, that the apostle, in injoining obedience to the civil magistrate, had no thought of injoining obedience to him in religious matters. For all the supreme magistrates then in the world were *Pagan* ; and idolatry was the religion by law established. And certainly we cannot suppose that the apostles could injoin it as a christian duty to embrace the established religion, when that was directly opposite to Christianity. To have threatened damnation to those who disobeyed in this case, would have been to threaten damnation to themselves, and to denounce an anathema against all the christians in the world, and even against Jesus Christ himself ; for these were all dissenters from the established religion ; and thousands gloriously suffered martyrdom, for refusing to comply with the religion of the state, and for asserting that right of private judgment which we are now endeavouring to defend.

According

According to St. *Paul*, the magiftrate is *ordained of God for a terror to evil doers ; and for a praife to them that do well.* His office is to preferve the liberties and natural rights of his fubjects, one of the moft important of which rights is that of private judgment, and an unmolefted enjoyment of a man's own religion, let it be what it will, provided he is a peaceable fubject and a good member of fociety. Thefe and fuch like are the ends for which, according to fcripture, the magiftrate is ordained of God, and not to make a religion for his fubjects. This would be to invade, and incroach upon, thofe natural rights of his fubjects, which it is his bufinefs to preferve inviolable. As the *Jews* faid occafionally to *Pilate, We have no king but Cæfar* ; fo chriftians, as fuch, may fay, *We have no king but Jefus Chrift :* And they are *traitors* to him their lawful fovereign if they fwear allegiance to any other as the lord of their faith, and the director of their religious conduct. And indeed the very mention of *articles of faith eflablifhed by law,* is as great a folecifm as *mathematicks eflablifhed by law* ; and deferves a worfe name than I chufe to give in this place.

Thus I have endeavoured with all poffible brevity and plainnefs to anfwer the moft material objections againft freedom of thought, and the rights of confcience in religious concerns. I have aimed at provoking no fect of chriftians whatever ; nor at pleafing any ; but have fpoken my fentiments, fuch as they are, with the honeft fimplicity that I think becomes a chriftian : And with fuch *freedom* as I apprehend is agreeable to the caufe I have been attempting to defend ; the caufe of *religious liberty* ; that liberty which God and the gofpel of his Son have granted to us ; that liberty, for the fake of which our pious fore-fathers forfook their native land, where, they had a *goodly heritage,* and

fought

sought a safe retreat in this western world, a wilderness inhabited by savage beasts and more savage men ; though both were less savage than some of those episcopal blood-thirsty tyrants from whose rage they fled. This is a cause of no less importance even to the present happiness of human society, than that of civil liberty, in opposition to arbitrary power. And here I beg leave to use the words of a truly catholic prelate of *the church of England*—" To liberty and property, says he, I " add the free exercise of religion as necessary to " the happiness of a governed society ; because as " there is no tyranny so odious to God, as tyran- " ny over the conscience ; so is there no slavery so " uneasy and ignominious, as a forced religion, or " a worship imposed upon—men by the fear or " application of outward inconveniencies : besides " that nothing promotes the flourishing condition " of a nation more than the indulgence of this " freedom to all whose principles are not manifestly " inconsistent with the publick safety." Thus the Bishop of *Winchester*, the noted scourge of civil and ecclesiastical tyranny.

I shall now close with a few words by way of application. And

1*st*, Let us all *stand fast in the liberty wherewith Christ has made us free* ; and not suffer ourselves to be *intangled with any yoke of bondage*.. If we have submitted to the yoke hitherto, and ingloriously subjected ourselves to any human impositions in religious matters ; it is better to throw off the yoke even now, than to let it gall us all our life-time : it is not yet too late to assert our liberty, and free ourselves from an ignominious slavery to the dictates of men.

Let us take pains to find out the truth, and after we are settled in our judgment concerning any religious tenet or practice, adhere to it with con-

stancy

stancy of mind, till convinced of our error in a rational way. Let us despise the frowns and censures of those vain conceited men who set themselves up for the oracles of truth and the standard of orthodoxy ; and then call their neighbours hard names—We have not only a right to think for ourselves in matters of religion, but to act for ourselves also. Nor has any man whatever, whether of a *civil* or *sacred* character, any authority to controul us, unless it be by the gentle methods of argument and persuasion. To Christ alone, the supreme and only head of the christian church, and the final judge of mankind ; to him alone we are accountable for not believing his doctrines, and obeying his commandments, as such. And whosoever attempts to restrain or controul us, takes it upon him to rule *another man's servants*, forgetting that he also is *a man under authority* ; and must hereafter stand or fall by a sentence from the same mouth with ourselves.

Did I say, we have a *right* to judge and act for ourselves ? I now add—it is our *indispensable duty* to do it. This is a right which we cannot relinquish, or neglect to exercise, if we would, without being highly culpable ; for it is absolutely unalienable in its own nature. We may dispose of our temporal substance if we please ; but God and nature and the Gospel of Christ injoin it upon us a duty to maintain the right of private judgment, and to worship God according to our consciences, as much as they injoin us to give an alms to the poor, to love God and our neighbour, and practise universal righteousness ; and we may as well talk of giving up our right to the *latter*, as the *former*. They are all *duties*, and not *rights* simply ; duties equally founded in the reason of things ; duties equally commanded by the same God ; duties equally injoined by the same Lord ; duties equally required

in

in the fame gofpel. And a neglect of the duty of private judgment may poffibly be attended with worfe confequences to ourfelves and others, than the neglect of almoft any other. For he that does not examine for himfelf what is true and right, acts intirely in the dark, and fo may run into the moft irregular and deftructive practices that can be conceived of, juft as his weak or wicked guides are pleafed to prompt him. He is fit only for a tool to the devil and his emiffaries : and may flatter himfelf that he is *doing God good fervice*, while he is imbruing his hands in the blood of the innocent, and perfecuting the church of Chrift.

But

2dly. And to conclude, while we are afferting our own liberty and chriftian rights, let us be confiftent and uniform ; and not attempt to incroach upon the rights of others. *They* have the fame right to judge for themfelves and to chufe their own religion, with ourfelves. And nothing is more incongruous than for an advocate for liberty to tyrannize over his neighbours. We have all liberty to think and act for ourfelves in things of a religious concern ; and we ought to be content with that, without defiring a liberty to opprefs and grieve others. However we have fome ignorant railing zealots amongft us, fired with a furious party fpirit, who are not fatisfied that they enjoy their own liberty; but mourn that their neighbours enjoy the fame, and that they have it not in their power to afflict them for their righteous fentiments. They groan under the righteous *act of toleration,* as much as our fathers groaned under the unrighteous one of *uniformity*. However, through mercy, we have but a few men of this ftamp amongft us ; and thofe are fuch ignorant and defpicable creatures, that they are more proper objects of pity, than of anger. My brethren, God forbid

bid that we should discover any thing of this same unchristian temper; or begrudge others the enjoyment of those rights which we ourselves esteem so dear, sacred and valuable. Let us, *as much as in us lies, live peaceably with all men*; but suffer none to lord it over our consciences. Let us avoid a contracted, censorious spirit in ourselves, and pity and despise it in others. Let us be courteous and friendly to all men of what denomination soever they be; and how much soever their religious principles may differ from our own. If we think them erroneous, let us not rail at them, but reason with them in the spirit of meekness. Let us use no methods but those of sober argument and kind persuasion, in order to bring men over to a belief and practice of *the truth as it is in Jesus:* and let us scorn those who are for using any other methods with us. God grant that how different soever our sentiments are, we may be united in love and charity; and that christians of all persuasions, and all churches, may live and behave in such a manner, as to meet at last above: and join in the *general assembly and church of the first-born which are written in heaven.* *Amen.*

SERMON

SERMON V.

On the Love of God.

MATTHEW XXII. 37——41.

JESUS *said unto him, Thou shalt love the Lord thy
God with all thy heart, and with all thy soul,
and with all thy mind.*
This is the first and great commandment.
*And the second is like unto it, Thou shalt love thy
neighbour as thy self.*
*On these two commandments hang all the law and
the prophets.*

THAT which renders it a matter of the highest importance to examine with freedom into
moral and religious subjects, is not so much the advantage simply of *knowing* what is *true* and *right*,
as the necessity of this in order to true and right *action*. It is scarce of any importance to us to gain a
speculative knowledge of true religion, but as this
has a relation to practice; and may teach us what
temper of mind towards our Creator, and one a-
nother, we ought to cultivate; and what an external conduct we ought to adorn our lives with, in
order to answer the end of our being; in order to
our filling up our place in the creation, and acting
our part well in the great *drama* of the world. This
is the view which ought to accompany all our inquiries into religious subjects. If we are sollicitous
only about knowing what is true and right, and terminate

minate our defires in fuch knowledge, we purfue
as an end what ought to be looked upon only a'
means to fomewhat farther and beyond, *viz.* fuch a
conduct as may render us acceptable to our creator,
and lay the foundation for rational happinefs here
and hereafter. Knowledge can hardly be faid
to be valuable for its own fake, but only as it may
be improved to good and excellent purpofes: Nor
is it eventually advantageous to us, any farther than
we conform ourfelves to truth and right in our behaviour.

For what end does the *mariner* ftudy the art of
navigation? Not, furely, for this only or chiefly,
that he may pleafe and amufe himfelf with the *theory* of it: but rather, that he may be able to *fteer
his courfe aright* through the ocean, and arrive fafe
at length at the port for which he is bound.   Without applying his knowledge in this way, all the advantage it will be to him, is that of being *fhipwrecked
with his eyes open,* while others run upon ruin *blindfold,* and purely through *ignorance.*—We alfo are
mariners; bound to *another country,* to *another
world.*   We fail at prefent upon a boifterous ftor-
my ocean, in which we are in danger of fuffering
fhipwreck.   For the moral world, as well as the
natural, has its *rocks* and *whirlpools;* its *fcylla* and
charybdis, and a thoufand enchanting *firens.*   To
know the *middle* and *fafe way,* will not fecure us,
unlefs we keep in it, and avoid the danger on either hand.   And to be *caftaways* through our own
negligence, while we know the courfe we fhould
fteer, inftead of diminifhing, will augment our forrow.   Religious knowledge applied to its true ends
and purpofes, is the only knowledge that can be
finally profitable and gainful; for, to ufe the words
of St. *James* with a little variation, *as the body without the fpirit is dead,* fo knowledge *without* practice,
is dead alfo: And it is the voice of reafon as well as
revelation,

revelation, That *the servant that knows his Lord's will, and doth it not, shall be beaten with many stripes.* What, then, has *our Lord* declared to us to be his will? And what does he require of us? One of the most comprehensive accounts of our duty towards our Maker, and each other, is contained in the words which I have chosen for the subject of the present discourse. They are the words of our Lord Jesus Christ to a person whom the historian stiles *a lawyer*, in answer to an important question, but proposed by *him*, perhaps, with no very good intention. The question to be resolved was this— *Which is the great commandment in the law?* And our Lord determines it in this manner—*Thou shalt love the Lord thy God with all thy heart, and with all thy soul, and with all thy mind. This is the first and great commandment. And the second is like unto it, Thou shalt love thy neighbour as thy self. On these two commandments hang all the law and the prophets.* In discoursing upon these words I shall inquire

I. Into the nature and obligation of the two duties here mentioned—*The love of God,* and of our *neighbour.*

II. In what sense, and upon what account it is said, that to love God, is the *first* and *great commandment.*

III. What our Lord intends by the assertion, That *on these two commandments,* viz. the love of God and of our neighbour, *hang all the law and the prophets.*

IV. And *lastly,* I shall endeavour to shew, that these two commandments have the same *place* and *preheminence* under the *gospel dispensation,* which they had under the *legal:* Or, that *all the Gospel of Jesus Christ hangs on these two commandments,* in the same sense in which *all the law and the prophets* did.

I. Then, let us inquire distinctly into the nature and obligation of the two duties here mentioned;
the

the firſt of which is expreſſed thus, *Thou ſhalt love the Lord thy God with all thy heart, and with all thy ſoul, and with all thy mind.*

We know that in ſcripture language and indeed in common diſcourſe, it is uſual for one duty or virtue to ſtand for all the reſt. *A righteous, a godly, a merciful, a juſt,* or *an upright man,* often ſignifies *a good man in general.* And ſo, when we are commanded to love or fear God, or to work righteouſneſs, the meaning is not that we ſhould practiſe only the particular duty mentioned, as diſtinguiſhed from others; but often at leaſt, that we ſhould become good men in general, and *walk in all the commandments and ordinances of the Lord blameleſs.* And this is the ſenſe which is ſometimes put upon the precept now under conſideration. However it ſeems plain, that this cannot be the true intention of it. For were it to be underſtood in this latitude, as injoining obedience to the commandments in general, it would include in it the *love of our neighbour,* which is expreſly diſtinguiſhed, in this place, from the *love of God.* Here is plainly a compariſon made betwixt two commandments, one of which is ſaid to be *the firſt and great commandment,* and the other to be *like unto it.* This, therefore, which is ſtiled *the firſt,* muſt be altogether diſtinct from that with which it is compared. Love is, indeed, the duty injoined in both; but the object of the *firſt,* is *our Creator* only; of the latter, only *our fellow-creatures.* This precept, therefore, does not include any of the duties of the *ſecond table* of the moral law, as they are commonly called. The moſt it injoins, is, *all* the duties of the *firſt table,* as diſtinguiſhed from thoſe of the *ſecond.* But, if I miſtake not, this command ſtill admits, and requires a farther *limitation.* It injoins certain diſpoſitions and affections of the *heart,* towards God, as diſtinguiſhed from all *external acts of of devotion and religion*; such as *praying, offering sacrifices, fasting,* observing *sabbaths* and *ordinances,* &c. The manner in which the precept is expreſſed, seems to shew, that the duty it injoins is wholly *internal*—*Thou shalt love the Lord thy God with all thy heart*; i. e. sincerely and unfeignedly—*and with all thy soul*—in the exercise of thy underſtanding, and rational faculties—*and with all thy mind*—freely, voluntarily, without reluctance or conſtraint. Theſe expreſſions seem to relate wholly to the mind. And that which determines this to be the true intention of the command, is what we find in the parallel place in another *Evangeliſt.* St. *Mark* relates the ſtory of a perſon's coming to our Saviour with the ſame queſtion which is here anſwered; and the anſwer to it is in effect the ſame. Upon which the *Scribe* (as he is called in St. *Mark*) replied thus—*Maſter, thou haſt said the truth; for there is one God; and to love him with all the heart—is more than* all whole burnt offerings and sacrifices—From this reply of the *Scribe*, it appears, that in propoſing his queſtion juſt before, he had a particular eye to the *external* ſervices required under the Law, compared with an *inward* regard to God, and sincere benevolence to mankind: And that he accordingly underſtood our Lord in his anſwer, as making a diſtinction and compariſon, not only betwixt the duties of the *firſt* and *second table*; but alſo, betwixt the ſeveral duties of the *firſt table*; and preferring the *internal* love and reverence of God, *to all burnt offerings and sacrifices*; and conſequently, *to all external acts of piety and devotion,* as injoined in the ceremonial law. This is plainly the ſenſe of the *Scribe*; and it is equally evident that our Lord approved his ſenſe: For it follows immediately in the next verſe—*And when Jeſus saw that he anſwered diſcretely, he said unto him, Thou art not far from the kingdom of God.* I ſhall, therefore, take it for granted,

granted, or rather proved, That the precept which our Lord calls the *firſt and great commandment*, is diſtinguiſhed not only from all the duties of the *ſecond table*, but likewiſe from many of the firſt; particularly, from all external acts of devotion; from all rites and ceremonies and legal inſtitutions; and in ſhort from all duties whatever, beſides thoſe internal ones of the *heart* and *affections*; and of which God is the *only* and the *immediate object*. The duty here required, is wholly a *ſpiritual ſacrifice*; and the *heart* is the only *altar* upon which it is to be *offered*. Accordingly, in the following diſcourſe, we ſhall have no concern with any thing beſides the inward ſentiments of the heart; the diſpoſitions and ſallies of the ſoul towards its Creator; the *Father of ſpirits*. But let none think I am going to inculcate *enthuſiaſm*, becauſe I ſpeak of the *religion* and *devotion* of the *heart*. I propoſe to ſpeak of nothing but what has its foundation in ſcripture, and the nature of things: Nor will any *enthuſiaſm* be incouraged, beſides that which *ſober reaſon* requires.

What then is it to *love the Lord our God*, in the ſenſe of the text? Or wherein does this duty conſiſt? I anſwer in general, That it conſiſts in exerciſing thoſe internal regards towards our Maker, which the perfections of his nature, and our relation to him require. And here I ſhall not ſpend time to prove, but take it for granted, That God is infinite in *power*, *knowledge* and *goodneſs*;—That he is able to perform whatever he pleaſes?—That he knows univerſally what is wiſeſt and beſt;—And that the moral rectitude of his nature is ſuch, that his will and actions are always conformable to truth and right:—That as he created all things, ſo he conſtantly upholds them, and governs them with perfect wiſdom and equity, accommodating and attempering his laws to the *common good* of his creatures
　　　　　　　　　　　　　　　—That

—That as he is the *father of all*, fo his government is *paternal*, free from all unneceffary rigor;—uniform and fteady, in oppofition to all capricioufnefs and arbitrary proceedings; And *finally*, in the words of the *Pfalmift*, That he *is good to all, and his tender mercies, over all his works.*

It is fufficient to our prefent purpofe, juft to have hinted in this general way at the character and perfections of God : For it being fuppofed that he is really *fuch a Being*, it will not, perhaps, be very difficult to point out the principal of thofe movements of mind, and internal regards, which are due to him : and fo to afcertain the nature of the duty under confideration. And I think the various things included in this important and comprehenfive duty of loving God, may not unfitly be reduced to the following heads—*Love, in a ftrict reftrained fenfe—Gratitude—Defire of the divine approbation, and delight in the confcioufnefs of it—Truft in, and dependence upon God—Abfolute refignation of heart to his will—*And laftly, *Joy in the confideration of our filial relation to him.*

What I mentioned *firft*, was the *love of God in the ftrict reftrained fenfe of the word.* By this I do not intend thofe flafhy and rapturous fallies of the heart towards God, which may proceed only from a fond conceit, that we are fingled out to be the peculiar favourites of heaven. We may eafily fall into an extafy, and run mad in religious contemplation, without having any thing of that divine love which is due to the perfections of our Creator. The love of God is a fteady, fober, calm and rational thing, the refult of thought, and confideration—It is indeed a *paffion*, but a paffion excited by reafon prefenting the proper object of it to the mind. Nor ought we to be fo follicitous about avoiding one extreme, as to fall into the contrary. We ought not to run fo far from *enthufiafm*, as to lofe fight of

H *real*

real devotion; we ought not to be so fond of a *rational religion*, as to suppose that religion consists wholly in cold dry speculation, without having any concern with the *affections*. Real piety necessarily supposes, that the heart is touched, affected, warmed, inflamed: and not barely that we have right speculative notions concerning God. A religion consisting in nothing but a knowledge of God's attributes, and an external conduct agreeable to his laws, would be a lifeless insipid thing: It would be neither a source of happiness to ourselves nor recommend us to the approbation of him, who requires us to *give him our heart*.

Indeed St. *John* says, That *this is the love of God, that we keep his Commandments.* But it is plain, both from the nature of the thing itself, and from the design of the apostle in this place, that his meaning is no more than this—That the *natural effect* or *consequence* of love to God, is *obedience to his commandments*: And not strictly speaking, that keeping the commandments is a proper definition of the love of God. These are evidently two distinct things; as distinct as love and obedience to any other being or person; or as any two things whatever. And how close a connection soever there may be betwixt them, they ought not to be confounded. It is evident at first view, that this command, *Thou shalt love the Lord thy God with all thy heart, and with all thy soul, and with all thy mind*, carries in it something altogether different from an injunction of *external obedience*. The precept relates to the heart and affections, as distinguished even from the understanding, whereby we discern and contemplate the divine perfections: and much more distinct from all external actions of what kind soever. Let any one see whether the following passages in the writings of the *royal poet and prophet*, do not carry in them the warmest expressions of inward esteem, approbation

and

and love. *Whom have I in heaven but thee? and there is nothing upon earth that I desire besides thee. My flesh and my heart faileth me; but God is the strength of my heart, and my portion for ever. Like as the hart panteth after the water-brooks, so longeth my soul after thee, O God. My soul is athirst for God; yea even for the living God. When shall I come and appear before him!*—It is plain that this is the language not barely of *reason*; but of *passion* and *fervour* and *emotion of spirit*. Nor can any tolerable account be given of these, and such like expressions in the devotional parts of scripture, without supposing that the affections of those who uttered them, were raised to a great degree of warmth; and that they terminated in God himself, as their proper and ultimate object, without regard to any farther or future advantage: they terminated in him as their end, in much the same manner that our animal affections and appetites center in their respective objects. Nor is there any thing that is absurd or romantic in this supposition; any thing that will not approve itself to our understandings upon the closest examination.

There is a natural distinction betwixt actions and characters, some being in themselves morally good, and others evil. Mankind have faculties for discerning these moral differences: and what is in itself right and good, is also in itself amiable in the eye of every rational being: it is in itself *right* to approve and love what is right, and *wrong* to approve and love what is wrong. Our Creator, besides endowing us with reason to distinguish betwixt moral good and evil, has moreover given us another faculty, which is sometimes called a *moral sense*; and which St. *Paul* speaks of under the titles of *the law written in the heart*, and *the law of the mind*. By virtue of this faculty, moral good and evil, when

H 2   they

they are objects to our minds, affect us in a very different manner; the first affording us pleasure, the other pain and uneasiness: And this, as unavoidably as the eye is differently affected with regular and irregular figures in body; or the ear, with the most grateful harmony, and the most harsh and grating discord: I say *as unavoidably*; but neither of them is absolutely unavoidable. There are some who have no *ear* for *music*, and others who have no *eye* for *architecture, painting* or *statuary*. And so there are some, perhaps, who have little or no *taste* in *morals*. However, as to the latter, this is not the natural state of their minds; but proceeds from their abusing and perverting *nature*. (And all our animal senses may be viciated also.) But take a man who has not violated frequently the *natural law of his mind*; and he can no more approve of what is commonly called *malevolence, cruelty* and *injustice*, than a *skilful architect* can approve of the most *irregular* and *aukward* pile of building: And on the other hand, he can no more hate and nauseate what appears to be *honest, generous and benevolent*, than the other can be displeased at the sight of an edifice, all the parts of which are *adjusted* by the exactest *rules of proportion*, and the whole brought to the greatest *perfection of art*. What man for example, who is not become depraved to a great degree in his own moral character, can read the contrary characters of *Cataline* and *Socrates* with the same complacency? Can he that has any remains of virtue, help being fired with indignation at the baseness and perfidy of the *former*; and with love, at the virtue and integrity of the *latter?* Does a man that lives by plunder; that swells his stores by rapine, and fattens on the blood of the innocent, appear as amiable as one, that, as *Job* elegantly expresses it, is *eyes to the blind, and feet to the lame?* One whose benevolence is diffused

to

to all about him? None can avoid looking upon the *former* as the proper object of difpleafure, and upon the *latter* as the proper object of love and complacency, although his own intereft is no ways affected by the conduct of either.

But what relation, it may be afked, has all this difcourfe to the love of God? I anfwer, a very near relation: For God, according to the fuppofition mentioned above, is perfect in all thofe moral qualities and excellencies which we efteem amiable in mankind: and which if any man does not efteem and admire and love, he is looked upon as a monfter, debafed below humanity, and unworthy to be reckoned among rational creatures. Now if it be reafonable to efteem and love our fellow-men in proportion to their juftice, integrity and benevolence, muft not he who is perfect in all moral excellence be in proportion the proper object of thofe fame affections? The goodnefs of God fo far tranfcends that of the beft of his creatures, that our bleffed Saviour has told us, *There is none good but one, that is God.* The moft that any can pretend to without arrogating too much to themfelves, is a faint refemblance of the divine perfections. And can it be reafonable to love and admire the mere portrait of moral excellence, and to let the fubftance, the fource and ftandard of it, remain unregarded? If goodnefs in a limited degree be worthy the efteem of all rational beings, fhall not that goodnefs that is without bounds, and abfolutely perfect, be thought worthy to excite in all, a real inward efteem alfo? an hearty and fincere complacency? an ardent inextinguifhable love? *A love ftrong as death? A love which many waters cannot quench, nor the floods drown?* In this there is no *enthufiafm*: in this there is nothing unreafonable and fanciful: For undoubtedly thofe qualities which being found in a limited degree, are really amiable, do not ceafe to

H 3   be

be fo, when they become infinite; but inftead of this, become *infinitely* amiable.

Were it poffible for us to contemplate the divine perfections without confidering *our own* relation to God; *our own* dependence upon him, and his providential care of *us*; could we confider him only as exercifing his moral perfections towards other beings with whom we have no concern, ftill it would be rational to love and efteem him. For thefe perfections are in themfelves amiable, and confequently they are fo to all beings who are capable of difcerning them. And we find ourfelves in a manner neceffitated to love thofe virtuous characters which we meet with in hiftory;—characters of men who lived in remote ages, and diftant parts of the globe; although our own intereft neither has, nor can be, any ways affected by their virtue. And thus alfo the moral perfections of God demand our love, feparate from the confideration of our own particular relation to him. But when we confider him under the notion of being *our* Creator, *our* moral Governor, *our* Father, *our* Friend, *our* Patron; this brings the matter *home to ourfelves*, and tends ftill farther to endear him to us.

And this naturally brings us to another of thofe religious regards which we owe immediately to God: I mean *gratitude.* This is nearly allied to the former; but intirely diftinct from it. The love of God, in the moft proper fenfe of it, is an inward efteem, and delightful admiration of the divine perfections, without the confideration of any good we have either received or expect from them. But gratitude has refpect to fomething paft; 'tis a thankful fenfe and recognition of certain benefits which we have actually received. And it is plain that if the moral attributes of God, are in themfelves a proper object of love, their being exerted in pofitive acts of goodnefs and beneficence to us, calls

for

for the returns of gratitude. Ingratitude is always looked upon as an indication of a bafe, fordid and degenerate mind: It is what we cannot avoid condemning in thofe to whom we have fhewn favour in any inftance: we expect, at leaft, that they fhould retain in their minds a fenfe of our munificence. All the world are agreed that this is what every man owes to his neighbour who has proved a benefactor to him. Why then fhould not the fame temper of mind take place in us with relation to God? If we think ourfelves obliged to thank our fellow-men for thofe inconfiderable favours, which they are fcarce more than the *inftruments* of conveying to us, what degree of gratitude can be fufficient for us to exercife towards our conftant and *infinite Benefactor?* towards that Being to whom we are indebted for our exiftence; for all the faculties of our minds and bodies? that Being who is the *original, voluntary* beftower of all that is valuable and dear to us? that Being from whom defcends *every good and every perfect gift?* And as we are *chriftians*, I may add, that Being who *fo loved the world as to give his only begotten fon that whofoever believeth in him fhould not perifh, but have everlafting life?*— *What fhall I render to the Lord for all his benefits? Blefs the Lord, O my foul; and all that is within me praife his holy name. Blefs the Lord, O my foul, and forget not all his benefits.* He hath *redeemed thy life from deftruction:* he hath *crowned thee with loving kindnefs and tender mercies.*

But to proceed—Another branch of that religious temper of mind which is implied in the love of God, is a *defire of his approbation and delight in the confcioufnefs or the profpect of it.* We defire to be thought favourably of, by mankind; and to be thought fo by the wife and good, yields no fmall fatisfaction to ingenuous and virtuous minds. But as God is the only perfect judge of real merit, to

H 4

gain

gain his approbation ought to be the higheſt ambition of every reaſonable creature. We are apt to lay traps and ſnares to catch the fluttering applauſes of the multitude; and delight to be *hoſanna'd* by them. But are *they* the ſupreme judges of what is really worthy of applauſe? Is it reaſonable to be ſollicitous about the ſentiments of the world concerning us, and to take no thought about the approbation of the great *Inſpector* and *Cenſor* of that world whoſe eſteem we court? No man that has any juſt conceptions of God's perfections can be regardleſs with what eye he views his conduct upon that ſtage where his place of action is aſſigned him. God himſelf is a *ſpectator* in this great *theatre* of the univerſe. A deſire of his applauſe, therefore, and of the *honour that comes from him*, ſhould in a manner exclude all lower ambition from our breaſts. And the proſpect of it muſt afford the higheſt ſatisfaction to every virtuous man, without the conſideration of any reward conſequent thereupon. The approbation of a *perfect judge*, is itſelf a *reward.* Nor is there really any pious regard to the ſentence that God paſſes upon our behaviour, any farther than our hope and delight terminates in that ſentence itſelf. This is *divine ambition.* But to look forward to ſome conſequent advantage beſide and beyond this, is *religious ſelfiſhneſs.* However, even this is not to be condemned, although it does not ſtrictly fall under the notion of *piety.* Piety *reſpects God himſelf, and him alone.*

To proceed—*Truſt in God and dependence upon him* as our portion and happineſs, is a duty which his perfections, and our own weakneſs, requires we ſhould live in the conſtant exerciſe of. None of us need to be informed of the internal want and poverty of our nature: we all *feel* it in a greater or leſs degree. It is the ſenſe of this inſufficiency at *home,* that makes us rove *abroad* after ſome foreign
ſup-

fupport. * We have commonly recourfe to di-
verfions and amufements ; to the company and converfation of our Friends, to *mammon*, and animal
pleafures. Upon things of this nature we lean for
fupport ; upon thefe we depend for that fedate
happinefs and fatisfaction, which our penurious
nature craves. But they are found to be abfolutely infufficient to anfwer this purpofe. Our inborn
thirft of happinefs is not to be allayed with fuch
fhallow draughts as thefe. *Vanity of vanities*, faid
Solomon, all is vanity and vexation of fpirit, after he
had fearched a long time for fubftantial happinefs in
worldly poffeffions and enjoyments. The moft that
thefe things have it in their power to do, is to *intox-
icate* us for a little while, and fo to make us think
ourfelves great and happy. But as foon as we grow
fober, and *come to ourfelves again*, the *fool's paradife*,
and the *airy caftles difappear :* we find our wants remaining, and folliciting for *fcmething elfe*. The conftant language of our hearts is—*who will fhew us
any good ?* — Who will do the friendly office to
point us to our happinefs ? Now whither fhall we
go to find fomething that may fill our minds, and
afford us a fincere, conftant and uniform fatisfaction ? Is there no object that is *adequate* to our wants
and capacities ? none that may be firmly relied and
depehded on, as a certain fource of quiet and happinefs ? Doubtlefs there is ; and indeed that Object
*is not far from every one of us: for in God we live,
and move and have our being.* His power, wifdom
and goodnefs, may be a prop to our tottering and
defponding fpirits ; and if we pleafe we may enjoy
prefent happinefs in relying upon the care of his
providence. We may thus get rid of all our wants
at once : of all our anxiety and follicitude about
what may be on the morrow. He, without whom

---

* See the Bifhop of *Briftol's* Sermon on the Love of God.

a fpar-

a sparrow cannot fall to the ground; He that *opens his hand, and satisfieth the desire of every living thing*; He that even *heareth the young ravens when they cry*; cannot fail to provide suitably for *us who are his offspring. The very hairs of our head are all numbered by him*: And we may *cast all our cares upon him*, as the apostle expresses it; *for he careth for us.* — *Behold the fowls of the air*, says our blessed Saviour; *for they sow not, neither do they reap*; *nor gather into barns*; *yet your heavenly father feedeth them. Are ye not much better than they?* — *Consider the lillies of the field, how they grow*; *they toil not, neither do they spin: And yet I say unto you that even* Solomon *in all his glory was not arrayed like one of these*—*Therefore take no thought for the morrow*; *for the morrow shall take thought for the things of itself: sufficient unto the day is the evil thereof.* Obedience to this command, understood with such limitations as common sense suggests, would disburthen us of a thousand fruitless cares, and be a source of constant serenity to our minds, in this various scene, this inconstant ocean we are passing through. The consideration of an universal kind providence presiding over the world, is, to them that will give themselves time to attend to it, a ground of continual peace, and composure of soul. All we need concern ourselves about is to do our own duty: the rest belongs to God; and he will doubtless do his part well; and they that *put their trust in him* will have no cause *to be ashamed*; but find their expectations answered to the full. He that is conscious of the integrity of his own heart, may have confidence towards God; and exult in the language of *David*, in hope of happiness both here and hereafter — *God is my refuge and strength, a very present help in trouble. Therefore will not I fear, though the earth be removed, and though the mountains thereof be carried into the midst of the sea*; *though the waters thereof roar and be troubled*;

troubled; though the mountains shake with the swelling thereof —— There is a river, the streams whereof shall make glad the city of God — Because he is at my right hand, I shall not be moved — Therefore my heart is glad, and my glory rejoiceth; my flesh also shall rest in hope——

Near akin to that trust and confidence in God now mentioned, is *absolute resignation to his will in all cases and circumstances.* There are indeed some things which, in one sense, will unavoidably give us uneasiness, such as sickness, the *loss* of our *deceased Friends,* and *ill usage* from our *surviving ones,* and the like. It is in vain to attempt to throw off human nature so far as not to be in any measure moved with things of this kind. But it is our indispensable duty to discharge our minds of all murmurings at providence; and to acquiesce patiently in the lot assigned us. Things could not, upon the whole, have been better ordered than they are, if the world be really under the government of a perfect Being. When we consider that *known unto God are all his works from the beginning;* his whole scheme and plan of government; and that by the goodness of his nature, he is disposed to order every event through the boundless universe, and through all periods of time, so that all shall *finally* concur, to promote the *common happiness* of his creatures, what reason have we to be submissive in all circumstances; and to say with our blessed Saviour, *not my will, but thine, be done!*

Upon this subject of resignation to the will of God, I shall beg leave to use the words of an admirable writer—— " The consideration, says he, " that the course of things is unalterable, hath a " tendency to quiet the mind under it, to beget a " submission of temper to it. But when we can " add, that this unalterable course is appointed " and continued by infinite wisdom and goodness;

" how

" how abfolute fhould be our fubmiffion, how in-
" tire our truft and dependence ? "

" This would reconcile us to our condition;
" prevent all the fupernumerary troubles arifing
" from imagination, diftant fears, impatience; all
" uneafinefs befides that which neceffarily arifes
" from the calamities themfelves we may be under.
" How many of our cares fhould we by this means
" be difburthened of ? cares not properly our own,
" how apt foever they may be to intrude upon us,
" and we to admit them; the anxieties of expecta-
" tion, follicitude about fuccefs and difappointment,
" which in truth are none of our concern. How
" open to every gratification would the mind be,
" which was clear of thefe incumbrances ? " Our
" refignation to the will of God, may be faid to
" be perfect, when our will is loft, and refolved
" up into his; when we reft in his will as our end,
" as being in itfelf moft juft and right and good.
" And where is the impoffibility of fuch an affec-
" tion to what is juft and right and good, fuch a
" loyalty of a heart to the governor of the uni-
" verfe, as fhall prevail over all finifter indirect de-
" fires of our own ? Neither is this at bottom any
" thing more than faith and honefty and fairnefs
" of mind; in a more enlarged fenfe indeed than
" thofe words are commonly ufed. And as in
" common cafes, fear and hope and other paffions
" are raifed in us by their refpective objects, fo this
" fubmiffion of heart and foul and mind, this re-
" ligious refignation, would be as naturally pro-
" duced, by our having juft conceptions of al-
" mighty God, and a real fenfe of his prefence
" with us. In how low a degree foever this tem-
" per ufually prevails amongft men, yet it is a
" temper right in itfelf; It is what we owe to our
" Creator : It is particularly fuitable to our mortal
" condition, and what we fhould endeavour after
" for

" for our own fakes in our paffage through fuch a
" world as this ; where is nothing upon which we can
" reft or depend : nothing but what we are liable to
" be deceived or difappointed in. Thus we might
" *acquaint ourfelves with God, and be at peace.* This
" is piety and religion in the ftricteft fenfe, confider-
" ed as an habit in the mind : An habitual fenfe of
" God's prefence with us ; being affected towards
" him as prefent, in the manner his fuperior nature
" requires from fuch a creature as man : This is to
" *walk with God.*" Thus the Bifhop of *Briftol.*

But to fubmiffion to the divine will, we may fit-
ly add even *joy and triumph of heart,* in the confideration of our relation to God. The fuperinten-
dency of divine providence, if conceived of in a
right manner, is one of the moft pleafurable and
delightful confiderations that can enter into the mind
of a reafonable creature, fenfible of his own weak-
nefs and various imperfections. Indeed, if inftead
of a wife and infinitely gracious Being, one whofe
kind regards are extended to all his intellectual creatures ; and one who governs the world with a view
at promoting the moral rectitude, and fo of advancing the happinefs of his creatures and offspring ;
I fay, if inftead of fuch a Being as this, we, in our
imaginations, place, at the head of the univerfe, a
capricious, humourfome and tyrannical Being ; one
who loves and hates at random, and has no uniform, confiftent, and benevolent defign ; we form
a fcheme of principles, more deftructive of rational
happinefs than that of *Atheifm* itfelf. For any man
had rather be left to the mercy of *atoms,* and *fate,*
and *chance,* or any other *chimerical Deity,* than be
fubjected to the pleafure of fuch a monfter, as an
all-knowing, infinitely powerful Being, deftitute of
a fteady, uniform principle of juftice and goodnefs ;
delighting himfelf in the exercife of a wanton, licentious omnipotence—But whatever fchemes of religion

gion have been propagated, in which the fupreme
ruler of the univerfe is reprefented in fuch a gloomy
and formidable drefs as this, they are equally inconfiftent with the religion of nature, and the religion
of Jefus Chrift. Thefe teach us to look upon God
as tranfcending all his creatures in mercy and goodnefs, no lefs than in power and greatnefs. Nor
fhall we behave ourfelves as becomes our relation to him, unlefs we always think of him with
inward joy and pleafure. What can be more unreafonable than for thofe who in God have a Father and Friend and Patron; one who is tenderly
concerned for their welfare, and does what he can
confiftently with the rules of wifdom, to promote
their beft interefts; what is more unreafonable than
for fuch, to entertain gloomy and melancholy
thoughts; and indulge fuperftitious fears, and
groundlefs fufpicions? Were God a malevolent Being; were he an unreafonable Tyrant; were he an
hard Mafter; were he an implacable and revenge-
ful Being; inftead of a merciful and faithful Creator; a compaffionate Parent; a gentle Mafter; a
righteous Judge; we might well think of him with
horror and dread; and even wifh a period put to
his exiftence. For whilft fuch a Being fways the
fcepter of the univerfe, no one can be fecure a moment; but had better, were it poffible, vanifh into
nothing, than have his future welfare depend upon
the precarious pleafure of fuch a Sovereign. Such
a Being were unworthy of any love, truft, confidence or reverence; and would be the proper object of dread and horror, and hatred to every rational creature. But God forbid that we fhould conceive of him in this manner. While God is our Father; while we are the objects of his love and care;
while he looks on all our involuntary failings with an
eye of pity, *remembering we are duft*, and even paffes
by our wilful fins upon our fhewing the tokens of
con-

contrition; while his liberal hand supplies our wants in this world; and while he offers us eternal happiness hereafter, upon the gracious terms of the gospel; what is there in this *idea* of God to make us fearful and uneasy? Does the idea of a Father carry any terror in it? Do we dread the thoughts of our gracious benefactor? Do we look upon our Father, as our executioner, as *Isaac* looked upon *Abraham*? Do we tremble at being in his presence? imagining that he inspects our conduct with the sagacious malice of an *Inquisitor*; instead of the bowels of a parent? While the *Fool says in his heart, there is no God*, do we *wish* there was none? If so we are Fools also. The doctrine of God's Being and providence is the most delightful and elevated subject of contemplation, that can enter into the mind of man.* Upon the truth or falshood of these great principles of natural and revealed religion, depends the just idea of the universe; and of our own situation, business, end, and expectations in it. And the whole system of nature immediately puts on a quite different face, if the notion of an over-ruling benevolent mind be excluded. The world, in that case, appears like a forlorn desolate wilderness; nor can we have any security; or safe dependence upon any thing—We know not to what infinite disorders and irregularities, the whole world may run the next moment; and how soon all rational beings may be involved in ruin and misery—Thoughts that excite the most terrible apprehensions in the mind of every considerate man—Such is the world without a providence—an helpless Orphan—deprived of its vital animating principle—the support of the virtuous—the hope of the distressed—and a restraint upon unbridled lust and violence—But once establish the doctrine of a superintending providence,

* See Mr. *Foster's* Sermon on Providence.

and

and creation revives; it puts on its former chearful countenance. If the world be under the government of a perfect Being, from this confideration naturally fprings peace, tranquility, joy and fatisfaction to every confiderate man—*The Lord reigneth, let the earth rejoice—Let the multitudes of the ifles be glad thereof.—Righteoufnefs and judgment are the habitation of his throne*—This is a confideration, which inftead of dejecting our minds, and filling us with gloomy fears, ought to put us upon anticipating that triumphant fong of the *bleffed*—Rev. xix.—*And I heard a great voice of much people in heaven, faying alleluia—Salvation and glory, and honour and power be unto the Lord our God ; for true and righteous are his judgments—Alleluia, for the Lord God omnipotent reigneth. Let us be glad and rejoice and give honour to him.*

Thus I have endeavoured to give fome account of that religious temper of mind which I take to be injoined in that precept which our Lord calls *the firft and great commandment.* The next thing to be confidered, is the nature and obligation of the duty commonly called *the love of our neighbour.* But this muft be left to another opportunity.

If it be poffible that any one fhould doubt of our obligation to love God in the fenfe above explained, let us reverfe the fcene, and try whether we can approve a temper of mind *contrary* to this. Let us fuppofe the divine attributes and conduct to be the fame with refpect to mankind, as we have hitherto fuppofed them, and made the ground of our obligation to the duty we have been difcourfing upon. But let us fuppofe that a people in fome *remote part of the globe,* inftead of making thofe returns of love, gratitude, &c. to God, thought it their duty to *hate* his infinite perfections,—to *blafpheme* their Creator for his goodnefs to them—to *dread* his approbation—to *court* his difpleafure—to be continually *fufpicious*

picious of him—to be *difcontented* at the methods of his providence, and to mourn when they confider-ed their filial relation to him, and his paternal go-vernment over them—Could we approve of fuch a fcheme as this? Could we think that thofe who em-braced it were in their right minds? Or fhould we think that they were not barely deftitute of what is called reafon and common fenfe, but had fome ac-tive principle directly contrary to it.—A fort of an-ti-rational faculty?—Well then, there is no medium between thefe two, unlefs we fuppofe that God is not to be regarded by us in any manner at all; than which, nothing can be more abfurd.—If he be the object of any affections in the human conftitution, it muft either be of thofe of love, efteem, honour, reverence; or the contrary one's of hatred, refent-ment, anger, contempt, and the like. But we at firft fight fee the fhocking abfurdity of the latter fuppofition; the former therefore muft be true——

Wherefore to conclude, Let us confider of the relation which God ftands in to us, and of our ob-ligations to him; and give him the glory that is due unto his name—*Great and marvellous are thy works, Lord God Almighty! Juft and true are all thy ways, O thou King of nations! Who fhall not fear thee, and glorify thy name!* Who fhall not admire thee, thou eternal, inexhauftible fountain of all good! Who fhall not love thee, thou fovereign beauty! Thou great original of all perfection! *Bleffing and glory and wifdom and thankfgiving, and honour and power and might, be unto our God for ever and ever,* through Jefus Chrift our Lord. *Amen.*

SERMON

I

SERMON VI.

On the Love of our Neighbour.

***

MATTHEW XXII. 37——41.

JESUS *said unto him, Thou shalt love the Lord thy
God with all thy heart, and with all thy soul,
and with all thy mind.*

This is the first and great commandment.

*And the second is like unto it, Thou shalt love thy
neighbour as thy self.*

*On these two commandments hang all the law and
the prophets.*

***

IN the preceeding discourse we inquired into the
nature and obligation of the love of God. The
love of our neighbour is to be the subject of the
present. The precept injoining this duty, is thus
expressed in the text—*Thou shalt love thy neighbour
as thy self.* Now the general question, What is implied in this precept, naturally resolves itself into
these three particular and subordinate inquiries.

1*st.* Who is here intended by our *neighbour?*

2*dly.* What *the love* of our neighbour implies in
it?

And, *lastly,* what is intended by our loving our
neighbour *as ourselves?* A resolution of these three
particular inquiries will give us a full idea of the nature and extent of the duty under consideration.

1*st.* Then, who is intended by our *neighbour?* I
answer, primarily and strictly, those who dwell *near
us ;*

us; with whom it is to be suppofed we have a frequent intercourfe;—and fo have more opportunities
either to *ferve* or *injure* them, than we have to ferve
or injure thofe that are far feparated from us. But
the term alfo includes all thofe with whom we have
any thing to do—all who come within the reach of
our abilities, fo that we can do them good either by
communicating pofitive happinefs of any kind to
them, or by removing the caufes of their mifery. Any
perfon with whom we have any kind of intercourfe,
whether he be one of our kindred or not; whether
he be an acquaintance or a ftranger; whether he be
a friend or an enemy; whether he profefs the fame
religion with ourfelves, or a different one; whether
he be in a private or a publick ftation; whether he
be our own countryman, or a foreigner; let him be
who he will, he is our neighbour in the fenfe of the
text, when providence puts it in our power to relieve his wants, and render him happy. That this
is the fenfe in which our Lord ufes the word *neighbour*, appears by St. *Luke*'s account of what paffed
betwixt *him* and a certain *lawyer* upon this fame
fubject. Our Lord had told him that if he *loved
God with all his heart, and his neighbour as himfelf,
he fhould live.* Upon this the *lawyer* afked the queftion which we are now endeavouring to anfwer—
And who is my neighbour? Luke x. 29. Upon this
our Lord relates a ftory concerning a *Jew* who fell
into the mercilefs hands of robbers. He was found
in the road by two travellers, a bigotted hard-hearted *prieft*, and a *levite* of the fame difpofition. Nei-
of them afforded the pitiable object any relief, although he were one of their own nation and religion.
But when a *Samaritan*, a man of another country,
and a different religion, a man who had *lefs orthodoxy* and *more charity*, than the other, found this
unhappy ftranger, he had compaffion on him, and
relieved him. *Which now*, fays our Saviour, *of thefe*
I 2 *three*

*three was neighbour unto him that fell among thieves.
And he said, he that shewed mercy on him : Then said
Jesus unto him, go thou and do likewise.* Go thou,
and act the same neighbourly part : Look upon thy
self to be a neighbour to every man, and every man
a neighbour to thee, who has any wants and calamities to recommend him to thee. Think not that
thou dischargest the duty of loving thy neighbour,
by returning the kind offices of thy friends ; by doing good to thy acquaintance ; to thy country-men ;
to those of thine own sect in religion ; but extend
thy friendship to all whom thou art capable of serving.

From this piece of history, or this *moral fable,*
(call it which you please) it appears, in general, that
the charity which is injoined in revelation, is infinitely more noble, generous, and disinterested than
the *love of our country,* as such, so much extolled
by some deistical writers : And than that *friendship*
which is recommended by writers of the same stamp
—A friendship confined to a particular knot of men,
whom humour or interest, or perhaps only a similitude of vices, has tied and united together. To
be a friend in the usual sense of the word, is to act
a kind part to some one, or more particular persons ;
but to love our neighbour, in the sense of scripture,
is to love the world ; and to be *that* to *all* with
whom we have any concern, which friendship is to
one or *two.*

Lest we should take up a notion that the proper
objects of our love were our friends, our kindred,
those of our own party, or our country only, our
blessed Saviour took care particularly to enjoin upon his disciples the love of their *enemies,* after his
own example, who died for us while we were *enemies in our minds by wicked works* ; and after the example of *his God and our God* ; *his Father and our
Father, who maketh his sun to rise on the evil and on
                                                    the*

the good, and fendeth rain on the juft, and on the un-
juft. Our *enemies* are included in the general term
neighbour; but it was highly proper and neceffary
that *they* fhould be particularly and exprefly pointed out to the *Jews*, becaufe they were generally
fuch blind narrow-hearted bigots, that they looked
upon all the world befides their own nation to be
the proper objects of their contempt and hatred.
This national hardnefs and ftinginefs of foul, was
continually increafed by the influence of the *Scribes*
and *Pharifees*, who, like too many modern teachers and doctors, inftead of inculcating the great duty of univerfal charity, expended their zeal upon
frivolous matters; and laboured more abundantly
to make the populace adore themfelves; and to
raife their indignation againft all fuch as dared to
fay any thing againft their *old traditions*, or *new*
whims, by which they made void the law of God.
And that which made it neceffary for our Saviour
particularly to recommend to his hearers the love
of their enemies, makes it proper for every other
preacher to do the fame, where bigotry and a party fpirit prevails; and would to God, that there
were not enough of this wretched fpirit to be feen in
our own land, at the prefent day, to make the fame
thing neceffary now!

Having thus confidered the *object* and *extent* of
the love recommended in the text; we proceed to
inquire,

2dly. Into the *nature* of the thing itfelf. What
then is implied in the *love* of our neighbour? I anfwer, it is the fame thing with benevolence, good-
will, or charity; a difpofition to do good and com-
municate happinefs. The fame word that is ufed
in the text to exprefs that temper of mind which
becomes us towards our Maker, is ufed alfo to exprefs the temper and difpofition of heart which is
required towards our neighbour. Both are expref-

fed

fed by the word *love*—*Thou fhalt love the Lord thy God with all thy heart*—*and thou fhalt love thy neighbour as thy felf.* However, although the words are the fame, the things intended by them are very different; as different as the objects of this love. When it is referred to God, no one imagines it means benevolence, or wifhing well, or doing good to our Creator; but efteem, complacency, admiration, reverence, fubmiffion, and the like. The reafon of the thing, confidering God's independency, power and wifdom and moral perfections, and our own relation to him, plainly points out thefe to be the things intended, when we are commanded to love *him.* And it is equally plain that when our neighbour is propofed to us as the object of our love, it cannot intend that we fhould pay him that fame internal reverence, honour, refignation, *&c.* which we pay to our Maker. This would be *idolatry* inftead of *charity.* So far as our neighbours refemble God, fo far indeed they are proper objects of the fame kind of internal regards which we owe to him: And it is doubtlefs our duty to efteem and reverence them in proportion to their real greatnefs and merit. For God requires us to *give honour to whom honour is due.* However, this is not what is primarily or principally intended by the love of our neighbour. This is a duty which we owe to all in common, with whom we have any concern; too many of whom have little or nothing in them that renders them the proper objects of delight, complacency, efteem and reverence. Nor can they be all in common the object of any other paffion befides that of benevolence or good-will: This, therefore, is what the precept in the text injoins upon us. And our blefled Saviour plainly leads us to this general idea of the duty, in his difcourfe with the lawyer before referred to, *Luke* x. When the *lawyer* afked, who was intended by his neighbour

whom

whom he was to love as himfelf, our Lord told
him the ftory of the *Jew* who was neglected in his
mifery by the *prieft* and *levite* ; and kindly relieved
by the *fchifmatical Samaritan*—and then added, *Go
thou, and do likewife.* This fhews that the primary and moft proper notion of the love of our neighbour, which he had juft before recommended, is a
kind and charitable difpofition. It alfo fhews farther, that the love of our neighbour, as the word
is ufed by our Saviour, is not reftrained to the heart
and affections, in the fame manner with the love of
God: but is ufed in fuch a large complex fenfe as
to include benevolent *action* as well as benevolence
of *mind.*—" Go thou, and *do likewife.*" As the
natural, and perhaps unavoidable, confequence of
God's being good, is his doing to his creatures ;
fo there is a clofe connexion betwixt thefe, in all o-
ther beings. We cannot conceive of a man's being
truly charitable in his heart towards his neighbour,
without doing good to him alfo, when it is in his
power, and the proper occafions prefent for calling
forth this internal principle into action. What a
man really wills and wifhes in his heart, he effects
alfo, when it does not exceed his abilities. So that
benevolent action will always be in proportion to the
ftrength of the benevolent principle, allowing for the
different powers, talents, and opportunities for doing
good, which take place in the world. ' This I take
to be the intention of St. *John*, in his 1 *Epift.* iii. 7.
*Little children, let no man deceive you : he that doth
righteoufnefs, is righteous, even as he is righteous.* He
that acts well, is really good to the degree that he
acts well ; and he doth righteoufnefs in proportion to
the righteous principle in his heart: thefe things
keep pace, and the one is always the meafure and
ftandard of the other.

Love is, in its own nature, an active and vigorous principle. This godlike gueft does not lie
dozing in that breaft where it takes up its abode,

I 4 and

and conceal itſelf from the obſervation of mankind, like eaſtern monarchs in their palaces. Its *light ſhines before men, and they ſee its good works.* It is conſtantly exerting itſelf for the benefit of thoſe we love : The charitable man *loves not in word and in tongue* only, *but indeed and in truth.* Charity contents not itſelf with good wiſhes ; with kind ſpeeches, and a courtly addreſs ; but does ſubſtantial acts of beneficence, according to the exigences of our neighbours, and our own abilities. It contents not itſelf, with ſaying to the naked, *be ye clothed* ; and to the hungry, *be ye filled* ; but adminiſters to their neceſſities. Love is infinite and the methods of its acting various, and innumerable. It originates in the heart, and from thence points every way, like various lines drawn from the center of a circle, or rays iſſuing from the ſun. It ſhines with its benign influence upon all that come in its way. It is *eyes to the blind* ; *and feet to the lame* ; it draws upon it the *bleſſing of him that is ready to periſh, and cauſes the widow's heart to ſing for joy.* It is inſtruction to the ignorant ; and conſolation to the ſorrowful ; it is a timely redreſs to the injured and oppreſſed ; and liberty to the captive. *Charity ſuffereth long and is kind* ; *charity envieth not* ; *charity vaunteth not itſelf, is not puffed up, doth not behave itſelf unſeemly* ; *ſeeketh not her own* ; *is not eaſily provoked, thinketh no evil* ; *rejoiceth not in iniquity, but rejoiceth in the truth : Beareth all things, believeth all things, hopeth all things, endureth all things.*

The apoſtle deſcribes charity, or the love of our neighbour, as comprehending all theſe virtues in it : And very naturally ; for they are plainly but ſo many different branches of the ſame tree. *Charity ſuffereth long*—We naturally bear a great while with thoſe whom we ſincerely love — It *is kind*— It is benign, courteous, obliging ; and ſweetens our manners, purging away all roughneſs, moroſeneſs and

and afperity—It *envieth not*—does not grieve and fret at the profperity of others, but rejoices in their happinefs—*It vaunteth not itfelf*—It is not infolent or affuming, but is meek and condefcending to others — *It is not puffed up*—It does not fwell a man with vain thoughts of his own goodnefs and importance, compared with others ; but leads him to *think others better than himfelf* — It *doth not behave itfelf unfeemly*—It prevents men from all indecencies in behaviour ; fuch as may be fhocking and offenfive to his neighbours ; and leads him to fuch a deportment of himfelf as may be agreeable to thofe with whom he converfes — *It feeketh not its own* —It is not felfifh, but excites a perfon to confult the benefit of others — *Is not eafily provoked* — or rather is not *greatly provoked* (as the word fignifies) —It is not angry to an excefs upon any occafion, violently inraged, and beyond meafure ; but obferves a mean, where there is real ground for refentment and anger. *It thinketh no evil*—It puts the moft favourable conftruction upon the conduct of others : and is not apt to impute to them ill defigns and intentions—*It rejoiceth not in iniquity*— It is not pleafed and delighted with the vices and mifconduct of mankind ; but pities and laments them—*It rejoiceth in the truth*—It is pleafed to fee truth and righteoufnefs prevail in the world, they being the foundation of happinefs—It *beareth all things*—or rather, it *covereth all things,*—agreeably to 1 *Pet.* iv. 8. *Charity fhall cover the multitude of fins.* — *It believeth all things* — It is not fufpicious that our neighbours defign to deceive and impofe upon us ; but is prone to believe what they fay, prefuming upon their honefty and integrity. —It *hopeth all things* — It will not fuffer us to defpair of our neighbour's repentance and reformation, although he may have wandered far in the ways of error and fin ; but hopes he may ftill be reclaimed
—Once

— Once more — *Charity endureth all things* — It is
patient and fedate; not fretful and tumultuous;
it bears calamities and injuries; it bears with the
faults and follies that are to be feen in the world,
fo far as is confiftent with the love of truth and
virtue and piety : It is a calm and unruffled felf-
enjoyment ; a compofed temper of foul, amidft all
the tumults and diforders of the world. Thus comprehenfive is the duty of charity, or the love of
our neighbour, in the fcripture fenfe of it ; neither,
indeed, have we yet carried it to its full extent.
Charity, confidered in its greateft latitude, com-
prehends in it all moral and focial virtues. He
that is a real lover of mankind will, from this fimple uniform principle, practife all thofe virtues
upon which the good order and happinefs of the
world depends : Benevolence naturally and neceffarily leads to this; *i. e.* to the practice of every virtue without exception. For there is not any particular one that can be omitted, nor any vice that
can be indulged, without detriment to the world.
The connexion betwixt the practice of all moral
virtues, and publick happinefs, is clofe and inti-
mate : Nor are thofe more private virtues, that fall
under the denomination of *temperance*, exceptions to
this general affertion. It would take us too long à
time to fhew how all particular virtues, (or if you
pleafe *chriftian graces*) that refpect either ourfelves or
our neighbour, may be derived from this one fource
of benevolence : But St. *Paul's* authority will be
fufficient to juftify the affertion, without any farther proof. *He that loveth another*, faith the apoftle, *hath fulfilled the law: For this, Thou shalt not
commit adultery ; thou shalt not steal ; thou shalt not
bear false witness ; thou shalt not covet ; and if there
be any other commandment, it is briefly comprehended
in this saying, namely, Thou shalt love thy neighbour
as thyself. Love worketh no ill to his neighbour ; therefore*

fore love is the fulfilling of the law. And for this reason the same apoftle calls charity by that emphatical
name—*The bond of perfectnefs*, Col. iii. 14.—The
tie and *nexus*, the common fource and fountain of
all moral perfections and excellencies: From that
they all flow, and into that they may all be refolved
again: As benevolence in the fupreme Father and
Lord of all things comprifes in it all the moral perfections of God: And as that fimple principle, under the direction of infinite wifdom, exerting itfelf
in a variety of ways, in order to accomplifh the
greateft poffible good in the whole, receives the various denominations of *goodnefs, grace, mercy, forbearance, juftice,* &c. fo all particular focial virtues,
may be only the various *modifications* of charity, exerted into action.

When we are fpeaking of the virtue of charity
in mankind, it fhould always be remembered that
we are not fpeaking of a blind impulfe or inftinct;
a fort of mad—good nature, that diffufes itfelf a-
broad without prudence, fore-thought or difcretion;
but of the benevolence of rational beings towards
their fellow-creatures; which fuppofes, that benevolence is always under the direction of reafon point-
ing out to it the ways in which it is to exert itfelf,
and the channels in which it ought to flow. Simple
benevolence, not directed by knowledge, would be
only a *loving, kind* fort of *phrenzy* or *diftraction,*
which it is probable might do as much hurt as good.
For a being without reafon to govern his actions by,
would be as likely to do wrong as right; to make
the object of his kindnefs miferable, as happy. But
he that is wife as well as benevolent, will obferve
thofe methods of acting, which are the moft conducive to happinefs; that is, he will ufe the moft effectual *means* to bring about his *end.*

There is no conceiveable goodnefs or evil in the
actions of an intelligent creature, but as they con-
duce

duce to fome good or bad end. And fince happinefs, in a large fenfe of the word, is the only good
end, the only thing that is valuable for its own fake,
it follows that an action is fo far good, and no farther, than it produces happinefs: And this is the
general rule which we ought to govern ourfelves
by in our intercourfe with the world. To do good
is what we fhould aim at. But then there are other
particular and fubordinate rules of conduct, flowing
from this general one, which ought to be the more
immediate regulators of our actions, in order to our
doing the greateft good we are capable of; fuch as
adhering to *truth, juftice*; doing good to a *benefactor* rather than to another; providing for our *own
families* and *kindred* rather than for others; and the
like: For there are certain peculiar ties and relations, which make it reafonable to give the preference
to fome in our kind offices, rather than to others.
And this is fo far from being inconfiftent with univerfal charity, that it is upon the whole moft advantageous to the world. Our benevolence would
be too vague, and diffufe; it would be in danger
of evaporating without doing much fervice to any,
had not the wife author of our nature by the conftitution he has given us, and certain particular affections, pointed it to fome *particular objects more
efpecially*. In general our kindred demand our firft
concern; our other friends and benefactors the next;
thofe of our neighbourhood the next—and fo on to
our country, our nation; and from our own nation,
to all others. This feems to be the order which
God and nature have pointed out to us; and if fo;
then to obferve it, and to arife in our good-will by
thofe *gradations*, muft certainly be the moft conducive
to the general happinefs of mankind; for the order
eftablifhed by God can never thwart, or interfere
with, the good of his creatures. To break in upon the *order of nature*, or to act out of our *proper
fphere,*

fphere, can never iffue in greater happinefs to ourfelves or others, than keeping ftrictly to *both.* And
the method of being ferviceable to mankind, whatever our ftation and circumftances in life are, is
ordinarily plain enough to thofe who have any real
inclination to follow it. But I muft haften to the
third and laft inquiry under this head, *viz.*

3*dly.* What is intended by our loving our neighbour *as ourfelves ?*

It has been obferved † by fome, That this ex-
preffion is capable of three different fenfes — It may
intend that we fhould love our neighbour with *as
great a degree of intenfenefs* as we do ourfelves : and
be as follicitous about his happinefs as about our
own. This would indeed be a glorious temper of
mind. But it may be reafonably queftioned whether it is poffible for mankind in this world, or
perhaps in any other, to be fo benevolent, as not
to have a peculiar feeling for themfelves. And as
the poffibility of this may be queftioned, it may,
in the fame degree, be queftioned whether this is
the true intention of the precept. For all God's
commands are adapted to our ftate, circumftances,
and capacities. Again, the precept may intend
that we fhould have a love to our neighbour *of the
fame kind* with that which we bear to ourfelves : *i. e.*
that as we are all naturally concerned for our own
welfare, fo we fhould alfo have *a real concern* in
fome degree for the welfare of others. But this in-
terpretation feems to be as much too low and jejune,
as that above mentioned was too fublime and elevated. For a man may have a real love to mankind in this fenfe, and yet be a wicked and unjuft
man, by reafon that his benevolence is not ftrong
enough to be a balance for his principle of felf-
love. All men have doubtlefs fome degree of real

† See the Bifhop of *Briftol's* Sermon on this fubject.

benevolence ;

benevolence; but a regard to their own private good may be so strong as to counter-act and defeat it; and so lead them habitually to the most cruel and inhuman practices.

It seems necessary, therefore, that we pitch upon some third way of interpreting the precept before us. And perhaps the sense of it may be this—That we should not barely love our neighbour; but that our love to him *bear some certain proportion* to our self-love; that we love him to such a degree, as shall prevent us from doing any injury to him for the sake of private interest; that in all our intercourse with him, we should *do to him, as we would that he should do to us.* More cannot be well intended in the precept; and it is certain that less cannot. And such a love to our neighbour as this, does not only imply that we abstain from all acts of injustice towards him; but also that we are active in serving him when he stands in need of our assistance; for certainly this is what we should expect of him. It is impossible exactly to determine *how far* we ought to go in acts of beneficence to our neighbour; but certainly something is justly expected of us, besides *not injuring* him. I shall beg leave to use the words of the Bishop of *Bristol* upon this subject, who seems to prefer the last-mentioned sense of the words. " Both our nature and condition, says he, require " that each particular man should make particular " provision for himself: And the inquiry what pro- " portion benevolence should have to self-love, when " brought down to practice, will be, what is a com- " petent care and provision for ourselves. And " how certain soever it be, that each man must de- " termine this for himself; and how ridiculous so- " ever it would be for any to attempt to determine " it for another; yet it is to be observed that the " proportion is real; and that a competent provi- " sion has a bound; and that it cannot be all which

" we

" we can poffibly get, and keep within our grafp,
" without legal injuftice.   Mankind almoft univer-
" fally bring in vanity, fupplies for what is called
" a life of pleafure, covetoufnefs, or imaginary no-
" tions of fuperiority over others, to determine this
" queftion : But every one who defires to act a pro-
" per part in fociety, would do well to determine
" how far any of them come in to determine it in a
" way of moral confideration. All that can be faid
" is, fuppofing, what as the world goes is fo much
" to be fuppofed that 'tis fcarce to be mentioned,
" that perfons do not neglect what they really owe
" to themfelves ; the more of their care and thought,
" and of their fortune they employ in doing good
" to their fellow-creatures, the nearer they come
" up to the law of perfection, *Thou fhalt love thy*
" *neighbour as thy felf.*"

We have now done with the three inquiries which
we propofed to anfwer—Who is our *neighbour?*
what is it *to love* our neighbour? what is it to love
him *as ourfelves?* We fhall conclude the prefent
difcourfe with a few words concerning our obligation to the duty, the nature of which we have been
confidering.   And if it be afked *why* we fhould live
in the exercife of benevolence, I anfwer

1*ft*. No man wants, that any one fhould point
out the particular grounds of the obligation that o-
thers are under to love and affift *him*.   Every man
naturally and unavoidably expects, and thinks he
has a right to expect, kind ufage from thofe about
him.   But will any man be fo vain as to imagine
that himfelf is the only perfon in the world that has
any title to fuch treatment? Can he, if he tries, perfuade himfelf, that all are obliged to love and do
good to him, according to *their* abilities, and *his*
own wants ; and yet that he is under obligation to
none? No man can ferioufly believe this, 'till *the*
light that is in him is become darknefs. Let us deal
fairly

fairly with ourselves: Let the same reason, whatever it be, that satisfies us, that others ought not
to injure us, but to be beneficent and humane to us,
satisfy us also, that we ought not be injurious to
them, but studious of their happiness. Happiness
is what each man desires for himself as a real good;
and he cannot be ignorant that others desire it also,
and have a right to expect it upon the same terms
with himself. Either no one has a right to expect
kindness, candour, and good-will; or all men have
the same. And then mutual benevolence, and an
intercourse of good offices, ought to take place in
the world universally.—But

2*dly*. God has required us to be benevolent, and
friendly to each other. He that commands us to
love himself with all our heart, commands us also
to love our neighbour as ourselves. And the will
or law of a perfect Being, a Being who is in all respects fit to be obeyed, is what constitutes obligation in the primary and most formal notion of obligation. We cannot properly be said to be under
obligation, but *to some Being*, who has a right to
give us law; and the more perfect that right is, the
stronger is our obligation. But

3*dly*. To inquire why we are obliged to be beneficent just and charitable, is to inquire why we are
obliged to be morally good; a question that seems
to carry its own answer with it—To suppose there
is such a thing as moral goodness and excellence, is
to suppose that all rational beings are under obligation to conform to the rules of it. It is a contradiction to suppose that any particular temper, or
course of action, is *right*, and yet that it may be
right for us *to deviate* from it. It is eternally right
to conform to what is right: Nor need we look out
for any farther obligation after we are satisfied that
a thing is really right: This of itself supposes we are
under obligation to do it; and that we cannot do

the

the contrary without acting a wrong and unreasonable part.

4thly. The nearer we conform to the great law of benevolence, the nearer we conform to the perfections of the Deity. God is infinite in goodness. In this the moral perfection of the divine nature consists. And if this be what renders God perfect, it must in proportion render us perfect also. And so far as we fall short of it, so far we fall short of perfection.

5thly. The order and the common good of the world evidently depend upon the exercise of mutual benevolence. From what proceed the tumults and principal calamities that are daily seen in the world, but from a neglect of this duty, and from the indulgence of a narrow selfish spirit? Were men to *put on, as the elect of God, bowels of love and compassion*; did they feel for others as well as themselves; we should no more hear of strife and debate betwixt private families; there would be no longer those contentions and animosities that disturb the peace either of church or state: We should no longer hear of the tyranny and oppression of princes; or the envy and rebellion of subjects; we should hear no more of *wars and rumours of wars*; of fields drunk with human gore, and *garments rolled in blood*; we should hear no more of cities stormed; countries laid desolate; men devoured by their fellow-men; or carried into inglorious captivity and slavery; but all the world would be hushed into peace, *every one sitting securely under his own vine, and under his own fig-tree*. It is selfishness, prevailing over charity and humanity, that has spread destruction and desolation through the world; that has depopulated the earth; that has turned the whole ocean into a *red sea*; and the whole world into *Golgotha* and *Aceldama, the place of a scull,* and a *field of blood.*

K   The

The conftitution of the world is fuch, that plenty, peace, and happinefs can prevail no farther than a foundation is laid for them in mutual benevolence, and an exchange of good offices. Love is the fpirit that cements mankind together; and preferves that order and harmony amongft them, which is requifite in order to the general fafety and welfare; juft as the regular motions and harmony of the heavenly bodies depend upon their mutual gravitation towards each other: Let this catholic and univerfal principle be once deftroyed, and confufion, difcord, and the crufh of worlds inevitably follow: And diforders fimilar to thefe unavoidably fucceed in the moral world, upon the neglect of thofe focial duties that have their foundation in love.

It is this divine principle that makes a good king; a good fubject; a good mafter, and a good fervant. This is fuch a temper of mind as would lead every man to fill up his own particular ftation in life with honour to himfelf; and fo as to contribute to the general happinefs of mankind; it would fweeten the naufeous draught of life, and make us all pafs the days of our pilgrimage in this world with pleafure; it would fpread joy throughout the earth. How glorious would it be if that time fhould come, that every man was fure, that he faw his *friend* every time he faw *his neighbour !* Would men take as much pains to do good, as they do to afflict and grieve and devour one another, the fociety of men on earth would refemble that of angels in heaven : But as things generally are, there is fo much ftrife and envy, and malice, and revenge, that a good man is fick of the world : And is ready to cry out with the prophet, *Oh that I had wings like a dove; for then would I fly away and be at reft.* But

6*thly.* An argument for charity may be taken from felf-love. That which tends to publick good, tends to private good alfo. To fuppofe the contrary is

a maa manifeſt contradiction. For *publick* happineſs is increaſed no farther than the happineſs of *individuals* is ſo. The temper of love is in itſelf, the temper of happineſs, and ſerene, ſelf-enjoyment: And if the world be under the government of a righteous and wiſe providence, thoſe muſt, in the final reſult of things, be found beſt to have conſulted their own intereſt, who have been the moſt induſtrious to advance the happineſs of others. Wherefore, let theſe conſiderations laid together excite us to put on the divine temper of love. That charity which reaſon dictates, is ſo far from being the love of any ſect or party of men, that it ought not to be confined even to the whole human ſpecies. It ought to extend to every order of beings that is capable of happineſs. There are none ſo high and ſo much above us, as not to have a juſt claim to it ; none ſo low and deſpicable as not to deſerve our kind regards. The reaſon why we are not commanded to extend our love to the angels, and all the glorious inhabitants of the other world, is not becauſe they are a different order of beings ; but becauſe they are out of the reach of our abilities ; becauſe their happineſs is not placed in our power, like that of our neighbour. And as to the lower animal world, it is as truly a tranſgreſſion of the laws of benevolence and humanity to put them to miſery out of mere wantonneſs, and when no good end can be anſwered by it, as it is groundleſly to afflict our fellow-men. Nothing ought to be below our notice, that is not ſo low in the ſcale of being, as to be exempted from pain, and incapable of happineſs. The lower animals are not ; and *Solomon* makes it one part of the character of *a righteous man*, that he *regardeth the life of his beaſt.* They are all, in a good ſenſe, *the offspring of God:* God is the common parent to us and them: And we may ſay, without a metaphor, even to the worm, *Thou art my ſiſter.* Although

we

we may be apt to think that our great superiority to the other inhabitants of this earth, sets us above an obligation to regard their happiness; yet God had a particular regard to them in the institution of the *sabbath*; he even *heareth the young ravens when they cry; and not a sparrow falleth to the ground without him.* If we would avoid a narrow, selfish disposition, we should consider the whole universe as one magnificent building, with different apartments for different inhabitants, all subjects of the same King, and children of the same Father, whose general law is benevolence and kindness. *Him* we should consider as sitting upon *the circuit of heaven*, and saying with a loud voice to *all*, what St. *John* said only to a *few—My children! Love one another; for love is of God.*

This earth, where mankind have their residence, bears but a small proportion to the universe. And this earth is again divided into different countries and nations; these countries and nations, into different cities and towns; into distinct societies and corporations and families. This is necessary and convenient; and every one ought to be principally concerned for the welfare of those to whom he is the most nearly allied. But he ought not to let any *part* ingross *the whole* of his benevolence. As a man's belonging to a particular family, does not destroy his relation to the whole common-wealth of which he is a member; so his particular relation to one political or civil society, does not destroy his relation to the greater society of mankind in general; not this, his relation to the whole rational creation. He that seriously considers himself in this light, as a member and part of one stupendous whole, will find little need of any farther arguments to convince him of the folly of being selfish, and contracted: He will be ashamed of any thing that looks like a *party spirit*: A vitious self-love will

naturally

naturally be weakened in him: Benevolence will spring up in his heart; it will diffuse itself like light from the sun, it will spread from kindred to a country; from a country to a kingdom; and from one kingdom to another, till it reach not only all the inhabitants of this little spot of ground called *the earth*, but till it grasp the universe; and then a man bears the nearest resemblance to that *one God and Father of all*, who *is good to all, and whose tender mercies are over all his works*.

Speculations of this kind may sometimes be of service to us, in order to open and enlarge our hearts: But our *proper business* lies chiefly much *nearer home*. It is our *neighbour* that we are more immediately concerned with; it is him that we are commanded to love as we do ourselves; and if we comply with this precept, according to its true intention, we cannot be deficient in our kind regards to those that are more remote from us. Benevolence and charity will be the general turn and bent of our mind; and will naturally be felt towards all beings when they present themselves to our thoughts. What connexion and dependence there may be of the various parts of the universe upon each other, we cannot tell; our *goodness*, perhaps, *may not extend to all*, so as to influence their happiness. But this we are certain of, that the happiness of mankind depends upon mutual kindness and charity. And this being the case, it is a call from God and nature, to improve all the powers and capacities we are endowed with, in doing good to those about us.— God grant that we may all be inspired with this divine principle of love, that so we may be *the children of our Father which is in heaven*; and the faithful followers of *Jesus Christ*, who has said, *By this shall all men know that ye are my disciples, if ye love one another*.

K 3   SERMON

SERMON VII.

The Love of God, the firſt and great
Commandment, &c.

MATTHEW XXII. 37——41.

JESUS *ſaid unto him, Thou ſhalt love the Lord thy*
God with all thy heart, and with all thy ſoul,
and with all thy mind.
This is the firſt and great commandment.
And the ſecond is like unto it, Thou ſhalt love thy
neighbour as thy ſelf.
On theſe two commandments hang all the law and
the prophets.

HAVING, in two former diſcourſes, conſidered the nature and obligation of the two duties
here mentioned, *viz.* The love of *God,* and of our
Neighbour, I proceed now, in the *ſecond* place, to
inquire,

II. In what ſenſe, and upon what account, it is
ſaid, That to love God, is the *firſt* and *great* commandment.

We may obſerve, that this aſſertion of our Lord
contains an expreſs and poſitive anſwer to the queſtion propoſed juſt before by the *lawyer.* It ſeems
that the *Jews* (as was obſerved in the firſt diſcourſe
upon this ſubject) were not agreed amongſt themſelves which commandment in the law [of *Moſes*]
was the greateſt, or moſt important. Some pitched
upon

upon *that* relating to *circumcifion* ; others *that* concerning the obfervation of the *fabbath* ; and fo on.
Now it was a refolution of this point, which the
lawyer, in his query, defired of our Lord.   And
confequently, the fenfe of our Lord's anfwer will
be this— " In making a *comparifon* betwixt the
" various precepts of the *mofaic inftitution*, the *pre-*
" *eminence* ought to be given to that which refpects
" the love of God ; this is the *principal*, the moft
" *important* and *fundamental* of all duties ; and
" which, therefore, demands your *chief* care and
" attention."

This is the purport of our Lord's anfwer. Now
the inquiry which naturally arifes here, is, What is
the *reafon* and *ground* of this preference ? Or, upon
what account does our Lord ftile this, the firft and
great commandment ? The reafon is too obvious to
need mentioning, why the pre-eminence or firft
place fhould be given to this commandment, had
the competition been only betwixt the internal love
and reverence of the one true God, and the *rituals*
of religion ordained in the ceremonial law.   But
it appears that the comparifon is made betwixt all
the commandments in general, *moral* as well as *ritual*.   And that which may feem ftrange to fome,
is, That the love of *God* fhould be looked upon as
of more importance than the love of our *neighbour :*
As *God is not* externally *worfhipped of men's hands,
as though he needed any thing* ; fo neither can our
loving him *with all our heart*, be any advantage to
him, he being abfolutely independent.   But our
righteoufnefs and charity may profit men like ourfelves: our neighbour may be really benefited by
our love and good offices.   And as we muft fuppofe that the *end* of all God's commandments,
muft be the advancement of the happinefs of his
creatures, and not his own, fo one might poffibly
think that thofe commandments fhould be efteemed

ed the moſt important, and claim our primary regard, in which the good of mankind is the moſt
immediately concerned, ſuch as juſtice, charity,
and, in ſhort all thoſe particular duties which are
comprehended in the general one of love towards
our neighbour. It might, therefore, have been expected, that our Lord's anſwer ſhould have run
thus— *Thou ſhalt love thy neighbour as thyſelf*; *this
is the firſt and great commandment.* But we find,
on the contrary, that he has aſſigned only the *ſecond*
place to this duty, and reſerved the *firſt* for the
love of God. Now if this ſhould appear a difficulty to any, as probably it does, the difficulty may
poſſibly be removed by the following conſiderations, which I ſhall ſcarce have more than time
enough to mention.

1. If it be our duty to love God at all, this is the
duty which is plainly *firſt* in the *order* of offices.
Our obligation to our Creator is prior in the order
of nature to our obligation to our fellow-men.
This appears particularly from hence, That our
obligation to love our neighbour ariſes principally
from the will and command of God : but we could
not have been under any obligation to comply with
his will in this *particular inſtance,* had we not been
under ſome antecedent obligation to him in general.
It is the perfections of God that induce upon us an
obligation to obey him at all. Our obligation,
therefore, to acknowledge the divine perfections,
to cultivate a proper regard to our Maker, or in
the words of the text, to *love the Lord our God
with all our heart,* is, in the nature of things,
prior to all others : And upon this account it may
be ſaid, that *this is the firſt and great commandment.* If, in our imaginations, we diveſt God of
thoſe perfections, which at preſent we ſuppoſe him
to be poſſeſſed of, our obligation to obey him in
any inſtance vaniſhes of courſe. But ſuppoſe him
                                            infinitely

infinitely wiſe, good and powerful, and our obligation to love, honour, and obey him, takes place
immediately. So that our obligation to God is
the *firſt* which we are under; it is, indeed, that into which all others may be reſolved. There is no
duty which we owe to our neighbour, conſidered
as a *religious* duty, but what derives its obligatory
force from the will and authority of God. And
as the divine perfections are the original and ſole
ground of all religious obligations in general, ſo
to have a ſuitable internal love and eſteem of, and
regard, towards, thoſe perfections, is the primary
and principal of all duties and obligations. But
I ſhall explain myſelf farther upon this head,
under a *ſecond* obſervation, *namely,*

2. That the whole of *religion,* in the largeſt
ſenſe of the word, ought to be conſidered as *the
ſervice of God,* the ſupreme Governor of the univerſe: and in this light it is uſually conſidered in
ſcripture. Now 'tis apparent, that the *firſt* thing,
not only in point of *order,* but of importance alſo, is
to form juſt ſentiments concerning the Being whom
we ſerve; to be ſuitably affected towards him; to
cultivate thoſe regards of eſteem, love, reverence,
&c. which the perfections of his nature, and his
relation to us, demand. Religion muſt originate
here; there can be really no religion, no ſervice,
that God can look upon as done in obedience to
him, but what proceeds from this principle of love
to him; and ſuch a principle does, as it were, in-
ſure our obedience to him in all other inſtances.
Loyalty of heart to our earthly *ſovereign;* a proper
ſenſe of our duty to him, in general, is the foundation of obedience to him in all particular inſtances.
The more our hearts are attached to our *prince,* the
better prepared, and, the more likely, are we, to
yield a thorough and univerſal obedience to his
laws. I ſpeak now of a temporal prince; but this
holds

holds equally with regard to God, the King of
kings and Lord of lords. Piety, or the love of
God, is the firſt and principal thing in religion, as
much as loyalty to our earthly ſovereign, is the
firſt and principal thing in the character of a good
ſubject. And this is, doubtleſs, the reaſon why
the *decalogue*, that ſummary of man's duty, begins
with our immediate duty to our Creator. When
the *law* was given at *mount Sinai*, it was uſhered in
thus, *I am the Lord thy God*, &c. *Thou ſhalt have
no other gods before me*. This injunction of loyalty to the one true God prepared the way to, and
uſhered in, all the other commandments. Nor
was this order, in delivering the law, *accidental*, or
without any particular *deſign*. It would be pre-
poſterous for a legiſlator to promulge any particular laws to his ſubjects, without firſt aſſerting
his own authority, and requiring his ſubjects to
own, acknowledge, and honour him as their prince,
or lawgiver. This is the purport of the firſt commandment in the decalogue : it requires thoſe to
whom it was given, to own, acknowledge, and honour the only true God; or, in the words of my
text, to *love the Lord their God with all their heart*.
And there is ſomething analogous to the divine conduct in this particular, in the conduct of earthly
princes, who, in the firſt place, require *an oath of allegiance* from their ſubjects, in order to make way
for their laws to be cordially received and obeyed.
This is a cuſtom which has prevailed pretty generally in the world; and it is plain that it anſwers
good ends in government. Nor is it leſs proper in
the divine government, than in human, that we
ſhould be required in the firſt place, and as the
ground-work, the ſum and ſubſtance of all, to have
a ſuitable regard towards him, whoſe ſubjects we
are; *i. e.* to honour and reſpect him as our prince.
The general reaſon of this, is the ſame in both
caſes,

caſes, *viz.* the neceſſity of our acknowledging the legiſlator, in order to our obeying his laws. And this brings me to obſerve, in the *third* place,

3. That the love of God is the only ſure and ſteady principle of virtue and righteouſneſs in our conduct towards our fellow-men. The moral and ſocial virtues are, indeed, amiable in themſelves ; worthy to be practiſed ; and it would (ordinarily at leaſt) be the intereſt of mankind to practiſe them, even although there were no God at all. But conſidering the weakneſs of human reaſon, the ſtrength of human paſſion, and the force and variety of temptation ; conſidering what men are in themſelves, and what a world they live in ; it cannot well be ſuppoſed that they ſhould uniformly act a virtuous part, from thoſe conſiderations alone. Virtue is amiable, and excellent in itſelf : But the bulk of mankind are not formed to be ſo powerfully ſtruck with the beauty and amiableneſs of it, as to diſarm temptation, and cauſe them to adhere to truth and right at the expence of their preſent eaſe and pleaſure. To the conſideration of the *fitneſs* of righteouſneſs, and all other moral virtues ; and the *uſual* tendency of them towards happineſs, it is neceſſary that the conſideration of a righteous Governor of the world ſhould be added ; whoſe poſitive will and command it is, that we ſhould invariably practiſe thoſe virtues which are in themſelves good ; and who will finally *render to every man according as his work ſhall be*— To exclude a God, and a righteous providence from the world, is (I will not ſay, wholly to break down the fence betwixt vice and virtue, and to make it wholly indifferent whether we practiſe the former or the latter ; but it is) to deprive virtue of one of its greateſt ſupports and guards. And it is to be remembered, that not to love God, not to cultivate thoſe religious regards towards him, which the

perfections

perfections of his nature demand, is to *exclude* him to all intents and purposes, as to any influence which the knowledge and belief of him, can have upon our behaviour. The acknowledging of a God can have no good effect upon our conduct any farther than our hearts are suitably affected towards him. So that there can be little or no real *virtue* without *piety.* If any thing puts men upon doing their duty towards their neighbour, and deters them from vice, when the eye of the world is not upon them, and when their temporal interest is forfeited thereby, it must be a sense of the divine perfections upon their hearts; *i. e.* a principle of love to God, in the large sense in which that duty was before explained. Without this, they will be continually in danger of relapsing into vice, whenever a present advantage is to be gained thereby, notwithstanding the beauty and amiableness of a contrary conduct. But let a man once have a suitable sense of the Deity upon his mind; let him really *love the Lord his God with all his heart,* and this will be a constant principle of virtuous conduct in all conditions and circumstances of life. It amounts to little less than a contradiction to suppose that a man should really love God, and yet indulge himself in the practice of those sins which God has forbidden; and which he knows are contrary to the divine perfections. The connexion betwixt the love of God, and obedience to his commandments,. is so close and inseparable, that St. *John* tells, That *this is the love of God, that we keep his commandments:* and again, *Hereby do we know that we know him, if we keep his commandments— He that saith, I know him, and keepeth not his commandments, is a lyar, and the truth is not in him—* The love of our neighbour (which includes all moral virtues in it) necessarily flows from the love of God, according to the same apostle— *If*
any

any man say, I love God, and hateth his brother, he is a lyar.—Nor is this less evident from reason than revelation. The love of God is the love of the divine perfections; 'tis the love of truth, goodness, justice, holiness, and all moral excellencies. And he that loves these perfections, cannot indulge himself in those vices which are contrary to them: but will, of course, practise all the moral virtues in his own life. It is a common observation, *that similitude begets love*; and it is equally true, *that love begets similitude.* What we love and admire in others, we imitate, as naturally as we love in others those dispositions and humours that prevail in ourselves. So that if a man love God, who is possessed of all moral perfections, he must, of course, be moulded into the same image himself; he will naturally conform his own temper and behaviour to the moral character of God, and *be perfect, even as his Father which is in heaven is perfect.*

From these considerations it follows, that although the ultimate design of all the divine commandments, were to bring us to a suitable temper and behaviour towards each other, in order to our mutual happiness; yet still, to *love the Lord our God with all our heart*, would be *the first and great commandment*; upon account of the influence which the performance of this duty must necessarily have upon our moral conduct towards our neighbour; and the impossibility of our adhering stedfastly to the practice of virtue without such a principle of divine love. Where the love of God takes place, the love of mankind and all the virtues that are comprehended in it, must necessarily take place also: Nor can the latter take place to any good purpose or degree, where the former is wanting. The love of God is the fountain from whence the love of our neighbour flows: and to expect to find the latter in the breast where the former is not, is

as

as vain as to expect to find a stream which has no source from whence it is derived. All moral excellencies in mankind have their origin here, in a proper regard and disposition of heart towards God: and this is sufficient, of itself, to intitle this command to the place which our Lord has assigned it. But

4. And *lastly* here, This may be said to be *the first and great commandment*, because the happiness of good men in this world consists principally in exercising those religious regards which are intended by the love of God. The duty consists in delight and complacency in God; in contemplating his perfections; in resignation of heart to his will; in trust and dependence upon him; and hope and confidence in his goodness. And he that is formed to such a divine and heavenly temper as this, has the temper of happiness. He has within him a secret spring of peace and consolation, that not only forbids him to be miserable, but also causes him to *rejoice with joy unspeakable and full of glory.* Without this principle of divine love, and trust in God, there can be but little happiness enjoyed in such a world of confusion and disorder as this, where every thing is in a fluctuating condition; where nothing can be depended upon. God is the adequate, the only adequate, object of our affections; and our supreme felicity in this world, as well as in the next, consists in the *enjoyment* of him. So that had God consulted only our present happiness, he could not have commanded us to do any thing which has so great a tendency to promote it, and is so closely connected with it, as *loving him with all our heart.* This will, indeed, appear wild and fanciful to some men, who value themselves much upon their *reason,* but have no *parts* or *capacity* for devotion. However the happiness of those whose souls are formed to the love of God, the supreme

and

and everlasting good, is not the less, because some men have no *taste* or *relish*, for the sublime and exalted pleasures of piety.

Having thus briefly shewn some of the grounds of that pre-eminence which our Lord gives to this commandment, I proceed

III. To inquire what our Lord intends by the assertion, that *on these two commandments*, viz. the love of God, and of our neighbour, *hang all the law and the prophets?* Now the full sense of this assertion may possibly be comprehended in the following particulars.

1. Under the *Mosaic* institution, and during the ministry of the *Jewish* prophets, the love of God and man, were the *principal* and *most important* duties; more excellent in themselves, more acceptable to God, and more beneficial to mankind, than the most punctilious observation of the ceremonial parts of the law. The love of God, comprehending a sincere regard to, and hearty complacency in, all the divine perfections; and the love of our neighbour, comprehending all moral, social, and relative virtues, were the *sum* and *substance* of religion under the legal dispensation. This is plainly implied in the assertion, That *on these two commandments hang all the law and the prophets.* Every thing was of little account when put in competition with these great and excellent duties. And this is plainly the light in which the prophets constantly taught the *Jews* to look upon the various precepts of the law. I shall have time to quote only two or three passages, where such a pre-eminence is evidently given to the unalterable duties of inward piety, and a life of charity and holiness. To this effect are the words of the prophet *Isaiah*, chap. i. *To what purpose is the multitude of your sacrifices unto me, saith the Lord?—Bring no more vain*

vain oblations—your hands are full of blood. Wash ye, make ye clean, put away the evil of your doings from before mine eyes, cease to do evil, learn to do well, seek judgment, relieve the oppressed, judge the fatherless, plead for the widow. So *Micah* vi. 5, and onwards—*Hear O my people! remember now what* Balak *king of* Moab *consulted—Wherewith shall I come before the Lord, and bow myself before the high God? Shall I come before him with burnt offerings, with calves of a year old? Will the Lord be pleased with thousands of rams, or with ten-thousands of rivers of oil? Shall I give my first born for my transgression; the fruit of my body for the sin of my soul? He hath shewed thee, O man, what is good; and what doth the Lord thy God require of thee, but to do justly, and to love mercy, and to walk humbly with thy God?* These duties are the same with those in the text; and the same which our blessed Saviour stiled *the weightier matters of the law,* Matt. xxiii. 23. and with the omission of which, he upbraids the *Pharisees,* Luke xi. 42. *But woe unto you* Pharisees; *for ye tythe mint and rue, and all manner of herbs; and pass over judgment and the love of God; these ought ye to have done, and not to leave the other undone.*

2. The affertion before us may carry fomething more in it, than that the love of God and man, were the *moft important* of any duties of the law— *On thefe two commandments hang all the law and the prophets*—This may poffibly intend, that thefe two general precepts, do in effect, and in fome fenfe, comprehend all other duties in them, of what kind foever.—Not ftrictly, indeed; for then no comparifon could properly be made betwixt them, and others—But as he that obeys them, he that has a real principle of love to God and man in his heart, will naturally be led to do his duty in every other inftance—to worfhip God in fuch manner as he requires,

quires, and to difcharge all the duties which he owes to himfelf, and to his neighbour, in his particular ftation. Thefe two virtues, as it were, comprehend all others in them. For he that fincerely loves and honours God in his heart, cannot fail to perform all the external acts of piety which God has injoined, all the duties of the *firft table* ; and from the love of our neighbour naturally flow, all the duties of the *fecond,* all the duties which we owe to one another. So that to love God and our neighbour, is, in effect, to obey the whole law and the prophets ; and to do all that God requires of us. And thus do *all the law and the prophets, hang on thefe two commandments.*

3. And *laftly* ; In this pofition it may be implied, That the *end* and *defign* of all pofitive inftitutions ; of all precepts not ftrictly comprehended in thefe natural and unalterable duties of piety and charity, was to bring men to the practice of them. All the rituals of religion, as appointed under the law, had fome reference to thefe effential duties ; they were not injoined under the notion of having any natural and inherent excellence or goodnefs in them ; but as means to bring men to a proper temper of mind towards their Maker, and one another ; neither were they valuable or beneficial any farther, than as they promoted this end, even fincere piety, and a life of holinefs and charity. In thefe things confifted real religion ; and every thing befides had no other relation to religion, but that of *means* to an *end.* The rituals of religion, though obferved with the greateft exactnefs, were rather an abomination, than a pleafure, to the Lord, when they were not accompanied or followed, by thefe natural and effential duties. Thus much is plainly implied in thofe words of the prophet, *Ifai.* lxvi. 2—5.—*To this man will I look, even to him that is poor and of a contrite fpirit, and trembleth at my*

L *word.*

word. He that killeth an ox, is as if he flew a man ; he that facrificeth a lamb, as if he cut off a dog's neck ; he that offereth an oblation, as if he offered fwine's blood ; he that burneth incenfe, as if he bleffed an idol: yea, they have chofen their own ways, and their foul delighteth in their abominations. I alfo will chufe their delufions,—becaufe when I called, none did anfwer ; when I fpake they did not hear ; but they did evil before mine eyes, and chofe that in which I delighted not.

Thus do *all the law and the prophets hang on thefe two commandments*—They are the moft important duties of the law and the prophets—All duties and virtues naturally flow from them—And all the ceremonials of religion were defigned as a means for promoting the practice of them. They were the fum and fubftance, the *alpha* and *omega,* the beginning and end, of the *Jewifh* religion.

Such was the religion of the *Old Teftament* ; and fuch alfo is the religion of the *new.* Which brings me to the *fourth* and *laft* thing propofed, *namely,*

IV. To fhew, that thefe two commandments have the fame place and pre-eminence, under the *gofpel-difpenfation,* which they had under the *legal:* Or, in other words, That *all the gofpel of Jefus Chrift hangs on thefe two commandments,* in the fame fenfe that *all the law and the prophets did.*

Now, that I may avoid obfcurity, and obviate fome objections which the ignorant, or the cavilling, might, perhaps, raife againft this affertion, I fhall briefly premife two or three things for the explanation of it, before I proceed to prove it.

Firft then, it may be obferved, That this affertion relates only to *duty,* or *practical religion,* as diftinguifhed from *faith* or *belief.* When our Saviour faid, that *all the law and the prophets hang on thefe two commandments,* he fpake of the *preceptive*

part

part of the law, and the *duty* of *Jews,* who were ſuppoſed already to *believe* the law and the prophets, and to be fully convinced of their divine original. To ſuch perſons as theſe he ſays, that there were no commands of ſo much importance, as thoſe which related to the love of God, and of their neighbour. In theſe things conſiſted the ſum and ſubſtance of duty under the *Jewiſh* œconomy. Our Lord was not ſpeaking of what was the ſubſtance of *natural* religion, but of the *moſaic,* which was of divine inſtitution, and received as ſuch by the poſterity of *Abraham.* And accordingly, when it is now ſaid under the goſpel-diſpenſation, that *all the goſpel of Jeſus Chriſt hangs on theſe two commandments, the love of God and man,* it is preſuppoſed that chriſtianity is believed; that Chriſt is received as *a teacher ſent from God.*; as the *promiſed Meſſiah*; and that the doctrines of his *incarnation, death, reſurrection,* and *aſcenſion* into heaven; and, in ſhort, all the doctrines delivered either by himſelf, or his inſpired apoſtles, are firmly believed. This being ſuppoſed, if the queſtion were aſked, *Which is the great commandment in the goſpel?* The true anſwer to it (putting only the term *goſpel,* inſtead of *law* and *prophets*) would be the ſame our Lord gives to the *lawyer* in the text —*Thou ſhalt love the Lord thy God with all thy heart, and with all thy ſoul, and with all thy mind. This is the firſt and great commandment: And the ſecond is like unto it, Thou ſhalt love thy neighbour as thy ſelf: on theſe two commandments hangs all the Goſpel.*

Secondly, It is not implied in this, that it is of no importance, whether *chriſtians* obey the *poſitive inſtitutions* of the goſpel or not, provided they practiſe the natural duties of piety and charity. As our Lord did not ſet aſide the rituals of religion under the law intirely, by giving the preference to

the

the love of God, and of mankind; so neither are they set aside by those who apply his assertion concerning the law and prophets, to the gospel. The contrary is rather implied. And it is a truth obvious to common sense, that all God's commandments, without exception, are to be obeyed; those of a *ritual,* as well as those of a *moral,* nature. But still, as there were *the weightier matters of the law* under the *Mosaic* dispensation, when a comparison was made betwixt the several commandments of it; so there are *the weightier matters of the gospel* also; and these are exactly the same under both dispensations.

Lastly here: When I speak of the substance of *christian duty,* and the weightier matters of the gospel, as consisting in the natural duties of piety and charity; or the love of God, and man; I would be supposed to intend, that these duties should be performed upon *evangelical* principles. The duties in themselves are really duties of *natural religion;* but being adopted into *christianity,* they are to be performed upon *christian principles,* and from *gospel motives;* with a proper *regard to,* and *dependence upon,* the *Mediator of this new covenant, who gave himself for us.*

With these explanations, I hope none will think the assertion strange, That these two commands contain the sum of christian duty; and that they ought to have the same pre-eminence under the gospel, which they had under the law.

The main design of the christian institution is evidently to bring men to that moral purity of heart and life, which is comprised in the love of God and of our neighbour. Neither the most exact compliance with the positive precepts of the gospel, nor any kind or degree of faith, unaccompanied with a principle of sincere piety and charity;

nor,

nor, indeed, any thing elfe, where the love of God and man are wanting, can intitle us to the divine acceptance hereafter; or *make us meet to be partakers of the inheritance of the faints in light.* If we believe in Chrift and his gofpel, fo far it is well: but this does but lay the foundation for our doing that, upon which our falvation finally turns. A right faith is an excellent and valuable thing; but it is advantageous no farther than it *purifies the heart*, and *works by love*; no farther than it transforms our minds into the divine likenefs; and leads us to live an holy and godly life. Thus the apoftle *Peter* exhorts us, to *give all diligence*, and to *add to our faith, virtue*; [conftancy, refolution, fortitude] *and to virtue, knowledge*; *and to knowledge, temperance*; *and to temperance, patience*; *and to patience, godlinefs*; *and to godlinefs, brotherly kindnefs*; *and to brotherly kindnefs, charity*. For, fays he, *if thefe things be in you, and abound, they make you that ye fhall neither be barren nor unfruitful in the knowledge of our Lord Jefus Chrift. But he that lacketh thefe things is blind* — 2 *Pet.* i. 5 — It is practical religion, the love of God, and a life of righteoufnefs and charity, proceeding from faith in Chrift and the gofpel, that denominates us good men, and good chriftians—Not wearing *the form of godlinefs*—Not the *belief* of any doctrines, however true, concerning the *atonement* of Chrift —Not a lazy *recumbency* upon the righteoufnefs of another— Not any *enthufiaftic fervors* of fpirit—Not a firm *perfuafion* that we are *elected* of God, and that our *names are written in the book of life*—Some of the worft men in the world, have as much *faith* as any in it—attend upon *fermons* and *facraments* as often—*rely* as confidently—have as *warm frames* and *lively imaginations*—and are as fully *perfuaded* of their being *chofen to falvation.*

But

But what does all this avail, if that *faith be without works?* if that *form of godliness be* without *the power?* if that *reliance* upon the righteoufnefs of Chrift, be thought to fuperfede *perfonal* and *inherent* holinefs ?—if thofe *fervors* of foul, are unattended by *divine love* and *charity?*—if thofe *towering imaginations,* are but the *vagaries of a wild fancy?*—and that *perfuafion* of their *election,* proceed from vanity only, and not from their having *given diligence to make their calling and election fure?*

The apoftle *Paul,* in the iid *chapter* of his epiftle to *Titus,* charges him to inculcate various moral and relative duties in his preaching; and then inforces this charge with an argument taken from the general defign of the gofpel.— *For the grace of God,* fays he, *has appeared unto all men, teaching us that, denying ungodlinefs and worldly lufts, we fhould live foberly and righteoufly and godly in this prefent world, looking for the bleffed hope, and the glorious appearing of the great God, and our Saviour Jefus Chrift, who gave himfelf for us, that he might redeem us from all iniquity; and purify unto himfelf a peculiar people, zealous of good works.* Thefe words are plainly expreffive of the main fcope and intention of Chrift's mediation, *viz.* the the bringing of mankind to real holinefs of heart and manners; or, in other words, to the love of God and of our neighbour. In the next chapter this fame apoftle commands *Titus* to teach the importance and neceffity of chriftian obedience, and good works. *This is a faithful faying, fays he, and thefe things I will that thou affirm conftantly, that they which have believed in God might be careful to maintain good works : thefe things are good and profitable unto men.* In what does St. *James* place the fubftance of Religion? *Pure religion and undefiled before God, even the Father, is this, to vifit the fatherlefs and widows in their affliction, and to keep a man's felf unfpotted from the world.*

world. Does he not tell us that *the devils believe
and tremble?* that *faith without works is dead?* that
faith cannot save us? and *that by works a man is
justified, and not by faith only?* The love of our
neighbour is fo effential, that St. *John* makes it a
certain evidence of a man's being in a ftate of favour with God; and the want of it as certain an
evidence that our religion is of no value. *We
know,* fays he, *that we are paffed from death to life,
becaufe we love the brethren—But whofo hath this
world's goods, and feeth his brother have need, and
fhutteth up his bowels of compaffion from him, how
dwelleth the love of God in him?* St. *Paul* alfo
makes the want of charity a certain mark of a
man's being *nothing* in *a religious eftimation,* whatever
faith, whatever gifts, whatever accomplifhments,
he may be endowed with. *Though I fpeak with
the tongues of men and of angels, and have not charity, I am become as founding brafs and a tinkling
cymbal. And though I have the gift of prophecy, and
underftand all myfteries, and though I have all faith,
fo that I could remove mountains, and have not charity, I am nothing. And though I beftow all my goods to
feed the poor, and though I give my body to be burned, and have not charity, it profiteth me nothing—
Now abideth faith, hope, charity, thefe three; but
the greateft of thefe is charity.* It would be endlefs
to quote all the paffages to this purpofe in the
writings of the apoftles.

Our Lord's preaching tended to the fame point.
What is his *fermon upon the mount,* but a moral
difcourfe wherein the excellency and neceffity of
internal piety, and holinefs of life, is declared in
the ftrongeft terms? Has he not made charity the
diftinguifhing character of his true difciples?—
*Hereby fhall all men know that ye are my difciples, if
ye love one another.* And *herein,* fays he, *is my
Father glorified, that ye bear much fruit. So fhall ye*

be

be my difciples. Has he not told us, that *not every one that faith unto him Lord, Lord, fhall enter into the kingdom of heaven; but he that doth the will of his Father which is in heaven?* Has he not affured us, that *many will fay unto him* in the laft day, *Lord, Lord, have we not prophefied in thy name; and in thy name have caft out devils; and in thy name have done many wonderful works? to whom he will then profefs, that he never knew them, becaufe they wrought iniquity?* Has he not faid, *If ye keep my commandments, ye fhall abide in my love, even as I have kept my Father's commandments, and abide in his love—This is my commandment that ye love one another as I have loved you?* If we look to the account which our Lord has given of the proceedings, at the final judgment, when he *fhall fit upon the throne of his glory, all nations being gathered before him* to receive their doom; I fay if we look to this account, what fhall we find reprefented as the ground and reafon, of the righteous being acquitted, but charity and good works? —*Come ye bleffed of my Father, inherit the kingdom prepared for you from the foundation of the world; for I was an hungred and ye gave me meat; thirfty, and ye gave me drink,* &c. And what, on the other hand, is reprefented as the ground and reafon of the condemnation of others, but the neglect of thefe fame duties?—*Depart from me ye curfed; for I was an hungred, and ye gave me no meat; thirfty, and ye gave me no drink,* &c. In fhort, the whole tenor of our Lord's preaching was *moral*: he feldom inculcated any thing upon his hearers befides piety towards God, and righteoufnefs and charity towards man: and all his difcourfes were juft as contrary to the *folifidian doctrines* which too many have given in to fince, as *light* is to *darknefs,* or *Chrift* to *Belial*; nor can the former any more *have communion* together, than the latter. Our Lord infifted fo much upon moral duties, that fome of late, in order to vindicate their own unfcriptural and irra-

tional

tional manner of preaching, have even been compelled to deny that he preached the *gofpel*, or defigned to do it; alledging that his doctrines and manner of preaching were *legal*. The irrefiftible conviction which thefe men have, that their own doctrines and difcourfes are of a very different caft and tenor from thofe of our bleffed Saviour, has put them upon making this wretched and impious evafion. They *apologize* for themfelves by *condemning* their Lord and mafter. And rather than acknowledge, as they ought, that they do not preach the real gofpel of Jefus Chrift, they deny that Jefus Chrift himfelf did. But notwithftanding *they* affert our Lord's preaching was *legal*, St. *John* the *Baptift* was plainly of a different opinion: for St. *John* the *Evangelift* informs us chap. i. that he *bare witnefs of him—faying— The* law *was given by* Mofes, *but* grace *and* truth *came by* Jefus Chrift. And our Lord himfelf, when the *Baptift* fent to inquire of him who he was, told the meffengers to tell *John*, among other things, that *the poor had the* gofpel *preached to them*; and this in order to fatisfy the *Baptift*, that he was the true *Meffiah*, and that *another* was not to be *looked for*. I muft, therefore, beg leave ftill to think, that our Lord really preached *his own gofpel*, although this may poffibly be looked upon by fome as an *heterodox* opinion; and a certain mark of my denying *the doctrines of grace*.

I hope it appears from what has been faid, that the love of God and of our neighbour; that fincere piety of heart; and a righteous, holy, and charitable life; are *the weightier matters of the gofpel*, as well as of *the law*. Indeed thefe are more evidently the fubftance of *chriftian* duty, than of *jewish*. Under the gofpel, rituals are of lefs account than they were under the law. It is not *on this mountain, or that*, that God is to be worfhipped;

shipped; every place is a *christian temple* ; for *the Father seeketh such to worship him*, as will *worship him in spirit and in truth.* Rituals were but *a yoke and a burthen, weak and beggarly elements* even under the law. And they are much more so under the Gospel, when compared to that *spiritual sacrifice* which christians are to offer to God. And as to charity, this is more peculiarly an *evangelical* than a *legal* duty. For which reason it is that St. *John* stiles this *a new commandment, that we love one another.*

Upon the whole then, the case seems to stand thus —Although the christian revelation brings us acquainted with many truths besides those which the light of nature suggests, or *Judaism* plainly taught; although it injoins us to do several things which would not have been obligatory without an explicit command; although it furnishes us with a great variety of new and excellent motives to excite us to the practice of our duty in all its branches; and although christianity cannot, for these reasons, with any sense or propriety, be said to be the same with natural religion, or only a re-publication of the law of nature ; yet the principal, the most important and fundamental duties required by christianity are, nevertheless, the same which were enjoined as such under the legal dispensation; and the same which are dictated by the light of nature. They are natural and moral duties, inforced with revealed and supernatural motives; and to be performed from principles peculiar to the gospel. And, indeed, it is plain beyond dispute, that the substance of true religion must necessarily be the same, not only under the *jewish* and *christian* dispensations, but also, in all countries, to all rational creatures, in all parts of the universe, in all periods of time. Modes and ceremonies of religion may, indeed, be various as the circumstances and conditions of men ; and God may afford different degrees of light and knowledge in dif-

different times and places : But the fum of our duty
refults from the nature of God, our relation to
him, and one another. And this muft therefore be
immutable as God himfelf, *with whom is no varia-*
blenefs, neither fhadow of turning. As God is the fame
in all times and places ; as mankind bear the fame
general relation to him in all times and places ; and
as our relation to each other is always the fame,
except as to fome trivial and merely circumftantial
differences ; fo the fubftance of human duty muft
neceffarily be the fame alfo in all times and places.
There cannot be any other than circumftantial differences in the duty, obligation and religion, of
creatures who are the offspring of the fame God ;
creatures endowed with the fame common nature ;
and creatures bearing the fame general relation to
each other. Now that religion which muft remain
invariably the fame, under every change of circum-
ftance, through all ages, in all places, and to all
rational beings, confifts in the love and veneration
of the fupreme Father and Lord of the univerfe,
and in the practice of righteoufnefs and charity.
This is the religion which is common to earth and
heaven : It is the religion of *angels* and *arch-angels*
above, as well as of *faints* below : This was the religion of paradife before the apoftafy of mankind :
This was the religion of *Noah* before the flood :
This was the religion of the *Patriarchs* afterwards :
This was the religion of the *Ifraelites* in *Egypt* before the law : This was the religion which was ra-
tified by God at mount *Sinai :* This was the religion of *the law and the prophets* to the day of the
Meffiah : This was the religion which *He* and his
apoftles principally inculcated upon mankind, under the gofpel difpenfation : And this will be the
religion, the employment and the happinefs of *the*
fpirits of juft men made perfect hereafter in the kingdom of heaven ; for the love of God and *charity*
shall

shall *never fail,* although *whether there be prophecies, they shall fail ; whether there be tongues, they shall ceafe ; and although, whether there be knowledge, it shall vanish away.*

Thus do these two duties claim the same place and pre-eminence under the evangelical difpenfation which they had in the law and the prophets : *On these two commandments hangs all the gofpel of Jefus Chrift.*

I have now done with the *four* particulars which I propofed to difcufs when I firft entered upon this fubjeft. There are various moral reflections and inferences which naturally arife from what has been now difcourfed ; and fo I muft beg your patience a few minutes longer.

1. Then, if the love of God and of our neighbour be the *weightier matters of the gofpel* as well of *the law,* we are naturally led to bewail the folly, and unhappy condition of thofe who, in a manner, leave thefe out of their religion. There are innumerable perfons even in the chriftian world, who, neglecting that fubftantial religion which confifts in the practice of thefe fublime and heavenly duties, employ all their zeal, care, and diligence about things of little or no importance. Chriftianity is principally an inftitution of life and manners ; defigned to teach us how to be good men, and to fhew us the neceffity of becoming fo. But there are multitudes who call themfelves chriftians, who content themfelves with an idle, fpeculative belief of certain notions and doctrines, without troubling themfelves about that *holinefs, without* which we are told, that *no man shall fee the Lord.* They *know* their duty *fo exactly,* and *believe* it *fo firmly,* that they imagine they may well be excufed from *doing* it. If they have but a great deal of faith, and rely ftrongly upon the righteoufnefs of Chrift, they think they cannot mifs of falvation, although, by their fins, they

they daily *crucify the son of God afresh, and put him to an open shame.* Some are pleasing themselves with a round of empty formalities, imagining that religion consists chiefly in frequent fastings, attending upon sacraments, and worshipping God with a great deal of outward pomp and ceremony. They forget that *God is a spirit*; and to be *worshipped* chiefly *in spirit:* and love all kinds of ordinances much better than they love their neighbours. There are many, were they asked, which was the first and great commandment, if they gave an answer agreeable to their own practice, must say—Thou shalt tell beads devoutly; visit the sepulchres of antient saints; fall down before relicks; pay homage to painted canvas, to carved stones, and moulded clay; pray frequently to the mother of God; or the like: and if they thought at all of the love of God, and our neighbour, would assign them only that low place, which our Lord gives to tything mint, anise, and cummin. Others place religion chiefly in having frequent raptures, and strange transports of mechanical devotion; in which the less they exercise their reason, the better and more glorious it is. For 'till they have lost all *human understanding*, they think it impossible they should get a *divine one*. Thus they go on, raising themselves from one degree of religious phrenzy to another, till they run quite *divinely mad*; and then they imagine, that with St. *Paul*, they are *caught up into the third heaven*; that they *hear unspeakable words*; that they *see visions*, and have *a multitude of revelations given to them*. And the consequence of this is, that they *are lifted up above measure.* They then look down with contempt upon all *moral duties*, as being below such *spiritual men*. They are for a religion that consists in something more refined and sublime, than the love of God and their neighbour; these are but barely rational and natural

ral

ral duties, and fit only for *carnal men,* or, at beft, babes in grace. Nothing can hit the refined tafte of thefe *Goliah's* in chriftianity, but what has fome myfterious fublimity in it, and is quite remote from reafon. What is plain and obvious is too low and vulgar for fuch great proficients in grace and fpiritual knowledge. God forbid that I fhould fay any thing to difcourage a lively and warm devotion. But fuch enthufiaftic flights as thefe, have no countenance from the gofpel of Chrift. And the almoft invariable confequence of indulging them, is the neglect of folid, fubftantial religion ; a rational love of God, of mankind, and the practice of moral virtue. When perfons once get to gafping thus eagerly after immediate infpiration, they generally bewilder themfelves, lofe fight of common fenfe, and neglect fober religion for the fake of having fermented fpirits, and fuperficial flafhes of joy. They impute all their ravings and follies and wild imaginations to the fpirit of God ; and ufually think themfelves *converted,* when the poor, unhappy creatures are only *out of their wits.*

2. Since the fubftance of chriftian duty confifts in the love of God and of our neighbour, and in the practice of morality, this fhews us what a gofpel-minifter's preaching ought chiefly to turn upon. When he is concerned with fuch as are already chriftians in *belief* and *fpeculation* ; that which he has to do ftill is to bring them to be chriftians in heart and behaviour——Not to dwell upon fpeculative points——upon trifling diftinctions, and upon metaphyfical niceties, which can only perplex his hearers, without bettering their minds and morals ——But to excite them to put on a temper of mind, and an outward converfation, which correfponds to their holy profeffion ; and, in the words of my text, to *love the Lord their God with all their heart, and their neighbour as themfelves.* However, this

is

is too plainly neglected by many. Their constant cry is—" Believe, believe"—" Come to Christ" —" Depend upon his righteousness." As for holiness and good works, they very rarely mention them; and when they do, it is rather with a design to undervalue them, and persuade people that they are good for nothing, than to inforce them as the indispensable condition of salvation. Nay, these things are not only spoken of very often, as being perfectly useless, but even hazardous to the souls of men. Good God! that the design of thy gospel should be thus frustrated by those whose immediate office it is, to inforce the holy precepts of it upon mankind!—

3. Hence it follows, that those people who are offended with moral discourses, under the notion that they are not *evangelical*, are grosly ignorant of the spirit and design of christianity—They *know not what they say, nor whereof they affirm*; and *need to be taught what* are the rudiments and *first principles of the oracles of God.* Such ignorant, licentious perverters of the gospel, the apostle speaks of in his second epistle to *Timothy. The time will come,* says he, *when they will not endure sound doctrine. But after their own lusts shall they heap unto themselves teachers, having itching ears; and they shall turn away their ears from the truth, and be turned unto fables.* And, indeed, of all the *fables* that ever were devised, there was never one that, either for sillinefs or impiety, equalled this, that faith without works, without the love of God and man, and a life of holiness, is sufficient to bring us to heaven.

4. From what has been said, we may see what those doctrines of the gospel are, which ought to be defended and propagated with the greatest zeal, *viz.* those which more immediately relate to practice; to the love of God and man—A zeal for all

such

fuch doctrines is *a zeal according to knowledge.* But
it is apparent, that thefe have been but little regarded by many chriftians, in comparifon of others
which a man might difbelieve, without hurting his
morals, or endangering his falvation. Thofe things
which have kept the chriftian world in an eternal
ferment ; which have fharpened the fpirits of men ;
and fet little angry bigots a fnarling and growling
at one another, are nice metaphyfical fooleries,
fcholaftic diftinctions without any difference, and
mere words without a meaning. Thefe are the
things (or rather the *nothings*) which have been dif-
puted about, to the neglect of *the weightier matters
of the gofpel*; and even to the deftruction of all piety and brotherly love ; of every thing becoming a man and a chriftian. So hot and furious
have many profeffed chriftians been in all ages, and
fo wrathful their contentions, about nothing, or
mere trifles, that one unacquainted with the genius of their religion, would be apt to think it a very different thing from what it is. He might be
apt to think that the mafter of thefe furious railing, and burning difputants, had left it in exprefs charge, as the diftinguifhing character of his
difciples, not that they fhould *be wife as ferpents,
and harmlefs as doves*—not that they fhould *love one
another* ; and practife mutual forbearance and condefcenfion—and do unto all men as they would
be done by—but that they fhould be venomous and
malicious as ferpents—hate one another with all
their hearts—do to every one as they would be
willing to be done to by none—go together by the
ears about words and founds—drag each other to
gaols and gibbets—to dungeons, and the flames—
and confign all over to hell-fire at laft, who could
not immediately pronounce their uncouth *fhibbo-
leths*—But O bleffed Jefus ! thou Saviour of the
world !

world! is this for *thy disciples to love one another as thou hast loved them?* Or didst thou mercifully *make peace* betwixt God and man *by the blood of thy cross,* that men being at peace with God, might thus make war upon one another, and inhumanly shed each others blood! But,

5. And to conclude : suffer me to beseech you all seriously to consider of the nature, the great end and design of the gospel, and principally to regard what is of the greatest importance. Content not yourselves with believing well—with being zealous either for, or against any particular doctrines—with practising the rituals of religion—with being sanguine in the vindication of any particular sect or party, or in opposing any—These things will not secure your salvation. 'Tis then, and then only, that you will be the real disciples of Christ, such as he will own and reward at the last day, when your faith has its genuine influence upon your hearts and lives ; when it inspires you with the love of God, and of your neighbour ; when it causes you to *break off your sins by repentance, and your iniquities by turning to the Lord.* This moral purity of heart and life, is that religion which our blessed Saviour has taught ; it is that religion which employed his lips ; and which all his behaviour preached to the world, more eloquently and louder than a thousand tongues. For God's sake, for your own sake, for the honour of the gospel, and your profession ; *let no man deceive you with vain words. He that doth righteousness,* and he only, *is righteous.* Let no man amuse you with idle, impious stories, as if faith, and reliance upon Christ, were all that the gospel made necessary, in order to your salvation. As surely as the gospel is a real revelation, so surely are these notions a mere dream—a fable—a fable wherein folly and wickedness seem to strive for precedency—As sure

M

as

as there is a God in heaven, no man will go thither *to behold his glory*, and to enjoy the everlasting pleasures that are at his right-hand, unless he forsakes his sins, and becomes holy as God is holy. I conclude with those words with which our blessed Saviour concluded his sermon upon the *mount*, Mat. vii. 24—28.—*Whosoever heareth these sayings of mine, and doth them, I will liken him unto a wise man which built his house upon a rock : And the rain descended, and the floods came, and the winds blew, and beat upon that house : and it fell not, for it was founded upon a rock. And every one that heareth these sayings of mine, and doth them not, shall be likened unto a foolish man which built his house upon the sand : And the rain descended, and the floods came, and the winds blew, and beat upon that house ; and it fell, and great was the fall of it.*

FINIS.

A

DISCOURSE,

CONCERNING
UNLIMITED SUBMISSION
AND
NON-RESISTANCE
TO THE
HIGHER POWERS

A

DISCOURSE,

CONCERNING

UNLIMITED SUBMISSION

AND

NON-RESISTANCE

TO THE

HIGHER POWERS;

WITH SOME REFLECTIONS ON THE RESISTANCE MADE TO

KING CHARLES I.

AND ON THE

ANNIVERSARY OF HIS DEATH:

In which the Mysterious Doctrine of that Prince's Saintship and Martyrdom
is unriddled :
The substance of which, was delivered in a Sermon preached in the *West
Meeting House*, in *Boston*, on the Lord's Day after the 30*th* of
January, 1749—50.

———

PUBLISHED AT THE REQUEST OF THE HEARERS,

BY JONATHAN MAYHEW, A. M.

Pastor of the West Church in Boston.

———

Fear GOD, honor the King——St. Paul.
He that ruleth over *Men* must be just, ruling in the fear of
GOD.——*Prophet* Samuel
I have said, ye are GODS——but ye shall die like Men, and
fall like one of the *Princes.——King* David.

Quid memorem infandas cædes ? Quid facta Tyranni
Effera ? Dii Capiti *ipsius* Generique *reservent.
Necnon Threïcius longa cum veste* Sacerdos,
Obloquitor.——Rom. Vat. Prin.

═══

BOSTON:

Printed and sold by D. Fowle, *in Queen Street,*
1750.

═══

BOSTON :

RE-PRINTED BY HALL & GOSS,
Congress Street, second Room over the Post Office.
1818.

PREFACE.

THE ensuing discourse is the last of three up-on the same subject, with some little alterations and additions. It is hoped that but few will think the subject of it, an improper one to be discoursed on in the pulpit, under a notion that this is preaching politics, instead of CHRIST. However, to remove all prejudices of this sort, I beg it may be remember-ed, that "all scripture—is profitable for doctrine, for reproof, for CORRECTION, for instruction in righteousness."* Why, then, should not those parts of scripture which relate to civil government, be examined and explained from the desk, as well as others? Obedience to the civil magistrate is a christian duty: and if so, why should not the nature, grounds and extent of it be considered in a christian assembly? Besides, if it be said, that it is out of character for a christian minister to meddle with such a subject, this censure will at last fall upon the holy apostles. They write upon it in their epistles to christian churches: and surely it cannot be deem-ed either criminal or impertinent, to attempt an ex-planation of their doctrine.

IT was the near approach of the *thirtieth* of *Jan-uary*, that turned my thoughts to this subject: on which solemnity, the *slavish* doctrine of passive obe-dience and non-resistance, is often warmly asserted; and the dissenters from the established church, repre-sented not only as schismatics, (with more of triumph than of truth, and of choler than christianity) but al-so as persons of seditious, traitorous and rebellious principles—GOD be thanked, one may, in any part of the *British* dominions, speak freely (if a decent regard be paid to those in authority) both of gov-ernment and religion; and even give some broad hints, that he is engaged on the side of Liberty, the BIBLE and Common Sense, in opposition to Tyran-ny, PRIEST-CRAFT and Nonsense, without being in danger either of the *Bastile* or the *Inquisition* :— Though there will always be *some* interested politi-

*2 Pet. iii. 16.

cians, contracted bigots, and hypocritical zealots for
a party, to take offence at such freedoms. *Their*
censure is praise: *their* praise is infamy—A spirit
of domination is always to be guarded against, both
in church and state, even in times of the greatest
security; such as the present is amongst US; at
least as to the latter. Those nations who are now
groaning under the iron sceptre of tyranny, were
once free. So they might probably have remain-
ed, by a seasonable caution against despotic measures. Civil tyranny is usually small in its beginning,
like "the drop of a bucket,"* till at length, like a
mighty torrent, or the raging waves of the sea, it
bears down all before it, and deluges whole countries
and empires. Thus it is as to ecclesiastical tyranny
also,—the most cruel, intolerable and impious, of
any. From small beginnings, "it exalts itself above
all that is called GOD, "and that is worshipped."†
People have no security against being unmercifully
priest-ridden, but by keeping all imperious BISH-
OPS and other CLERGYMEN who love to "lord
it over God's heritage," from getting their *foot* into
the *stirrup* at all. Let them be once fairly *moun-
ted*, and their "beasts, the laity,"‡ may *prance* and
flounce about to no purpose: and they will at length,
be so *jaded* and *hack'd* by these reverend *jockies*,
that they will not even have *spirits* enough to complain, that their *backs* are *galled*; or, like *Balaam's*
ass, to "rebuke the madness of the prophet."§

"THE mystery of iniquity began to work"¶ even
in the days of some of the apostles. But the kingdom of Anti-christ was then in one respect, like the
kingdom of heaven, however different in all others.
It was "as a grain of mustard-seed."* This grain
was sown in *Italy*, that fruitful field: and though it
were "the least of all seeds," it soon became a
mighty tree. It has, long since, overspread and
darkened the greatest part of *Christendom*, so that
we may apply to it, what is said of the tree which
Nebuchadnezzar saw in his vision—"The height
thereof reacheth unto heaven, and the sight thereof, to the end of all the earth—And THE BEASTS
OF THE FIELD have shadow under it." Tyran-

*Isa. xi. 15.   †2 Thes. ii. 4.
‡Mr. *Leslie*.   §2 Pet. ii. 16.   ¶2 Thes. ii. 7.   *Matt. xiii. 31.

ny brings *ignorance* and *brutality* along with it. It degrades men from their just rank, into the class of brutes. It damps their spirits. It suppresses arts. It extinguishes every spark of noble ardor and generosity in the breasts of those who are enslaved by it. It makes naturally strong and great minds, feeble and little ; and triumphs over the ruins of virtue and humanity. This is true of tyranny in every shape. There can be nothing great and good, where its influence reaches. For which reason it becomes every friend to truth and human kind, every lover of God and the christian religion, to bear a part in opposing this hateful monster. It was a desire to contribute a mite towards carrying on a war against this common enemy, that produced the following discourse. And if it serve in any measure, to keep up a spirit of civil and religious liberty amongst us, my end is answered.—There are virtuous and candid men in all sects ; all such are to be esteemed : there are also vicious men and bigots in all sects ; and all such *ought to be despised.*

"To virtue only and her friends, a friend ;
The world beside may murmur or commend.
Know, all the distant din that world can keep,
Rolls o'er my grotto, and but sooths my sleep."
                                                POPE.

JONATHAN MAYHEW.

CONCERNING UNLIMITED SUBMISSION AND NON-RESISTANCE TO THE HIGHER POWERS.

Rom. xiii. 1, 8.

1. *Let every soul be subject unto the higher powers. For there is no power but of God ; the powers that be, are ordained of God.*

2. *Whosoever therefore resisteth the power, resisteth the ordinance of God ; and they that resist, shall receive to themselves damnation.*

3. *For rulers are not a terror to good works, but to the evil. Wilt thou then not be afraid of the power ? Do that which is good, and thou shalt have praise of the same :*

4. *For he is the minister of God to thee for good. But if thou do that which is evil, be afraid ; for he beareth not the sword in vain : For he is the minister of God, a revenger to execute wrath upon him that doeth evil.*

5. *Wherefore ye must needs be subject, not only for wrath, but also for conscience sake.*

6. *For, for this cause pay you tribute also : For they are God's ministers, attending continually upon this very thing.*

7. *Render therefore to all their dues : tribute to whom tribute is due ; custom, to whom custom : fear, to whom fear ; honor to whom honor.*

IT is evident that the affair of civil government may properly fall under a *moral* and *religious* consideration, at least so far forth as it relates to the general nature and end of magistracy, and to the grounds and extent of that submission which persons of a private character, ought to yield to those who are vested with authority. This must be allowed by all who acknowledge the divine original of christanity. For although there be a sense, and a very plain and important sense,

in which Christ's *kingdom is not of this world ;*[*] his inspired apostles have, nevertheless, laid down some
general principles concerning the office of civil rulers,
and the duty of subjects, together with the reason and
obligation of that duty. And from hence it follows,
that it is proper for all who acknowledge the authority of Jesus Christ, and the inspiration of his apostles,
to endeavour to understand what is in fact the doctrine
which they have delivered concerning this matter.
It is the duty of *christian* magistrates to inform themselves what it is which their religion teaches concerning the nature and design of their office. And it is
equally the duty of all *christian* people to inform themselves what it is which their religion teaches concerning that subjection which they owe to *the high powers.*
It is for these reasons that I have attempted to examine into the scripture account of this matter, in order
to lay it before you with the same *freedom* which I
constantly use with relation to other doctrines and precepts of christanity; not doubting but you will *judge*
upon every thing offered to your consideration, with
the same spirit of *freedom* and *liberty* with which it is
spoken.

THE passage read, is the most full and express of
any in the New Testament, relating to rulers and subjects : and therefore I thought it proper to ground upon it, what I had to propose to you with reference to
the authority of the civil magistrate, and the subjection which is due to him. But before I enter upon an
explanation of the several parts of this passage, it will
be proper to observe one thing which may serve as a
key to the whole of it.

IT is to be observed, then, that there were some persons amongst the *christians* of the apostolic age, and particularly those at *Rome,*to whom St. *Paul* is here writing,
who seditiously disclaimed *all* subjection to civil author-

[*] John, xviii, 36,

ity ; refusing to pay taxes, and the duties laid upon
their trafic and merchandize ; and who scrupled not
to speak of their rulers, without any due regard to their
office and character. Some of these turbulent *christians* were converts from *Judaism* and others from *Paganism*. The *Jews* in general had long before this
time, taken up a strange conceit, that being the *peculiar* and *elect* people of God, they were, therefore, exempted from the jurisdiction of any *heathen* princes or
governors. Upon this ground it was, that some of them,
during the public ministry of our blessed Saviour came
to him with that question—*Is it lawful to give tribute
unto Cæser, or not ?** And this notion many of them re-
tained after they were proselyted to the *christian* faith.
As to the *Gentile* converts, some of them grossly mis-
took the nature of that *liberty* which the gospel prom-
ised; and thought that by virtue of their subjection
to Christ, the *only* King and Head of his church, they
were wholly freed from subjection to any other prince ;
as though Christ's *kingdom had been of this world,* in
such a sense as to interfere with the civil powers of the
earth, and to deliver their subjects from that allegiance
and duty, which they before owed to them. Of these
visionary *christians* in general, who disowned subjection to the civil powers in being, where they respectively lived, there is mention made in several places in
the New-Testament: the apostle *Peter* in particular,
characterizes them in this manner—*them that—despise
government—presumptuous are they, self-willed, they are
not afraid to speak evil of dignities.*† Now it is with reference to these doating *christians*, that the apostle
speaks in the passage before us. And I shall now
give you the sense of it in a paraphrase upon each
verse in its order, desiring you to keep in mind the
character of the persons for whom it is designed, that
so, as I go along, you may see how just and natural

* Matth. xxii. 17. †2 Pet. ii. 10.

2

this address is ; and how well suited to the circumstances of those against whom it is levelled.

The apostle begins thus—*Let every soul** *be subject
unto the higher powers ;*† *for there is no power*‡ *but of
GOD* : *the powers that be*§ *are ordained of GOD*‖ ver.
1. q. d. " Whereas some professed *Christians* vainly
imagine, that they are wholly excused from all manner
of duty and subjection to civil authority, refusing to hon-
or their rulers, and to pay taxes ; which opinion is not
only unreasonable in itself, but also tends to fix a lasting reproach upon the *christian* name and profession.
I now, as an apostle and ambassador of Christ, exhort
every one of you, be he who he will, to pay all dutiful
submission to those who are vested with any civil office. For there is, properly speaking, no authority
but what is derived from God, as it is only by his permission and providence that any possess it. Yea, I
may add, that all civil magistrates, as such, although
they may be *heathens,* are appointed and ordained of
God. For it is certainly God's will, that so useful an
institution as that of magistracy, should take place in
the world, for the good of civil society." The apostle proceeds—*Whosoever, therefore, resisteth the power,*

**Every soul.* This is an *hebraism,* which signifies *every man ;* so that the
apostle does not exempt the *clergy :* such as were endowed with the gift of
prophecy, or any other miraculous powers which subsisted in the church at
that day. And by his using the *Hebrew* idiom, it seems that he had the *Jewish*
converts principally in his eye.

†*The Higher Powers :* more literally, the *over-ruling powers :* which
term extends to all civil rulers in common.

‡By *power,* the apostle intends not lawless *strength* and brutal *force,*
without regulation or proper direction ; but just *authority ;* for so the word
here used properly signifies. There may be *power* where there is no *authority.* No man has any *authority* to do what is wrong and injurious, though he
may have power to do it.

§*The powers that be :* Those persons who are in fact vested with authority ;
those who are in possession. And who those are, the apostle leaves christians to determine for themselves ; but whoever they are, they are to be obeyed.

‖*Ordained of God :* As it is not without God's providence and permission,
that any are clothed with authority ; and as it is agreeable to the positive will
and purpose of God, that there should be *some persons* vested with authority
for the good of society : not that any rulers have their commission immediately from God, the supreme Lord of the Universe. If any assert, that kings,
or any other rulers, are ordained of God in the latter sense, it is incumbent
upon them to show the commission which they speak of, under the broad seal
of heaven. And when they do this, they will no doubt, be believed.

resisteth the ordinance of God ; and they that resist shall receive to themselves damnation. ver. 2. q. d. "Think not, therefore, that ye are guiltless of any crime or sin against God, when ye factiously disobey and resist the civil authority. For magistracy and government being, as I have said, the ordinance and appointment of God, it follows, that to resist magistrates in the execution of their offices, is really to resist the will and ordinance of God himself : And they who thus resist, will accordingly be punished by God for this sin in common with others." The apostle goes on—*For rulers are not a terror to good works, but to the evil.** *Wilt thou then, not be afraid of the power? Do that which is good, and thou shalt have praise of the same: For he is the minister of God to thee for good,* ver. 3d, and part of the 4th. q. d. "That you may see the truth and justness of what I assert, (viz. that magistracy is the ordinance of God, and that you sin against him in opposing it,) consider that even *pagan* rulers, are not, by the nature and design of their office, enemies and a terror to the good and virtuous actions of men, but only to the injurious and mischievous to society. Will ye not, then, reverence and honor magistracy, when ye see the good end and intention of it ? How can ye be so unreasonable ? Only mind to do your duty as members of society; and this will gain you the applause and favor of all good rulers. For while you do thus, they are, by their office, as ministers of God, obliged to encourage and protect you ; it is for this very purpose that they are clothed with power." The apostle subjoins—*But if thou do that which is evil, be afraid, for he beareth not the sword in vain. For he is the minister of God, a revenger, to execute wrath*

---

*For rulers are not a terror to good works, but to the evil. It cannot be supposed that the apostle designs here, or in any of the succeeding verses, to give the true character of *Nero*, or any other civil powers then in being, as if they were in fact such persons as he describes, a terror to evil works only, and not to the good. For such a character did not belong to them ; and the apostle was no sycophant, or parasite of power, whatever some of his pretended successors have been. He only tells what rulers would be, provided they acted up to their character and office.

upon him that docth evil.* ver. 4. latter part, q. d.
"But upon the other hand, if ye refuse to do your duty
as members of society; if ye refuse to bear your part
in the support of government; if ye are disorderly, and
do things which merit civil chastisement, then, indeed,
ye have reason to be afraid. For it is not in vain that
rulers are vested with the power of inflicting punishment. They are, by their office, not only the ministers of God for good to those that do well, but also
his ministers to revenge, to discountenance and punish
those that are unruly, and injurious to their neighbors."
The apostle proceeds—*Wherefore ye must needs be sub-*
ject not only for wrath, but also for conscience sake, ver.
5. q. d. "Since therefore, magistracy is the ordinance
of God ; and since rulers are, by their office, benefactors to society, by discouraging what is bad, and encouraging what is good, and so preserving peace and
order amongst men ; it is evident that ye ought to pay
a willing subjection to them; not to obey merely for
fear of exposing yourselves to their wrath and dis-
pleasure, but also in point of reason, duty and conscience : Ye are under an indispensable obligation, as
christians, to honor their office, and to submit to them
in the execution of it." The apostle goes on—*For,*
for this cause pay your tribute also ; For they are God's
ministers, attending continually upon this very thing, ver.

*It is manifest that when the apostle speaks of it, as the office of civil rulers,
to encourage what is *good,* and to punish what is evil, he speaks only of *civil*
good, and *evil.* They are to consult the good of society *as such ;* not to dictate in religious concerns ; not to make laws for the government of men's
consciences ; and to inflict civil penalties for religious crimes. It is sufficient
to overthrow the doctrine of the authority of the civil magistrate, in affairs of
a spiritual nature, (so far as it is built upon any thing which is here said by
St. Paul, or upon any thing else in the New-Testament) only to observe, that
all the magistrates then in the world, were *heathen,* implacable enemies to christianity : so that to give them authority in religious matters, would have been,
in effect, to give them authority to extirpate the christian religion, and to establish the idolatries and superstitions of paganism. And can any one reasonably suppose, that the apostle had any intention to extend the authority of rulers,
beyond concerns merely civil and political, to the overthrowing of that religion which he himself was so zealous in propagating? But it is natural for
those whose religion cannot be supported upon the footing of reason and
argument, to have recourse to power and force, which will serve a bad cause
as well as a good one ; and indeed much better.

6. q. d. "And here is a plain reason also why ye should pay tribute to them; for they are God's ministers, exalted above the common level of mankind, not that they may indulge themselves in softness and luxury, and be entitled to the servile homage of their fellowmen; but that they may execute an office no less laborious than honorable; and attend continually upon the public welfare. This being their business and duty, it is but reasonable, that they should be requited for their care and diligence in performing it; and enabled, by taxes levied upon the subject, effectually to prosecute the great end of their institution, the good of society." The apostle sums all up in the following words. *Render therefore to all their dues; tribute,* to whom tribute is due; custom,* to whom custom; fear, to whom fear; honor, to whom honor*, ver. 7. q. d. "Let it not, therefore, be said of any of you hereafter, that you contemn government, to the reproach of yourselves, and of the *christian* religion. Neither your being *Jews* by nation, nor your becoming the subjects of Christ's kingdom, gives you any dispensation for making disturbances in the government under which you live. Approve yourselves, therefore, as peaceable and dutiful subjects. Be ready to pay to your rulers all that they may, in respect of their office, justly demand of you. Render tribute and custom to those of your governors to whom tribute and custom belong: And cheerfully honor and reverence all who are vested with civil authority, according to their deserts."

THE apostle's doctrine, in the passage thus explained, concerning the office of civil rulers, and the duty of subjects, may be summed up in the following observations;† viz.

**Grotius observes that the greek words here used, answer to the *tributum* and *vectigal* of the *Romans*; the former was the money paid for the soil and poll; the latter, the duties laid npon some sorts of merchandize. And what the apostle here says, deserves to be seriously considered by all christians concerned in that common practice of carrying on an *illicit trade* and *running of goods*.

†The several observations here only mentionod, were handled at large in two preceeding discourses upon this subject.

THAT the end of magistracy is the good of civil society, *as such :*

THAT civil rulers, *as such,* are the ordinance and ministers of God ; it being by his permission and providence that any bear rule ; and agreeable to his will, that there should be *some persons* vested with authority in society, for the well-being of it :

THAT which is here said concerning civil rulers, extends to all of them in common : It relates indifferently to monarchical, republican and aristocratical government ; and to all other forms which truly answer the sole end of government, the happiness of society ; and to all the different degrees of authority in any particular state ; to inferior officers no less than to the supreme :

THAT disobedience to civil rulers in the due exercise of their authority, is not merely *political sin,* but heinous *offence against God* and *religion :*

THAT the true ground and reason* of our obligation to be subject to the *higher powers,* is the usefulness of magistracy (when properly exercised) to human society, and its subserviency to the general welfare :

*Some suppose the apostle in this passage enforces the duty of submission, with *two* arguments quite distinct from each other : one taken from this consideration, that rulers are the ordinance, and the ministers of God, (ver. 1. 2. and 4.) and the other, from the benefits that accrue to society from civil government, (ver. 3, 4 and 6.) And indeed these may be distinct motives and arguments for submission, as they may be separately viewed and contemplated. But when we consider that rulers are not the ordinance and the ministers of God, but only so far forth as they perform God's will, by acting up to their office and character, and so by being benefactors to society, this makes these arguments coincide, and run up into *one* at last : at least so far, that the former of them cannot hold good for submission, where the latter fails. Put the supposition, that any men bearing the title of a magistrate, should exercist his power in such a manner as to have no claim to obedience by virtue of tha argument which is founded upon the usefulness of magistracy : and you equally take off the force or the other argument also, which is founded upon his being the ordinance and the minister of God. For he is no longer God's ordinance and minister, than he acts up to his office and character, by exercising his power for the good of society—This is, in brief, the reason why it is said above, in the *singular* number, *the true ground and reason,* &c. The use and propriety of this remark may be more apparent in the progress of the argument concerning resistance.

THAT obedience to civil rulers is here equally requir=
ed under all forms of government, which answer the
sole end of all government, the good of society; and to
every degree of authority in any state, whether supreme or subordinate :

(From whence it follows,

THAT if unlimited obedience and non-resistance, be
here required as a duty under any one form of government, it is also required as a duty under all other
forms ; and as a duty to subordinate rulers as well as
to the supreme.)

AND lastly, that those civil rulers to whom the apostle enjoins subjection, are the persons *in possession; the
powers that be ;* those who are *actually* vested with
authority.*

THERE is one very important and interesting point
which remains to be inquired into ; namely, the *extent*
of that subjection *to the higher powers,* which is here
enjoined as a duty upon all christians. Some have
thought it warrantable and glorious, to disobey the civil powers in certain circumstances; and, in cases of
very great and general oppression, when humble re-
m onstrances fail of having any effect; and when the
pu lic welfare cannot be otherwise provided for and se-
cur ed, to rise unanimously even against the sovereign
himself, in order to redress their grievances ; to vindicate their natural and legal rights ; to break the yoke

*This must be understood with this *proviso,* that they do not grossly *abuse*
their power and trust, but exercise it for the good of those that are governed.
Who these persons were, whether *Nero,* &c. or not, the apostle does not say ;
but leaves it to be determined by those to whom he writes. God does not
interpose in a miraculous way, to point out the persons who shall bear rule,
and to whom subjection is due. And, as to the unalienable, indefeasible right
of *primogeniture,* the scriptures are entirely silent, or rather plainly, contradict
it : *Saul* being the first king among the *Israelites ;* and appointed to the royal
dignity, during his own father's life-time : and he was succeeded, or rather
superseded by *David, the* last *born among many brethren*—Now if *God* has not
invariably determined this matter, it must, of course, be determined by *men.*
And if it be determined by *men,* it must be determined either in the way of
force, or of *compact.* And which of these is the most *equitable,* can be no
question.

of tyranny, and free themselves and posterity from inglorious servitude and ruin. It is upon this principle that many royal oppressors have been driven from their thrones into banishment; and many slain by the hands of their subjects. It was upon this principle that *Tarquin* was expelled from *Rome*; and *Julius Cæsar*, the conqueror of the world, and the tyrant of his country, cut off in the senate house. It was upon this principle, that king *Charles* I, was beheaded before his own banqueting house. It was upon this principle, that king *James* II. was made to fly that country which he aimed at enslaving: And upon this principle was that *revolution* brought about, which has been so fruitful of happy consequences to *Great-Britain*. But, in opposition to this principle, it has often been asserted, that the scripture in general (and the passage under consideration in particular) makes all resistance to princes a crime, in any case whatever.—If they turn tyrants, and become the common oppressors of those, whose welfare they ought to regard with a paternal affection, we must not pretend to right ourselves, unless it be by prayers and tears and humble intreaties: And if these methods fail of procuring redress, we must not have recourse to any other, but all suffer ourselves to be robbed and butchered at the pleasure of the *Lord's anointed*; lest we should incur the sin of rebellion, and the punishment of damnation. For he has God's authority and commission to bear him out in the worst of crimes, so far that he may not be withstood or controled Now whether we are obliged to yield such an absolute submission to our prince: or whether disobedience and resistance may not be justifiable in some cases, notwithstanding any thing in the passage before us, is an inquiry in which we are all concerned; and this is the inquiry which is the main design of the present discourse.

Now there does not seem to be any necessity of supposing, that an absolute, unlimited obedience,

whether active or passive, is here enjoined, merely for
this reason, that the precept is delivered in *absolute
terms*, without any *exception* or *intimation* expressly
mentioned. We are enjoined, (ver. 1.) to be *subject
to the higher powers:* and (ver. 5.) to be *subject for
conscience sake.* And because these expressions are
absolute and unlimited, (or more properly, general)
some have inferred, that the subjection required in
them, must be absolute and unlimited also: At least
so far forth as to make passive obedience and non-resistance, a duty in all cases whatever, if not active
obedience likewise. Though, by the way, there is
here no distinction made betwixt active and passive
obedience; and if either of them be required in an
unlimited sense, the other must be required in the
same sense also, by virtue of the present argument;
because the expressions are equally absolute with respect to both. But that unlimited obedience of any
sort, cannot be argued merely from the indefinite expressions in which obedience is enjoined, appears from
hence, that expressions of the same nature, frequently occur in scripture, upon which it is confessed on all
hands, that no such absolute and unlimited sense ought
to be put. For example, *Love not the world; neither
the things that are in the world; *Lay not up for
yourselves treasures upon earth; †Take therefore no
thought for the morrow;‡* are precepts expressed in
at least equally absolute and unlimited terms: but it
is generally allowed that they are to be understood
with certain restrictions and limitations; some degree
of love to the world, and the things of it, being allow-
able. Nor, indeed, do the *Right Reverend Fathers in
God,* and other *dignified clergymen* of the established
church, seem to be altogether averse to admitting of
restrictions in the latter case, how warm soever any
of them may be against restrictions, and limitations,
in the case of submission to authority, whether civil or
ecclesiastical. It is worth remarking also, that patience

* 1 John ii. 15.   † Matt. vi. 19.   ‡ Matt. vi 34.

3

and submission under private injuries, are enjoined in much more peremptory and absolute terms, than any that are used with regard to submission to the injustice and oppression of civil rulers. Thus, *I say unto you, that ye resist not evil; but whosoever shall smite thee on the right cheek, turn to him the other also. And if any man will sue thee at the law, and take away thy coat, let him have thy cloak also. And whosoever shall compel thee to go a mile with him, go with him twain.** Any man may be defied to produce such strong expressions in favor of a passive and tame submission to unjust, tyrannical rulers, as are here used to enforce submission to private injuries. But how few are there that understand those expressions literally? And the reason why they do not, is because (with submission to the *quakers*) common sense shows that they were not intended to be so understood.

But to instance, in some scripture precepts which are more directly to the point in hand.—Children are commanded to obey their parents, and servants their masters, in as absolute and unlimited terms as subjects are here commanded to obey their civil rulers. Thus this same apostle—*Children obey your parents in the Lord ; for this is right. Honor thy father and mother, which is the first commandment with promise.—Servants be obedient to them that are your masters, according to the flesh, with fear and trembling, with singleness of your heart as unto Christ.*† Thus also wives are commanded to be obedient to their husbands—*Wives, submit yourselves unto your own husbands, as unto the Lord. For the husband is the head of the wife, even as* CHRIST IS THE HEAD OF THE CHURCH.—*Therefore, as the church is subject unto Christ, so let the wives be to their own husbands* IN EVERY THING.‡ In all these cases, submission is required in terms (at least) as absolute and universal, as are ever used with respect to rulers and subjects. But who supposes that the apostle ever intended to teach, that children, ser-

*Mat. v. 39, 40, 41.   †Eph. vi. 1, &c.   ‡Eph. v. 22, 23, 24.

vants and wives, should, in all cases whatever, obey their parents, masters and husbands respectively, never making any opposition to their will, even although they should require them to break the commandments of God, or should causelessly make an attempt upon their lives? No one puts such a sense upon these expressions, however absolute and unlimited. Why then should it be supposed, that the apostle designed to teach universal obedience, whether active or passive, to *the higher powers*, merely because his precepts are delivered in absolute and unlimited terms? And if this be a good argument in one case, why is it not in others also? If it be said, that resistance and disobedience to *the higher powers*, is here said positively to be a sin, so also is the disobedience of children to parents; servants, to masters; and wives, to husbands, in other places of scripture. But the question still remains, whether in all these cases, there be not some exceptions? In the three latter, it is allowed there are. And from hence it follows, that barely the use of absolute expressions, is no proof, that obedience to civil rulers, is, in all cases, a duty ; or resistance, in all cases, a sin. I should not have thought it worth while to take any notice at all of this argument, had it not been much insisted upon by some of the advocates for passive obedience and non-resistance : For it is, in itself, perfectly trifling; and rendered considerable, only by the stress that has been laid upon it for want of better.

THERE is, indeed, one passage in the New-Testament, where it may seem, at first view, that an unlimited submission to civil rulers, is enjoined.—*Submit yourselves to every ordinance of man for the Lord's sake.**—To *every ordinance of man.*—However, this expression is no stronger than that before taken notice of, with relation to the duty of wives—*So let the wives be subject to their own husbands*—IN EVERY THING. But

*1 Pet. 2. 13.

the true solution of this difficulty (if it be one) is *this* : by *every ordinance of man*,* is not meant every command of the civil magistrate without exception; but *every order of magistrates appointed by man ;*—whether *superior* or *inferior* : For so the apostle explains himself in the very next words—*Whether it be to the king as supreme, or to governors, as unto them that are sent*, &c. But although the apostle has not subjoined any such explanation, the reason of the thing itself would have obliged us to limit the expression [*every ordinance of man*]to such human ordinances and commands,as are not inconsistent with the ordinances and commands of God, the supreme lawgiver; or with any other higher, and antecedent obligations.

It is to be observed, in the next place, that as the duty of universal obedience and non-resistance to the *higher powers*, cannot be argued from the absolute unlimited expressions which the apostle here uses; so neither can it be argued from the scope and drift of his reasoning, considered with relation to the persons he was here opposing. As was observed above, there were some professed *christians* in the apostolic age,who disclaimed all magistracy and civil authority in general, *dispising government* and *speaking evil of dignities ;* some under a notion that *Jews* ought not to be under the jurisdiction of *Gentile* rulers; and others, that they were set *free* from the temporal powers, by Christ. Now it is with perons of this licentious opinion and character, that the apostle is concerned. And all that was directly to his point, was to show that they were bound to submit to magistracy *in general.* This is a circumstance very material to be taken notice of, in order to ascertain the sense of the apostle. For this being considered, it is sufficient to account for all that he says concerning the the duty of subjection, and the sin of resistance, to the *higher powers*, without

* Literally, *every human institution*, or *appointment.* By which manner of expression the apostle plainly intimates, that rulers derive their authority *immediately*, not from *God*, but from *men*.

having recourse to the doctrine of unlimited submission and passive obedience, in all cases whatever.
Were it known that those in opposition to whom the
apostle wrote, allowed of civil authority in general, and
only asserted that there were *some cases* in which obedience and non-resistance, were not a duty, there
would, then, indeed, be reason for interpreting this passage as containing the doctrine of unlimited obedience,
and non-resistance, as it must, in this case, be supposed
to have been levelled against such as denied that doctrine. But since it is certain that there were persons
who vainly imagined, that civil government, in general,
was not to be regarded by them, it is most reasonable
to suppose, that the apostle designed his discourse
only against *them*. And agreeably to this supposition,
we find that he argues the usefulness of civil magistracy in general; its agreeableness to the will and
purpose of God, who is *over all;* and so deduces from
hence, the obligation of submission to it. But it will
not follow, that because civil government is, in general, a good institution, and necessary to the peace and
happiness of human society, therefore there are no
supposeable cases in which resistance to it can be innocent. So that the duty of unlimited obedience,
whether active or passive, can be argued, neither from
the manner of expression here used, nor from the general scope and design of the passage.

AND if we attend to the nature of the argument with
which the apostle here enforces the duty of submission
to *the higher powers,* we shall find it to be such an one,
as concludes not in favour of submission to all who bear
the *title* of rulers, in common ; but only, to those who
actually perform the duty of rulers, by exercising a reasonable and just authority,for the good of human society.
This is a point which it will be proper to enlarge upon ;
because the question before us turns very much upon
the truth or falsehood of this position. It is obvious,
then, in general, that the civil rulers whom the apostle

here speaks of, and obedience to whom he presses upon christians as a duty, are *good rulers*,* such as are in the exercise of their office and power, benefactors to society. Such they are described to be, throughout this passage. Thus it is said, that they are not *a terror to good works, but to the evil;* that they are God's *ministers for good; revengers to execute wrath upon him that doeth evil;* and that *they attend continually upon this very thing.* St. *Peter* gives the same account of rulers: They are *for a praise to them that do well, and the punishment of evil doers.*† It is manifest that this character and description of rulers, agrees only to such as are rulers in fact, as well as in name: to such as govern well, and act agreeably to their office. And the apostle's argument for submission to rulers, is wholly built and grounded upon a presumption that they do in fact answer this character; and is of no force at all upon the supposition of the contrary. If *rulers are a terror to good works, and not to the evil;* if they are not *ministers for good to society,* but for evil and distress, by violence and oppression; if they *execute wrath upon* sober, peaceable persons, who do their duty as members of society; and suffer rich and honorable knaves to escape with impunity; if instead of *attending continually upon* the good work of advancing the public welfare, they *attend* only upon the gratification of their own lust and pride, and ambition, to the destruction of the public welfare; if this be the case, it is plain that the apostle's argument for submission does not reach them; they are not the same, but different persons from those whom he characterizes; and who must be obeyed according to his reasoning.— Let me illustrate the apostle's argument, by the following *similitude:* (it is no matter how far it is from any thing which has, in fact, happened in the world.) Suppose, then, it was allowed, in general, that the

---

* By *good rulers,* are not intended such as are good in a *moral* or *religious,* but only in a *political,* sense; those who perform their duty so far as their office extends; and so far as civil society, as such, is concerned in their actions.

†See the marginal note, page 11. See also the marginal note, p. 12.

clergy were an useful order of men; that they ought to be *esteemed very highly in love for their works' sake;** and to be decently supported by those whom they serve, *the laborer being worthy of his reward.*† Suppose farther, that a number of *Reverend* and *Right Reverend Drones*, who *worked not;* who preached, perhaps, but *once a year*, and *then*, not the *gospel* of Jesus Christ; but the *divine right of tythes;*—the *dignity of their office as ambassadors of Christ*, the equity of *fine cures*, and a *plurality of benefices;*—the excellency of the *devotions* in *that prayer book*, which some of them hired *chaplains to use for them;*—or some favourite point of *church tyranny*, and *antichristian* usurpation; suppose such men as these, spending their lives in effeminacy, luxury and idleness; (or when they were not idle, doing that which is worse than idleness; suppose such men) should, merely by the merit of *ordination* and *consecration*, and *a peculiar, odd habit*, claim great respect and reverence from those whom they civilly called the *beasts of the laiety;*‡ and demand thousands *per annum*, for that good service which they—*never performed;* and for which, if they had performed it, this would be much more than a *quantum meruit:* suppose this should be the case, (it is only by way of *simile*, and surely it will give no offence) would not every body be astonished at such insolence, injustice and impiety? And ought not such men to be told plainly, that they could not reasonably expect the esteem and reward, due to the ministers of the gospel, unless they did the duties of their office? Should they not be told, that their *title* and *habit* claimed no regard, reverence or pay, separate from the *care* and *work* and various *duties* of their *function?* And that while they neglected the *latter*, the *former* served only to render them the more ridiculous and contemptible?—The application of this *similitude* to the case in hand, is very easy.—If those who bear the title of civil rulers, do not perform the duty of civil rulers, but act directly

* 1 Thes. v. 13.   † 1 Tim. v. 18.   ‡ Mr. Leslie.

counter to the sole end and design of their office; if
they injure and oppress their subjects, instead of defending their rights and doing them good ; they have
not the least pretence to be honored, obeyed and re-
warded, according to the apostle's argument. For his
reasoning, in order to shew the duty of subjection to
the *higher powers*, is, as was before observed, built
wholly upon the supposition, that they do, *in fact*, perform the duty of rulers.

IF it be said, that the apostle here uses another argument for submission to the *higher powers*, besides
that which is taken from the usefulness of their office
to civil society, when properly discharged and execut-
ed; namely, that their *power is from God;* that they
are ordained of God; and that they *are God's ministers* : And if it be said, that this argument for submission to them will hold good, although they do not exercise their power for the benefit, but for the ruin, and
destruction of human society; this objection was ob-
viated, in part, before.* Rulers have no authority
from God to do mischief.   They are not *God's ordinance*, or *God's ministers*, in any other sense than as it
is by his permission and providence, that they are exalted to bear rule ; and as magistracy duly exercised,
and authority rightly applied, in the enacting and executing good laws,—laws attempered and accommodated to the common welfare of the subjects, must be
supposed to be agreeable to the will of the beneficent
author and supreme Lord of the universe ; whose *kingdom ruleth over all ;*† and whose *tender mercies are
over all his works.*‡ It is BLASPHEMY to call tyrants
and oppressors, *God's ministers*.   They are more properly *the messengers of* SATAN *to buffet us.*§   No rulers
are properly *God's ministers*,but such as are *just,ruling
in the fear of God.*‖ When once magistrates act contrary to their office, and the end of their institution;

when they rob and ruin the public, instead of being guardians of its peace and welfare ; they immediately cease to be the *ordinance* and *ministers of God ;* and no more deserve that glorious character, than common *pirates* and *highwaymen.* So that whenever that argument for submission fails, which is grounded upon the usefulness of magistracy to civil society, (as it always does when magistrates do hurt to society instead of good) the other argument, which is taken from their being the ordinance of God, must necessarily fail also ; no person of a civil character being *God's minister,* in the sense of the apostle, any farther than he performs God's will, by exercising a just and reasonable authority; and ruling for the good of the subject.

THIS in general. Let us now trace the apostle's reasoning in favor of submission to the *higher powers,* a little more particularly and exactly. For by this it will appear, on one hand, how good and conclusive it is, for submission to those rulers who exercise their power in a proper manner : And, on the other, how weak and trifling and inconnected it is, if it be supposed to be meant by the apostle to show the obligation and duty of obedience to tyrannical, oppressive rulers, in common with others of a different character.

THE apostle enters upon his subject thus—*Let every soul be subject unto the higher powers ; for there is no power but of God : the powers that be, are ordained of God.** Here he urges the duty of obedience from this topic of argument, that civil rulers, as they are supposed to fulfil the pleasure of God, are the ordinance of God. But how is this an argument for obedience to such rulers as do not perform the pleasure of God, by doing good ; but the pleasure of the devil, by doing evil ; and such as are not, therefore, *God's ministers,* but the devil's ! *Whosoever, therefore, resisteth the power, resisteth the ordinance of God ; and*

*Ver. 1.

4

they that resist, shall receive to themselves damnation. Here the apostle argues, that those who resist a reasonable and just authority, which is agreeable to the will of God, do really resist the will of God himself; and will, therefore, be punished by him. But how does this prove, that those who resist a lawless, unreasonable power, which is contrary to the will of God, do therein resist the will and ordinance of God? Is resisting those who resist God's will, the same thing with resisting God? Or shall those who do so, *receive to themselves damnation! For rulers are not a terror to good works, but to the evil. Wilt thou then not be afraid of the power? Do that which is good; and thou shalt have praise of the same. For he is the minister of God to thee for good.*† Here the apostle argues more explicitly than he had before done, for revereing, and submitting to magistracy, from this consideration, that such as really perform the duty of magistrates, would be enemies only to the evil actions of men, and would befriend and encourage the good; and so be a common blessing to society. But how is this an argument, that we must honor, and submit to such magistrates as are not enemies to the evil actions of men, but to the good; and such as are not a common blessing, but a common curse, to society! *But if thou do that which is evil, be afraid: For he is the minister of God, a revenger, to execute wrath upon him that doth evil.*‡ Here the apostle argues from the nature and end of magistracy, that such as did evil, (and such only) had reason to be afraid of the *higher powers;* it being part of their office to punish evil doers, no less than to defend and encourage such as do well. But if magistrates are unrighteous; if they are *respecters of persons;* if they are partial in their administration of justice; then those who do well, have as much reason to *be afraid,* as those that do evil: there can be no safety for the good, nor any peculiar ground of terror to the unruly and injurious. So that in this case, the main

*Ver. 2. †Ver. 3d. and part of the 4th. ‡Ver. 4th. latter part.

end of civil government will be frustrated. And what reason is there for submitting to that government, which does by no means answer the design of government? *Wherefore ye must needs be subject not only for wrath, but also for conscience sake.** Here the apostle argues the duty of a cheerful and conscientious submission to civil government, from the nature and end of magistracy as he had before laid it down, i. e. as the design of it was to punish evil doers, and to support and encourage such as do well; and as it must, if so exercised, be agreeable to the will of God. But how does what he here says, prove the duty of a cheerful and conscientious subjection to those who forfeit the character of rulers? to those who encourage the bad, and discourage the good? The argument here used no more proves it to be a sin to resist such rulers, than it does, to *resist the devil,* that he may *flee from us.*† For one is as truly the *minister of God* as the other. *For, for this cause pay you tribute also; for they are God's ministers, attending continually upon this very thing.*‡ Here the apostle argues the duty of paying taxes, from this consideration, that those who perform the duty of rulers, are continually attending upon the public welfare. But how does this argument conclude for paying taxes to such princes as are continually endeavoring to ruin the public? And especially when such payment would facilitate and promote this wicked design! *Render therefore to all their dues; tribute, to whom tribute is due; custom, to whom custom; fear, to whom fear; honor, to whom honor.*‖ Here the apostle sums up what he had been saying concerning the duty of subjects to rulers. And his argument stands thus—"Since magistrates who execute their office well, are common benefactors to society, and may, in that respect, be properly styled *the ministers and ordinance of God;* and since they are constantly employed in the service of the public, it becomes you to pay them tribute and custom; and to reverence,

*Ver. 5.   †James iv. 7.   ‡Ver. 6.   ‖Ver. 7.

honor, and submit to them in the execution of their respective offices." This is apparently good reasoning. But does this argument conclude for the duty of paying tribute, custom, reverence, honor and obedience to such persons as (although they bear the title of rulers) use all their power to hurt and injure the public? such as are not *God's ministers*, but SATAN's? such as do not take care of, and attend upon the public interest, but their own, to the ruin of the public? that is, in short, to such as have no natural and just claim at all to tribute, custom, reverence, honor and obedience? It is to be hoped that those who have any regard to the apostle's character as an inspired writer, or even as a man of common understanding, will not present him as reasoning in such a loose incoherent manner; and drawing conclusions which have not the least relation to his premises. For what can be more absurd than an argument thus framed? "Rulers are, by their office, bound to consult the public welfare and the good of society: therefore you are bound to pay them tribute, to honor, and submit to them, even when they destroy the public welfare, and are a common pest to society, by acting in direct contradiction to the nature and end of their office."

THUS, upon a careful review of the apostle's reasoning in this passage, it appears that his arguments to enforce submission, are of such a nature, as to conclude only in favor of submission *to such rulers as he himself describes;* i. e. such as rule for the good of society, which is the only end of their institution. Common tyrants, and public oppressors, are not entitled to obedience from their subjects, by virtue of any thing here laid down by the inspired apostle.

I NOW add farther, that the apostle's argument is so far from proving it to be the duty of people to obey, and submit to such rulers as act in contradiction to the public good,† and so to the design of their office, that

† This does not intend, their acting so in *a few particular instances,* which the best of rulers may do through mistake, &c. but their acting so *habitually ;*

it proves *the direct contrary.* For, please to observe. that if the end of all civil government, be the good of society; if this be the thing that is aimed at in constituting civil rulers; and if the motive and argument for submission to government, be taken from the apparent usefulness of civil authority, it follows, that when no such good end can be answered by submission. there remains no argument or motive to enforce it; if instead of this good end's being brought about by submission, a *contrary end* is brought about, and the ruin and misery of society effected by it; here is a plain and positive reason against submission in all such cases, should they ever happen. And therefore, in such cases, a regard to the public welfare, ought to make us withhold from our rulers that obedience and subjection which it would, otherwise, be our duty to render to them. If it be our duty, for example, to obey our king, merely for this reason, that he rules for the public welfare, (which is the only argument the apostle makes use of) it follows, by a parity of reason, that when he turns tyrant, and makes his subjects his prey to devour and to destroy, instead of his charge to defend and cherish, we are bound to throw off our allegiance to him, and to resist; and that according to the tenor of the apostle's argument in this passage. Not to discontinue our allegiance, in this case, would be to join with the sovereign in promoting the slavery and misery of that society, the welfare of which, we ourselves, as well as our sovereign, are indispensably obliged to secure and promote, as far as in us lies. It is true the apostle puts no case of such a tyrannical prince; but by his grounding his argument for submission wholly upon the good of civil society; it is plain he implicitly authorises, and even requires us to make resistance, whenever this shall be necessary to the public safety and happiness. Let me make use of this easy and familiar

and in a manner which plainly shows, that they aim at making themselves great, by the ruin of their subjects.

similitude to illustrate the point in hand—Suppose
God requires a family of children, to obey their father
and not to resist him; and enforces his command with
this argument; that the superintendence and care and
authority of a just and kind parent, will contribute to
the happiness of the whole family; so that they ought
to obey him for their own sakes more than for his :
Suppose this parent at length runs distracted, and attempts, in his mad fit, to cut all his children's throats :
Now, in this case, is not the reason before assigned,
why these children should obey their parent while he
continued of a sound mind, namely, *their common good*,
a reason equally conclusive for disobeying and resisting him, since he is become delirious, and attempts their
ruin? It makes no alteration in argument, whether this
parent, properly speaking, loses his reason, or does,
while he retains his understanding, that which is as
fatal in its consequences, as any thing he could do, were
he really deprived of it. This similitude needs no
formal application—

But it ought to be remembered, that if the duty
of universal obedience and non-resistance to our king
or prince, can be argued from this passage, the same
unlimited submission under a republican, or any other
form of government; and even to all the subordinate
powers in any particular state, can be proved by it
as well : which is more than those who alledge it for
the mentioned purpose, would be willing should be
inferred from it. So that this passage does not answer their purpose; but really overthrows and con-
futes it. This matter deserves to be more particularly considered.—The advocates for unlimited submission and passive obedience, do, if I mistake not, always speak with reference to kingly or monarchical
government, as distinguished from all other forms ;
and, with reference to submitting to the will of the
king, in distinction from all subordinate officers, acting beyond their commission, and the authority which
they have received from the crown. It is not pre-

tended that any person besides kings, have a divine
right to do what they please, so that no one may resist them, without incurring the guilt of factiousness
and rebellion. If any other supreme powers oppress
the people, it is generally allowed, that the people
may get redress, by resistance, if other methods prove
ineffectual. And if any officers in a kingly govern-
ernment, go beyond the limits of that power which
they have derived from the crown, (the supposed
original source of all power and authority in the state)
and attempt, illegally, to take away the properties
and lives of their fellow-subjects, they may be *forci-
bly* resisted, at least till application can be made to
the crown. But as to the sovereign himself, he may
not be resisted in any case ; nor any of his officers,
while they confine themselves within the bounds
which he has prescribed to them. This is, I think,
a true sketch of the principles of those who defend
the doctrine of passive obedience and non-resistance.
Now there is nothing in scripture which supports this
scheme of political principles. As to the passage under consideration, the apostle here speaks of civil rulers in *general ;* of all persons in *common,* vested with
authority for the good of society, without any particular reference to one form of government, more than
to another ; or to the supreme power in any particular state, more than to subordinate powers. The
apostle does not concern himself with the different
forms of government.† This he supposes left intire-

† The essence of government (I mean *good* government ; and this is the
only government which the apostle treats of in this passage) consists in the
making and *executing of good laws*—laws attempered to the common felicity
of the *governed.* And if this be, *in fact,* done, it is evidently, in itself, a thing
of no conseqnence at all, what the *particular* form of government is ;—whether the legislative and executive power be lodged in *one and the same* person,
or in *different* persons ;—whether in *one* person, whom we call an *absolute monarch ;*—whether in a *few,* so as to constitute an *aristocracy ;*—whether in
many, so as to constitute a *republic ;* or whether in *three co-ordinate branches,*
in such manner as to make the government *partake* something of *each* of these
forms ; and to be, at the same time, *essentially different* from them *all.* If the
end be attained, it is enough. But no form of government seems to be so un-
likely to accomplish this *end,* as *absolute monarchy*—Nor is there any one
that has so little pretence to a *divine original,* unless it be in this sense, that

ly to human prudence and discretion. Now the consequence of this is, that unlimited and passive obedience, is no more enjoined in this passage, under monarchical government; or to the supreme power in any state, than under all other species of government; which answer the end of government; or, to all the subordinate degrees of civil authority, from the highest to the lowest. Those, therefore, who would from this passage infer the guilt of resisting kings, in all cases whatever, though acting ever so contrary to the design of their office, must, if they will be consistent, go much farther, and infer from it the guilt of resistance under all other forms of government; and of resisting *any petty officer* in the state though acting beyond his commission, in the most arbitrary, illegal manner possible. The argument holds equally strong in both cases. All civil rulers, as such, are the *ordinance* and *ministers of God;* and they are all, by the nature of their office, and in their respective spheres and stations, bound to consult the public welfare. With the same reason therefore, that any deny unlimited and passive obedience to be here enjoined under a republic or aristocrasy, or any other established form of civil government; or to subordinate powers, acting in an illegal and oppressive manner; (with the same reason) others may deny, that such obedience is enjoined to a king or monarch, or any civil power whatever. For the apostle says nothing that is *peculiar to kings;* what he says, extends equally to *all* other persons whatever, vested with any civil office. They are all, in exactly the same sense, the *ordinance of God;* and the *ministers of God;* and obedience is equally enjoined to be paid to them all. For, as the apostle expresses it, *there is* NO POWER *but of God:* And we are required to *render to* ALL *their* DUES;

God *first* introduced it into, and thereby overturned, the common wealth of *Israel*, as a *curse* upon that people for their *folly* and *wickedness*, particularly in *desiring* such a government. (See 1 *Sam.* viii. chap.) Just so God, before, sent *Quails* amongst them, as a *plague*, and a *curse*, and not as a *blessing*. *Numb.* chap. xi.

and not MORE than their DUES. And what these *dues* are, and to *whom* they are to be *rendered*, the apostle *sayeth not ;* but leaves to the reason and consciences of men to determine.

THUS it appears, that the common argument, grounded upon this passage, in favor of universal and passive obedience, really overthrows itself, by proving too much, if it proves any thing at all; namely, that no civil officer is, in any case whatever, to be resisted, though acting in express contradiction to the design of his office; which no man, in his senses, ever did, or can assert.

IF we calmly consider the nature of the thing itself, nothing can well be imagined more directly contrary to common sense, than to suppose that *millions* of people should be subjected to the arbitrary, precarious pleasure of *one single man ;* (who has *naturally* no superiority over them in point of authority) so that their estates, and every thing that is valuable in life, and even their lives also, shall be absolutely at his disposal, if he happens to be wanton and capricious enough to demand them. What unprejudiced man can think, that God made ALL to be thus subservient to the lawless pleasure and phrenzy of ONE, so that it shall always be a sin to resist him! Nothing but the most plain and express revelation from heaven could make a sober, impartial man believe such a monstrous, unaccountable doctrine, and, indeed, the thing itself, appears so shocking—so out of all *proportion*, that it may be questioned, whether all the *miracles* that ever were wrought, could make it credible, that this doctrine *really* came from God. At present, there is not the least syllable in scripture which gives any countenance to it. The hereditary, indefeasible, divine right of kings, and the doctrine of non-resistance, which is built upon the supposition of such a right, are altogether as fabulous and chimerical, as transubstantiation; or any of the most absurd reveries of ancient or modern vissionaries. These notions are fetched neither from divine rela-

5

tion, nor human reason; and if they are derived from neither of those sources, it is not much matter from *whence they come, or whither they go.* Only it is a pity that such doctrines should be propagated in society, to raise factions and rebellions, as we see they have, in fact, been both in the *last,* and in the *present* REIGN.

But then, if unlimited submission and passive obedience to the *higher powers,* in all possible cases, be not a duty, it will be asked, "How far are we obliged to submit? If we may innocently disobey and resist in some cases, why not in all? Where shall we stop? What is the measure of our duty? This doctrine tends to the total dissolution of civil government; and to introduce such scenes of wild anarchy and confusion, as are more fatal to society than the worst of tyranny."

After this manner, some men object; and, indeed, this is the most plausible thing that can be said in favor of such an absolute submission as they plead for. But the worst (or rather the best) of it, is, that there is very little strength or solidity in it. For similar difficulties may be raised with respect to almost every duty of natural and revealed religion.—To instance only in two, both of which are near a kin, and indeed exactly parallel, to the case before us. It is unquestionably the duty of children to submit to their parents; and of servants, to their masters. But no one asserts, that it is their duty to obey, and submit to them, in all supposeable cases; or universally, a sin to resist them. Now does this tend to subvert the just authority of parents and masters? Or to introduce confusion and anarchy into private families? No. How then does the same principle tend to unhinge the government of that larger family, the body politic? We know, in general, that children and servants are obliged to obey their parents and masters respectively. We know also, with equal certainty, that they are not obliged to submit to them in all things, without exception; but may, in some cases, reasonably, and therefore innocently, resist them. These principles are acknowledged upon all hands, whatever difficulty there may be in fixing the exact limits of submission. Now there is at least as much difficulty in stating the measure of duty in these two cases, as in the case of rulers and subjects. So that this is really no objection, at least no reasonable one, against resistance to the *higher powers:* Or, if it is one, it will hold equally against resistance in the other cases mentioned.—It is indeed true, that turbulent, vicious-minded men, may take occasion from this principle, that their rulers may, in some cases, be lawfully resisted, to raise factions and disturbances in the state; and to make resistance where resistance is needless, and therefore, sinful. But is it not equally true, that children and servants of turbulent, vicious minds, may take occasion from this principle, that parents and masters may, in some cases be lawfully resisted, to resist when resistance is unnecessary, and therefore, criminal? Is the principle in either case false in itself, merely because it may be abused; and applied to legitimate disobedience and resistance in those instances, to which it ought not to be applied? According to this way of arguing, there will be no true principles in the world; for there are none but what may be wrested and perverted to serve bad purposes, either through the weakness or wickedness of men.†

†WE may very safely assert these two things in general, without underminding government: One is, That no civil rulers are to be obeyed when they enjoin things that are inconsistent with the commands of God: All such disobedience is lawful and glorious; particularly, if persons refuse to comply with any *legal establishment of religion,* because it is a gross perversion and corruption (as to doctrine, worship and discipline) of a pure and divine religion, brought from heaven to earth by the *Son of God,* (the only King and Head of the *christian* church, and propagated through the world by his inspired apostles. All commands running counter to the declared will of the supreme legislator of heaven and earth, are null and void: And therefore disobedience to them is a duty, not a crime. (See the marginal note, page 12.) Another thing that may be asserted with equal truth and safety, is, that no government is to be submitted to, at the *expence* of that which is the *sole end* of all government—the common good and safety of society. Because, to submit in this case, if it should ever happen, would evidently be to set up the *means* as more valuable, and above the *end:* than which there cannot be a greater solecism and contradiction. The only reason of the institution of civil government, and the only rational ground of submission to it, is the common safety and utility. If therefore, in any case, the common safety and utility would not be promoted by submission to government, but the contrary, there is no ground or motive for obedience and submission, but, for the contrary.

Whoever considers the nature of civil government, must, indeed, be sensible that a great degree of *implicit confidence,* must unavoidably be placed in those

A PEOPLE, really oppressed to a great degree by their sovereign, cannot well be insensible when they are so oppressed. And such a people (if I may allude to an ancient *fable*) have, like the *hesperian* fruit, a DRAGON for their *protector* and *guardian* : Nor would they have any reason to mourn, if some HERCULES should appear to dispatch him.—For a nation

that bear rule : This is implied in the very notion of authority's being originally a *trust*, committed by the people, to those who are vested with it, as all just and righteous authority is ; all besides, is mere lawless force and usurpation ; neither God nor nature, having given any man a right of dominion over any society, independently of that society's approbation and consent to be governed by him.—Now as all men are fallible, it cannot be supposed that the public affairs of any state, should be always administered in the best manner possible, even by persons of the greatest wisdom and integrity. Nor is it sufficient to legitimate disobedience to the *higher powers* that they are not so administered ; or that they are, in some instances, very ill managed : for upon this principle, it is scarcely supposeable that any government at all, could be supported, or subsist. Such a principle manifestly tends to the dissolution of government ; and to throw all things into confusion and anarchy.—But it is equally evident, upon the other hand, that those in authority may abuse their *trust* and power *to such a degree*, that neither the law of reason, nor of religion, requires, that any obedience or submission should be paid to them ; but on the contrary, that they should be totally *discarded ;* and the authority which they were before vested with, transferred to others, who may exercise it more to those good purposes for which it is given.—Nor is this principle, that resistance to the *higher powers*, is, in some extraordinary cases, justifiable, so liable to abuse, as many persons seem to apprehend it. For although there will be always some petulant, querulous men, in every state—men of factions, turbulent and carping dispositions,—glad to lay hold of any trifle to justify an l legitimate their caballing against their rulers, and other seditious practices ; yet there are, comparatively speaking, but few men of this *contemptible character*. It does not appear but that mankind, in general, have a disposition to be as submissive and passive, and tame under government, as they ought to be. Witness a great, if not the greatest part of the known world, who are now groaning, but not murmuring, under the heavy yoke of tyranny ! While those who govern, do it with any tolerable degree of moderation and justice, and, in any good measure act up to their office and character, by being public benefactors ; the people will generally be easy and peaceable ; and be rather inclined to flatter and adore, than to insult and resist them. Nor was there ever any *general* complaint against any administration, *which lasted long*, but what there was good reason for. 'Til people find themselves greatly abused and oppressed by their governors, they are not apt to complain ; and whenever they do, in fact, find themselves thus abused and oppressed, they must be stupid not to complain. To say that subjects in general, are not proper judges when their governors oppress them, and play the tyrant ; and when they defend their rights, administer justice, impartially, and promote the public welfare, is as great *treason* as ever man uttered ; it is treason,—not against one *single* man, but the state—against the whole body politic ;—'tis treason against mankind ;—'tis treason against common sense ;—'tis treason against GOD. And this impious principle lays the foundation for justifying all the tyranny and oppression that every any prince was guilty of. The people know for what end they set up, and maintain, their governors ; and they are the proper judges when they execute their *trust* as they ought to do it ;—when their prince exercises an equitable and paternal authority over them ;—when from a prince and common father, he exalts himself into a tyrant— when from subjects and children, he degrades them into the class of slaves ;— plunders them, makes them his prey, and unnaturally sports himself with their lives and fortunes.

thus abused to arise unanimously, and to resist their prince, even to the dethroning him, is not criminal ; but a reasonable way of vindicating their liberties and just rights ; it is making use of the means, and the only means, which God has put into their power, for mutual and self defence. And it would be highly criminal in them, not to make use of this means. It would be stupid tameness, and unaccountable folly, for whole nations to suffer *one* unreasonable, ambitious and cruel man, to wanton and riot in their misery. And in such a case it would, of the two, be more rational to suppose, that they that did **NOT** *resist*, than that they who did, would *receive to themselves damnation.*

OF KING CHARLES'S SAINTSHIP AND MARTYRDOM.

THIS naturally brings us to make some reflections upon the resistance which was made about a century since, to that unhappy prince, KING CHARLES I. ; and upon the ANNIVERSARY of his death. This is a point which I should not have concerned myself about, were it not that *some men* continue to speak of it, even to this day, with a great deal of warmth and zeal ; and in such a manner as to undermine all the principles of LIBERTY, whether civil or religious, and to introduce the most abject slavery both in church and state ; so that it is become a matter of universal concern.—What I have to offer upon this subject, will be comprised in a short answer to the following *queries ; viz.*

FOR what reason the resistance to king *Charles* the *First,* was made ?

BY whom it was made ?

WHETHER this resistance was REBELLION, † or not ?

† N. B. I speak of rebellion, treason, saintship, martyrdom, &c. throughout this discourse, only in the *scriptural* and *theological sense.* I know not how the *law* defines them ; the study of *that* not being my employment— ..

How the *Anniversary* of king *Charles's* death came at *first* to be solemnized as a day of fasting and humiliation ? And lastly,

WHY those of the episcopal clergy who are very high in the principles of *ecclesiastical authority*, continue to speak of this unhappy man, as a great SAINT and a MARTYR ?

FOR what reason, then, was the resistance to king *Charles*, made ? The general answer to this enquiry is, that it was on account of the *tyranny* and *oppression* of his reign. Not a great while after his accession to the throne, he married a *French catholic ;* and with her seemed to have *wedded* the politics, if not the religion of *France*, also. For afterwards, during a reign, or rather a tyranny of many years, he governed in a perfectly wild and arbitrary manner, paying no regard to the constitution and the laws of the kingdom, by which the power of the crown was limited ; or to the solemn oath which he had taken at his coronation. It would be endless, as well as needless, to give a particular account of all the illegal and despotic measures which he took in his administration ; —partly from his own natural lust of power, and partly from the influence of wicked councellors and ministers.—He committed many illustrious members of both houses of parliament to the *Tower*, for opposing his arbitrary schemes.—He levied many taxes upon the people without consent of parliament;—and then imprisoned great numbers of the principal merchants and gentry for not paying them.—He erected, or at least revived, several new and arbitrary courts, in which the most unheard-of barbarities were committed with his knowledge and approbation.—He supported that more than fiend, arch-bishop *Laud* and the clergy of his stamp, in all their church tyranny and hellish cruelties—He authorised a book in favor of *sports* upon the *Lord's day ;* and several clergymen were persecuted by him and the mentioned *pious* bishop, for not reading it to the people after *divine service.*—When the parliament complained to him of the arbitrary proceedings of his corrupt ministers, he told that *august body*, in a rough, domineering, unprincely manner, that he wondered any one should be so foolish and insolent as to think that he would part with the meanest of his servants *upon their account*—He refused to call any parliament at all for the space of twelve years together, during all which time, he governed in an absolute, lawless, and despotic manner—He took all opportunities to encourage the *papists*, and to promote them to the highest offices of honor and trust.—He (probably) abetted the horrid massacre in *Ireland*, in which two hundred thousand protestants were butchered by the Roman Catholics.—He sent a large sum of money, which he had raised by his arbitrary taxes, into *Germany*, to raise foreign troops, in order to force more arbitrary taxes upon his subjects.—He not only by a long series of *actions*, but also in *plain terms*, asserted an absolute uncontroulable power ; saying even in one of his speeches to parliament, that as it was blasphemy to dispute what God might do ; so it was sedition in subjects to dispute what the king might do.—Towards the end of his tyranny, he came to the House of Commons with an armed force,† and demanded five of its principal members to be delivered up to him.—And this was a prelude, to that unnatural war, which he soon after levied against his own dutiful subjects ; whom he was bound by all the laws of honor, humanity, piety, and I might add, of *interest* also, to defend and cherish with a paternal affection—I have only time to hint at these facts in a general way, all which, and many more of the same tenor, may be proved by good authorities : So that the *figurative* language which St. *John* uses, concerning the just and beneficent deeds of our blessed Saviour, may be applied to the unrighteous and execrable deeds of this prince, *viz. And there are also many other things which* king Charles *did the which, if they should be written every one, I suppose that even the world itself, could not contain the books that*

---

† Historians are not agreed, what number of soldiers attended him in this monstrous invasion of the priviledges of parliament—Some say 300, some 400 : And the author of *The history of the kings of Scotland,* says 500.

*should be written.** Now it was on account of king *Charles's* thus assuming a power above the laws, in direct contradiction to his coronation-oath, and governing the greatest part of his time, in the most arbitrary oppressive manner ; it was upon this account, that that resistance was made to him, which, at length, issued in the loss of his crown, and of *that head* which was unworthy to wear it.

BUT by whom was this resistance made ? Not by a private *junto ;*—not by a small seditious *party ;*—not by a *few desparadoes,* who, to mend their fortunes, would embroil the state ;—but by the LORDS and COMMONS of *England.* It was they that almost unanimously opposed the king's measures for overturning the constitution, and changing that free and happy government into a wretched, absolute monarchy. It was they, that when the king was about levying forces against his subjects, in order to make himself absolute, commissioned officers, and raised an army to defend themselves and the public : And it was they that maintained the war against him all along, till he was made a prisoner. This is indisputable. Though it was not properly speaking, the parliament, but the army, which put him to death afterwards. And it ought to be freely acknowledged, that most of their proceedings, in order to get this matter effected, and particularly the court by which the king was at last tried and condemned, was little better than a mere mockery of justice.—

THE next question which naturally arises, is, whether this resistance which was made to the king *by the Parliament,* was properly *rebellion,* or not ? The answer to which is plain, that it was not ; but a most righteous and glorious stand, made in defence of the natural and legal rights of the people, against the natural and illegal encroachments of arbitrary power. Nor was this a rash and too sudden opposition. The nation had been patient under the oppsessions of the crown, even to *long suffering ;*—for a course of many

* John xxi. 25.

years ; and there was no rational hope of redress in any other way.—Resistance was absolutely necessary, in order to preserve the nation from slavery, misery and ruin. And who so proper to make this resistance, as the Lords and Commons;—the whole representative body of the people ;—guardians of the public welfare; and each of which, was, in point of legislation, vested with an equal, co-ordinate power, with that of the crown ?* Here were *two* branches of the legislature against *one* ;—two of which, had law and equity, and the constitution on their side, against one which was impiously attempting to overturn law and equity, and the constitution ; and to exercise a wanton licentious *sovereignty* over the properties, consciences and lives of all the people :—Such a *sovereignty* as some inconsiderately ascribe to the Supreme Governor of the world.—I say, inconsiderately ; because God himself does not govern in an absolutely arbitrary and despotic manner. The power of this Almighty King (I speak it not without caution and reverence ;

* The *English* constitution is originally and essentially *free*. The character which *J. Cæsar* and *Tacitus* both give of the ancient *Britains* so long ago, is, That they were extremely *jealous of their liberties*, as well as a people of a *martial* spirit. Nor have there been wanting frequent instances and proofs of the same glorious spirit (in both respects) remaining in their posterity ever since, —in the struggles they have made for liberty, both against foreign and domestic tyrants.—Their kings hold their title to the throne, solely by grant of parliament ; i. e. in other words, by the voluntary consent of the people. And, agreeably hereto, the prerogative and rights of the crown are stated, defined and limited by law ; and that as truly and strictly as the rights of any inferior officer in the state ; or indeed, of any private subject. And it is only in this respect, that it can be said, that " the king can do wrong." Being restrained by the law, he cannot, while he confines himself within those just limits which the law prescribes to him as the measure of his authority, injure and oppress the subject.—The king, in his coronation oath, swears to exercise only such a power as the constitution gives him : And the subject, in the oath of allegiance, swears only to obey him in the exercise of such a power. The king is as much bound by his oath, not to infringe the legal rights of the people, as the people are bound to yield subjection to him. From whence it follows, that as soon as the prince sets himself up above law, he loses the king in the tyrant : he does to all intents and purposes, unking himself, by acting out of, and beyond, that sphere which the constitution allows him to move in. And in such cases, he has no more right to be obeyed, than any inferior officer who acts beyond his commission. The subjects' obligation to allegiance *then* ceases of course : and to resist him, is no more *rebellion*, than to resist any foreign invader. There is an essential difference betwixt *government and tyranny ;* at least under such a constitution as the *English*. The former consists in ruling according to law and equity ; the latter in ruling contrary to law and equity. So also, there is an essential difference betwixt resisting a tyrant, and rebellion ; the former

6

the power of this Almighty King) is *limited by law*; not indeed, by *acts of Parliament*, but by the eternal *laws* of truth, wisdom and equity ; and the everlasting *tables* of right reason ;—tables that cannot be *repealed*, or *thrown down* and *broken* like those of *Moses.*—But king *Charles* sat himself up above all these, as much as he did above the written laws of the realm; and made mere humor and caprice, which are no rule at all, the only rule and measure of his administration. And now, is it not perfectly ridiculous to call resistance to such a tyrant, by the name of *rebellion ?—the grand rebellion ?* Even that——parliament, which brought king *Charles II.* to the throne, and which run *loyally mad*, severely reproved one of their own members for condemning the proceedings of that parliament which first took up arms against the former king. And upon the same principles that the proceedings of this parliament may be censured as wicked and rebellious ; the proceedings of those, who since opposed king *James II.* and brought the Prince of *Orange* to the throne, may be censured as wicked and rebellious also. The cases are parallel.—But whatever *some* men may *think*, it is to be hoped that for their own sakes, they will not dare to *speak* against the REVO- LUTION, upon the justice and legality of which, depends (in part) his present MAJESTY'S right to the throne.

IF it be said, that although the parliament which first opposed king *Charles's* measures, and at length took up arms against him, were not guilty of rebellion ; yet certainly those persons were, who condemned, and put him to death ; even this perhaps is not true. For he had, in fact, *unkinged* himself long before, and had forfeited his title to the allegiance of the people. So that those who put him to death, were, at most, only guilty of *murder ;* which, indeed, is bad enough.

a just and reasonable self-defence ; the latter consists in resisting a prince whose administration is just and legal ; and this is what demonstrates it a crime.— Now it is evident, that king *Charles's* government was illegal, and very oppressive, through the greatest part of his reign : And, therefore, to resist him, was no more rebellion, than to oppose any foreign invader, or any other domestic oppressor.

if they were really guilty of *that ;* (which is at least disputable.) *Cromwell,* and those who were principally concerned in the *(nominal)* king's death, might possibly have been very wicked and designing men. Nor shall I say any thing in vindication of the reigning *hypocrisy* of those times, or of *Cromwell's* maleadministration during the *interregnum :* (for it is *truth,* and not a *party,* that I am speaking for.) But still it may be said, that *Cromwell* and his adherents were not, properly speaking, guilty of *rebellion ;* because he whom they beheaded was not, properly speaking, *their king ;* but a *lawless tyrant.*—Much less, are the whole body of the nation at that time to be charged with rebellion on that account ; for it was no *national act ;* it was not done by a *free* parliament. And much less still, is the nation at present, to be charged with the great sin of rebellion. for what their *ancestors* did, (or rather did NOT) a century ago.

But how came the *anniversary* of king *Charl s's* death, to be solemnized as a day of fasting and humiliation ? The true answer in brief, to which enquiry, is, that this fast was instituted by way of *court* and *compliment* to king *Charles* II. upon the *restoration.* All were desirous of making their court to him; of ingratiating themselves; and of making him forget what had been done in opposition to his *father,* so as not to revenge it. To effect this, they ran into the most extravagant professions of affection and loyalty to him, insomuch that he himself said, that it was a *mad* and *hair brained* loyalty which they professed. And amongst other strange things, which his first parliament did, they ordered the *Thirtieth* of *January* (the day on which his father was beheaded) to be kept as a day of solemn humiliation, to deprecate the judgements of heaven for the rebellion which the nation had been guilty of, in that which was no national thing ; and which was not rebellion in them that did it.—Thus they soothed and flattered their new king, at the expence of their liberties :—And were ready to yield up *freely* to *Charles* II. all that enormous power, which they had justly resisted *Charles* I. for usurping to himself.

THE last query mentioned, was, Why those of the *episcopal clergy* who are very high in the principles of *ecclesiastical authority*, continue to speak of this unhappy prince as a *great Saint* and a *Martyr?* This, we know, is what they constantly do, especially upon the 30th of *January;* a day sacred to the *extolling* of *him,* and to the *reproaching* of those who are not of the *established church.* Out of the same mouth on this day, *proceedeth blessing and cursing;†* therewith bless they their God, even Charles, and therewith curse they the dissenters: And their *tongue can no man tame; it is an unruly evil, full of deadly poison.* King *Charles* is, upon this solemnity, frequently compared to our Lord Jesus Christ, both in respect of the *holiness* of his life, and the greatness and injustice of his *sufferings;* and it is a wonder they do not add something concerning the *merits* of his death also—But *blessed saint* and *royal martyr,* are as humble titles as any that are thought worthy of him.

Now this may, at first view, well appear to be a very strange *phenomenon.* For king *Charles* was really a man black with guilt and *laden with iniquity,‖* as appears by his crimes before mentioned. He lived a tyrant; and it was the oppression and violence of his reign, that brought him to his untimely and violent end at last. Now what of saintship or martyrdom is there in all this! What of saintship is there in encouraging people to *profane* the *Lord's Day?* What of saintship in falsehood and perjury? What of saintship in repeated robberies and depredations? What of saintship in throwing real saints, and glorious patriots, into goals? What of saintship in overturning an excellent civil constitution;—and proudly grasping at an illegal and monstrous power? What of saintship in the murder of thousands of innocent people; and involving a nation in all the calamities of a civil war? And what of martyrdom is there, in a man's bringing an immature and violent death upon

†Jam. iii. 8, 9, 10. ‖Isai. i. 4.

himself, by *being wicked overmuch ?** Is there any such thing as grace, without goodness ? As being a follower of Christ, without following him ? As being his disciple, without learning of him to be just and beneficent ? Or, as saintship without sanctity ?† If not, I fear it will be hard to prove this man a saint. And verily, would be apt to suspect that *that church* must be but *poorly stocked* with saints and martyrs, which is forced to adopt such enormous sinners into her *callendar,* in order to swell the number.

But to unravel this *mystery of* (*nonsense* as well as of) *iniquity,* which has *already worked* for a *long time* amongst us ;‡ or, at least, to give the most probable solution of it; it is to be remembered, that king *Charles,* this *burlesque* upon saintship and martyrdom, though so great an oppressor, was a true friend to the *Church;* so true a friend to her, that he was very well affected towards the *Roman Catholics ;* and would, probably, have been very unwilling to unite *Lambeth* and *Rome.* This appears by his marrying a true *daughter* of that true *mother of harlots ;*‖ which he did with a dispensation from the *Pope,* that supreme BISHOP; to whom when he wrote, he gave the title of MOST HOLY FATHER. His queen was extremely bigotted to all the follies and superstitions, and to the *hierarchy,* of *Rome ;* and had a prodigious ascendency over him all his life. It was, in part, owing to this, that he (probably) abetted the massacre of the protestants in *Ireland ;* that he assisted in extirpating the *French* prot-

*Ecles. vii. 17.

†Is it any wonder that even persons who do not *walk after their own lusts,*should *scoff* at *such saints* as this, both in the *first* and in the *last days,* even *from everlasting to everlasting ?* 2 Pet. iii. 3, 4.--But perhaps it will be said, that these things are MYSTERIES, which (although very true in themselves) *lay-understandings* cannot comprehend: Or, indeed, any other persons amongst us, besides those who being INWARDLY MOVED BY THE HOLY GHOST, have taken a trip across the *Atlantic* to obtain *episcopal ordination* and *the indelible character.*—However, if these *consecrated gentlemen* do not quite despair of us, it is hoped that, in the abundance of their charity,they will endeavor to *illucidate* these *dark* points; and, at the same time, explain the creed of *another of their eminent saints,* which we are told, that unless we *believe faithfully,* (i. e. *believingly*) *we cannot be saved :* which creed, (or rather *riddle*) notwithstanding all the labors of the *pious* —— and *metaphysical* Dr *Waterland,* remains somewhat *œnigmatical,* still.

‡ 2 Thess. ii. 7.   ‖ Rev. xvii. 5.

estants at *Rochelle ;* that he all along encouraged *Papists,* and popishly effected *clergymen,* in preference to all other persons, and that he upheld that monster of wickedness, ARCHBISHOP LAUD, and the bishops of his stamp, in all their church-tyranny and diabolical cruelties. In return to his kindness and indulgence, in which respects, they caused many of the pulpits throughout the nation, to ring with the divine absolute, indefeasible right of kings; with the praises of *Charles* and his reign; and with the damnable sin of resisting the *Lord's anointed,* let him do what he would. So that not *Christ,* but *Charles,* was commonly preached to the people.—In *plain English,* there seems to have been an impious bargain struck up betwixt the *sceptre* and the *surplice,* for enslaving both the *bodies* and *souls* of men. The king appeared to be willing that the clergy should do what they would,—set up a monstrous hierarchy like that of *Rome,*— a monstrous inquisition like that of *Spain* or *Portugal,*—or any thing else which their own pride,and the devil's malice, could prompt them to: *Provided always,* that the clergy would be *tools* to the crown; that they would make the people believe, that kings had God's authority for breaking God's law; that they had a commission from heaven to seize the estates and lives of their subjects at pleasure; and that it was a damnable sin to resist them, even when they did such things as deserved more than damnation.—This appears to be the true key for explaining the *mysterious* doctrine of king *Charles's* saintship and martyrdom. He was a saint, not because he was in his life, a good *man,* but a good *churchman ;* not because he was a lover of *holiness,* but the *hierarchy ;* not because he was a friend to *Christ,* but the *Craft.* And he was a martyr in his death, not because he bravely suffered death in the cause of truth and righteousness, but because he died an enemy to liberty and the rights of conscience ; i. e. not because he died an enemy to *sin,* but *dissenters.* For these reasons it is that all bigotted clergymen, and friends to church-power, paint this man as a saint in life, though he was such a mighty, such a *royal sinner ;*

and as a martyr in his death, though he fell a sacrifice only to his own ambition, avarice, and unbounded lust of power. And from prostituting their praise upon king *Charles*, and offering him that incense which is not his due, it is natural for them to make a transition to the dissenters (as they commonly do) and to load them with that reproach which they do not deserve; they being generally professed enemies both to civil and ecclesiastical tyranny. WE are commonly charged (upon the *Thirtieth of January*) with the guilt of putting the king to death, under a notion that it was our ancestors that did it ; and so we are represented in the blackest colours, not only as scismatics, but also as traitors and rebels, and all that is bad. And these *lofty* gentlemen usually rail upon this head, in such a manner as plainly shows, that they are either grossly ignorant of the history of those times which they speak of ; or, which is worse, that they are guilty of the most shameful prevarication, slander and falsehood. —But every *petty priest*, with a *roll* and a *gown*, thinks he must do something in imitation of his *betters*, in *lawn*, and show himself a *true son* of the church : And thus, through a foolish ambition, to appear *considerable*, they only render themselves *contemptible*.

But suppose *our* fore-fathers did kill their *mock* Saint and Martyr, a century ago, what is that to *us* now ? If I mistake not, these gentlemen generally preach down the doctrine of the *imputation of Adam's sin to his posterity*, as absurd and unreasonable, notwithstanding they have solemnly subscribed what is equivalent to it in *their own articles of religion*. And therefore, one would hardly expect that they would lay the guilt of the kings death upon *us*, although *our fore-fathers* had been the only authors of it. But this conduct is much more surprising, when it does not appear that *our* ancestors had any more hand in it than *their own*.—However, bigotry is sufficient to account for this, and many other *phenomena*, which cannot be accounted for in any other way.

Although the observation of this *anniversary* seems to have been (at least) superstitious in its *original* :

and although it is often abused to very bad purposes by the established clergy, as they serve themselves of it, to perpetuate strife, a party spirit, and divisions in the christian church; yet it is to be hoped that one good end will be answered by it, quite contrary to their intention : It is to be hoped, that it will prove a standing *memento*, that *Britons* will not be *slaves ;* and a warning to all corrupt *councellors* and *ministers*, not to go too far in advising to arbitrary, despotic measures—

· To conclude : let us all learn to be *free*, and to be *loyal.* Let us not profess ourselves vessels to the lawless pleasure of any man on earth. But let us remember at the same time, government is *sacred*, and not to be *trifled* with. It is our happiness to live under the government of a *Prince§* who is satisfied with ruling according to law as every other *good prince* will. We enjoy under his administration all the liberty that is proper and expedient for us. It becomes us, therefore, to be contented, and dutiful subjects. Let us prize our freedom; but not *use our liberty for a cloak of maliciousness* * There are men who strike at *liberty* under the term *licentiousness.* There are others who aim at popularity under the disguise of *patriotism.* Be aware of both. *Extremes* are dangerous. There is at present amongst *us*, perhaps, more danger of the *latter*, than of the *former.* For which reason I would exhort you to pay all due Regard to the government over us; to the KING and all in authority; and to *lead a quiet and peaceable life.*† And while I am speaking of loyalty to our *earthly Prince*, suffer me to put you in mind to be loyal also to the supreme RULER of the universe, *by whom kings reign, and princes decree justice.*‡ To which king eternal, immortal, invisible, even to the ONLY WISE GOD,‖ be all honor and praise, DOMINION and thanksgiving, through JESUS CHRIST our LORD. AMEN.

§GEORGE the *Second.*

*Pet. ii. 16. †1 Tim. ii. 2. ‡Prov. viii. 15. ‖ Tim. i. 17.

The Snare broken.

A

Thankſgiving-Diſcourſe

The Snare broken.

A

Thankſgiving-Diſcourſe,

PREACHED

At the Deſire of the Weſt Church

IN

Boſton, *N. E.* Friday *May* 23, 1766.

OCCASIONED BY THE

REPEAL

OF THE

Stamp-Act.

BY

Jonathan Mayhew, D. D

Paſtor of ſaid Church.

——— Brethren, ye have been called unto LIBERTY *; only uſe not*
LIBERTY *for. an occaſion to the fleſh, but by love ſerve one*
another. Ap. PAUL.

BOSTON:

Printed and Sold by R. & S. DRAPER, in New-
bury-Street ; EDES & GILL, in Queen-Street ;
and T. & J. Fleet, in Cornhill. 1766.

THE
DEDICATION.

TO THE RIGHT HONORABLE

WILLIAM PITT, Efq;

ONE OF HIS

MAJESTY'S

MOST HONORABLE PRIVY COUNCIL,

AND AN ILLUSTRIOUS

PATRON OF AMERICA.

S I R,

DID not a wide ocean intervene, the Author of the enfuing Difcourfe would not prefume to prefix fo great a NAME to a littlePerformance of his, without firft humbly requefting the indulgence, and obtaining it. Nor would he truft to the fufficiency of that apology for taking

this

this liberty, did not some perfons perfwade him to hope, it will be kindly and con-defcendingly taken as a teftimony of that fincere gratitude and high veneration which not only he but his country has for ONE, who hath twice at leaft been a prin-cipal Inftrument in the hand of GOD, of faving GREAT BRITAIN and her Colonies from impending ruin: Once, by magnani-moufly conducting a juft and glorious war againft foreign nations; and once, by pre-ferving peace in His own;—by exerting Himfelf to prevent a fatal rupture between BRITAIN and her Colonies, and to re-eftab-lifh fuch an harmony as effentially con-cerns the welfare of both.

AT the late moft important CRISIS, You, SIR, whom no rewards could ever tempt, no frowns of the Great ever difmay, no dangers difconcert; and to whom, fo good and great in Yourfelf, no titles, however high, could poffibly add any new dignity or luftre; You, Great Sir, was not "afhamed of our chain", or reluctant at ftanding forth to plead the caufe of poor AMERICA; and to ftem the mighty torrent that was againft her,

her, which threatened to end in a deluge of blood ! When it was accounted criminal by many, even to lifp but a broken word or two in Her *favor*, You, Sir, was not afhamed or afraid to pour forth all Your unrivall'd eloquence in a ftrenuous vindication of Her infringed *Rights*. And, indeed, her caufe being fuppofed good, the more friendlefs She was, the more She needed, and in fome fort deferved, fo powerful a patronage. For, furely, great talents were given for great occafions ; to be employed in defence of the innocent and feeble. God made fome men ftrong, on purpofe to "· bear the infirmities of the weak"; that they might be able to affift and fupport them in their dangers and extremities; as You, Sir, have ever done, fince You adorned the British fenate ; and particularly in a late ever-memorable inftance.

To You, Great Sir, under GOD and the King, grateful America chiefly attributes it, that She is now happily re-inftated in the enjoyment of her former liberties and privileges ; tho' She has, at the fame time, a very deep fenfe of her obligations to other great and illuftrious Perfonages.

If,

IF, SIR, you could, at this diſtance, have an adequate conception of the univerſal joy of AMERICA, preceeded by the moſt alarming apprehenſions for Her liberties : If You could be fully ſenſible how much we aſcribe it to You, that they are not loſt; how, next to the KING, we bleſs You as our common FATHER, and ſend up ardent vows to Heaven for You ; this would, it muſt give You a ſublime, and truly Godlike pleaſure. It might even ſuſpend, for a while, the ſevereſt pangs of that excruciating diſorder, which has ſo often detain'd you from the BRITISH Senate, to the great detriment of the public ; particularly when the late dreadful STAMP-ACT was paſſed. Nay, it might, perhaps, without any other miracle, give You ſuch ſpirits and vigor, as to "take up Your bed and walk," like thoſe ſick and lame perſons inſtantly cured by the word of Him, who came from Heaven to make us " free indeed".

So univerſal, ſo great is our joy ; and ſo much, SIR, are we indebted for it to your good offices ! But, alas ! what can poor AMERICA do in return ? Nothing but acknowledge

knowledge the obligation with as much sincerity as a grateful country ever acknowledged one: Nothing but call you, over and over again, her FATHER, her FATHER; and endeavour to make goodYour generous engagements for her prudent, dutiful behaviour towards her Mother-country: Nothing but erect a few marble, brass or copper statues in honor to You; (for AMERICA has but little silver or gold) statues that will be of no service to You, since they will go to decay long before Your name and memory will need any such poor helps to preserve them.

Alas! AMERICA can do no more!— Yes, SIR, there is one thing more: She will pray that You may long live in health, happiness and honor, that if there should be any occasion hereafter, as in time past, You may step in and prevent Her's and BRITAIN's ruin, when no other man could; and that, when You must, according to the common lot of men, however great and good (O may it be late!) cease to plead the cause of LIBERTY on earth, You may in Heaven, as Your reward,

enjoy

enjoy " the glorious LIBERTY of the sons of God"!

I AM, with the warmest gratitude, and highest veneration, Right Honorable and Most Worthy

S I R,

Your most obedient,

Most Dutiful

And Most Humble Servant,

JONATHAN MAYHEW.

PSALM CXXIV. 7, 8.

Our foul is escaped as a bird from the snare of the fowlers ; the snare is broken, and we are escaped.

Our help is in the name of the Lord, who made heaven and earth.

THE late gracious appearance of divine providence for us, in the day of our trouble, seemed so seasonable, so signal, so important; in a word, so interesting to the present and future generations, that we of this Society thought it expedient to agree among ourselves upon a day, in order to take a particular, religious notice of it; and to praise the name of the Lord, in whom is our help. If there had been any probability of our being called together for this end by *Proclamation*, as upon some less memorable occasions, we should not have been desirous to anticipate the day; which might have had the appearance of ostentation. But of that, so far as I have heard, there was very little, if any, prospect. By this perfectly voluntary, and free-

B

will offering, I hope we shall render to God, in some poor measure, the glory due to his name; and that he will graciously accept it, thro' our Lord Jesus Christ the righteous, our mediator and advocate with the Father. At the same time it is supposed that, in proceeding thus, we give no just ground of offence to Jew or Gentile, or to the church of God; which we would by no means do. We only exercise that liberty, where-with Christ hath made us free, being desirous that all other persons and churches should do the same; and not chusing that either they or we should be "entangled with any yoke of bondage."

Having rendered our devout thanks to God, whose kingdom ruleth over all, and sung his high praises; permit me now, my friends and brethren, with unfeigned love to my country, to congratulate you on that interesting event, which is the special occasion of this solemnity: An event, as I humbly conceive, of the utmost importance to the whole British empire, whose peace and prosperity we ought ardenly to desire; and one, very peculiarly affecting the welfare of these colonies. Believe me, I lately took no inconsiderable part with you in your grief, and gloomy apprehensions, on account of a certain PARLIAMENTARY ACT, which you supposed ruinous in its tendency to the American plantations, and, eventually, to Great-Britain. I now partake no less in your common joy, on account of the REPEAL of that act; whereby these colonies are emancipated from a slavish, inglorious bondage; are re-instated in the enjoyment of
their

their ancient rights and privileges, and a foundation is laid for lasting harmony between Great-Britain and them, to their mutual advantage.

But when you requested me to preach a sermon on this joyful occasion, I conclude it was neither your expectation nor desire, that I should enter very particularly into a political consideration of the affair. Had I conceived this to have been your intention, I must, tho' with reluctance, have given you a refusal; partly from a conviction of the impropriety of minutely discussing points of this nature in the pulpit, and partly from a sense of my own inability to do it as it ought to be done. I suppose I shall best answer your expectation, as well as most gratify my own inclination, by waving political controversy, and giving you such counsels and exhortations respecting your duty to God and man, as are agreeable to the sacred oracles, to the dictates of sober reason, and adapted to the occasion. This is, therefore, what I chiefly propose to do in the ensuing discourse, as God shall enable me: And may the Father of lights teach me to speak, and you to hear in such a manner, that our assembling together at this time, out of the ordinary course, may be to his honor, and to christian edification.

However, if my discourse is to be particularly adapted to this great occasion, instead of being so general, as to be almost as suitable to any other, you are sensible it is necessary that the occasion itself should be kept in view. I shall therefore briefly premise a few things relative thereto by way of introduction to the main design; such

thing

things, I mean, as shall now be taken for granted.
In mentioning which, my aim will be to express,
in brief, what I take to be the general sense of
these colonies rather than to explain my own.
For it is on such commonly-received opinions,
that my exhortations and cautions will be grounded; leaving the paricular discussion of them to
others, who are better qualified for it, and to
whom it more properly belongs. And if I
should be mistaken in any of these particulars,
it is hoped candor will excuse it; seeing these
are matters out of the way of my profession.

I pursuance of this plan, it shall now be taken
for granted, that as we were free-born, never
made slaves by the right of conquest in war, if
there be indeed any such right, nor sold as slaves
in any *open lawful* market, for *money*, so we have
a natural right to *our own*, till we have freely
consented to part with it, either in person, or by
those whom WE have appointed to represent,
and to act for us.

It shall be taken for granted, that this natural
right is declared, affirmed and secured to us, as
we are British subjects, by Magna Charta; all
acts contrary to which, are said to be *ipso facto*
null and void: And, that this natural, constitutional right has been further confirmed to most
of the plantations by particular subsequent royal
charters, taken in their obvious sense; the legality and authority of which charters was never
once denied by either House of Parliament; but
implicitly at least acknowledged, ever since they
were respectively granted, till very lately.

It

It is taken for granted also, that the right of trial by juries, is a conftitutional one with refpect to all Britifh fubjects in general, particularly to the colonifts; and that the plantations in which civil government has been eftablifhed, have all along, till of late, been in the uninterrupted enjoyment of both the rights aforefaid, which are of the utmoft importance, being effential to liberty.

It fhall, therefore, be taken for granted, that the colonies had great reafon to petition and remonftrate againft a late act of Parliament, as being an infraction of thefe rights, and tending directly to reduce us to a ftate of flavery.

It is, moreover, taken for granted, whatever becomes of this queftion about *rights*, that an act of that fort was very hard, and juftly grievous, not to fay oppreffive; as the colonies are poor, as moft of them were originally fettled at the fole and great expence of the adventurers; the expence of their money, their toil, their blood; as they have expended a great deal from time to time in their wars with their French and Savage neighbours, and in the fupport of his Majefty's government here; as they have, moreover, been ever ready to grant fuch aids of men and money to the crown, for the common caufe, as they were able to give; by which means a great load of debt ftill lies on feveral of them; and as Great Britain has drawn vaft emolument from them in the way of commerce, over and above all that fhe has ever expended for them, either in peace or war: So that fhe is, beyond

all

all comparifon, richer, more powerful and refpectable now, than fhe would have been, if our
fathers had never emigrated: And both they and
their pofterity have, in effect, been labouring,
from firft to laft, for the aggrandizement of the
mother-country. In this light, that fhare of
common fenfe, which the colonifts have, be it more
or lefs, leads them to confider things.

It is taken for granted, that as the furprifing,
unexampled growth of thefe colonies, to the
extenfion of his Majefty's dominion, and prodigious advantage of Britain in many refpects,
has been chiefly owing, under God, to the liberty enjoyed here; fo the infraction thereof in two
fuch capital points as thofe before referred to,
would undoubtedly difcourage the trade, induftry and population of the colonies, by rendering
property infecure and precarious; would foon
drain them of all their little circulating money;
would put it abfolutely out of their power to
purchafe Britifh commodities, force them into
manufactures of their own, and terminate, if not
in the ruin, yet in the very effential detriment of
the mother-country.

It fhall, therefore, alfo be taken for granted,
that altho' the colonies could not juftly claim an
exclufive right of taxing themfelves, and the
right of being tried by juries; yet they had
great reafon to remonftrate againft the act aforefaid on the footing of inexpedience, the great
hardfhip, and deftructive tendency of it; as a
meafure big with mifchief to Britain, as well as
to themfelves; and promoted *at firft*, perhaps,
only by perfons who were real friends to neither.

But

But as to any methods of oppofition to that meafure, on the part of the colonies, befides thofe of humble petitioning, and other ftrictly legal ones, it will not, I conclude, be fuppofed, that I appear *in this place* as an advocate for them, whatever the general fenfe of the colonifts may be concerning this point. And I take for granted, that we are all perfectly agreed in condemning the riotous and fellonious pro- ceedings of certain *men of Belial*,† as they have been juftly called, who had the effrontery to cloke their rapacious violences with the pretext of zeal for liberty; which is fo far from being a new thing under the fun, that even Great Britain can furnifh us with many, and much more flagrant examples of it.

But, my Brethren, however unconftitutional, oppreffive, grievous or ruinous the aforefaid act was in its nature, and fatal in its tendency, his Majefty and the Parliament have been pleafed to hearken to the juft complaints of the colonies, feconded and enforced by the prudent, fpirited conduct of our merchants; by certain noble and ever-honored patriots in Great Britain, ef- poufing our caufe with all the force of reafon and eloquence, and by the general voice of the nation: So that a total repeal of that dreadful act is now obtained. His Majefty and the Par- liament were far too wife, juft and good to per- fift in a meafure, after they were convinced it was wrong; or to confider it as any point of honor, to enforce an act fo grievous to three million good fubjects, fo contrary to the intereft of the

British .

† The Book of America, Chap. II. v. 13.

British merchants and manufacturers, and to the general sense of the nation. They have been pleased, in the act of repeal itself, greatly to their honor, implicitly to acknowledge their fallibility and erroneous judgment in the other act, by saying, that " the continuance of the said act " would be attended with many inconveniences, " and *might* be productive of consequences great- " ly detrimental to the commercial interests of " *those* kingdoms." These being the reasons assigned for the repeal, we may justly conclude, that if those *many inconveniences* and *detrimental consequences* could have been foreseen, the act complained of would never have been passed. And as the same reasons will doubtless operate at least as strongly, probably much more strongly hereafter, in proportion to the growth of the colonies, than they do at present, we may naturally conclude also, that an act of the like nature will never again be heard of.

Thus " our soul is escaped as a bird from the snare of the fowlers ; the snare is broken, and we are escaped ;" tho' not without much struggling in the snare, before it gave way, and set us at liberty again. But when I speak of that pernicious act as a *snare*, and those who prepared it for us as *fowlers*, greedy of their prey, let it be particularly observed, that I intend not the least reflexion on our gracious Sovereign or the Parliament; who must not be supposed to have any evil designs against the colonies, which are so necessary to Great Britain, and by which so many thousands of her manufac-

turers

turers are fupported, who, but for them, muft actually ftarve, emigrate, or do what I chufe to forbear mentioning. No! I apply this, as I conclude you will, only to fome evil-minded individuals in Britain, who are true friends neither to her nor us ; and who accordingly fpared no wicked arts, no deceitful, no difhonorable, no difhoneft means, to pufh on and obtain, as it were by *furprife*, an act fo prejudicial to both ; and, in fome fort, to the *enfnaring* of his Majefty and the Parliament, as well as the good people of America : Being, not improbably, in the interefts of the Houfes of Bourbon and the Pretender, whofe caufe they meant to ferve, by bringing about an open rupture between Great Britain and her colonies ! Thefe, thefe men, my Brethren, are the cunning *fowlers*, thefe the *enfnarers*, from whofe teeth " our foul is efcaped as a bird :" And fuch traitors will, doubtlefs, e'er long be caught in another *fnare*, fuitable for 'them, to the fatisfaction of the King's good fubjects on both fides the Atlantic, if his Majefty and the Parliament fhould judge it neceffary for the vindication of their own honor, or for the public good, to bring them to condign punifhment.

Let me juft add here, that according to our lateft and beft advices, the King, his truly patriotic Miniftry and the Parliament have the intereft, particularly the commercial intereft of the colonies much at heart ; being *now* difpofed even to enlarge, inftead of curtailing their privileges, and to grant us every indulgence, confiftent

C

fiftent with the common good of the Britifh empire : More than which we cannot reafonably, and, I am perfuaded, do not defire.

Thefe things being premifed, let me now proceed to thofe reflections, exhortations and cautions relative to them, which were the chief defign of this difcourfe. And the prefent occafion being a very peculiar one, fuch as never before occurred in America, and, I hope in God, never will again; I fhall crave your indulgence if I am confiderably longer than is cuftomary on other occafions, which are lefs out of the ordinary courfe.

In the firft place then, it is evident from the preceding view of things, that we have the greateft caufe for thankfulnefs to Almighty God, who doeth his will among the inhabitants of the earth, as well as in the armies of heaven. He, in whofe hands are the hearts of all men, not excepting thofe of Kings, fo that he turneth them whitherfoever he will, as the rivers of water, hath infpired the people of America with a noble fpirit of liberty, and remarkably united them in ftanding up for that invaluable blefling. He hath raifed us up friends of the greateft eminence in Britain, in our perilous circumftances. He hath united the hearts of almoft all wife and good men there, to plead our caufe *and their own* fuccefsfully. He hath blefled the King with an upright Miniftry, zealous for the public good, and knowing wherein it confifts. He hath given the King wifdom to difcern, and integrity to purfue, the interefts of his people,

at

at the late alarming CRISIS, when so much depended on the measures that were then speedily to be taken! He hath changed his royal purpose, and that of his Parliament, in a matter which nearly and essentially concerned, at least *our* temporal happiness; disposing them to take off from our necks that grievous and heavy burden, which, to be sure, was not put upon us but with reluctance, and thro' the dishonest artifices of certain wicked men who, perhaps, intended, if possible, entirely to alienate the affections of the colonists from their common Father the King, and from their Mother-country. O execrable design! to the accomplishment of which, the pernicious measure aforesaid apparently tended. But blessed be He, who governeth among the nations, that he hath confounded the devices of such treacherous men. To allude to the psalm, a part of which I mentioned as my text; " If it had not been the Lord who was on our side, when men rose up against us," and if they could have had their wicked will, " then they had swallowed us up " quick;"—" then the waters had overwhel- " med us, the stream had gone over our soul; " then the proud waters had gone over our soul. " Blessed be the Lord, who hath not given us " as a prey to their teeth;" the ravening teeth of those cunning *fowlers*, from whose treacherous *snare* we have just escaped; " our help be- " ing in the name of the Lord, who made hea- " ven and earth." To Him, therefore, we justly owe the undissembled gratitude of our

hearts,

hearts, as well as the joyful praises of our lips : For I take it for granted, that you all firmly believe, that He who made the world, exerci- fes a providential government over it ; fo that the very hairs of our head " are all numbered by," and that " a fparrow doth not fall to the ground without" Him. How much more then, is his providence to be acknowledged in the rife, in the prefervation, in the great events, the re- volutions, or the fall of mighty ftates and king- doms ?

To excite our gratitude to God the more ef- fectually, let us confider the greatnefs of our late danger and of our deliverance : Let us take a brief retrofpective view of the perplexed, wretched ftate, in which thefe colonies were, a few months ago, compared with the joyful and happy condition, in which they are at pre- fent, by the removal of their chief grievances.

We have never known fo quick and general a tranfition from the depth of forrow to the height of joy, as on this occafion ; nor, indeed, fo great and univerfal a flow of either, on any other occafion whatever. It is very true, we have heretofore feen times of great adverfity. We have known feafons of drought, dearth, and fpreading mortal difeafes ; the peftilence walk- ing in darknefs, and the deftruction wafting at noon day. We have feen wide devaftations, made by fire ; and amazing tempefts, the hea- vens on flame, the winds and the waves roaring. We have known repeated earthquakes, threat- ning us with fpeedy deftruction. We have

been

been under great apprehensions by reason of
formidable fleets of an enemy on our coasts,
menacing fire and sword to all our maritime
towns. We have known times when the French
and Savage armies made terrible havock on our
frontiers, carrying all before them for a while ;
when we were not without fear, that some capital towns in the colonies would fall into their
merciless hands. Such times as these we have
known ; at some of which almost every " face
gathered paleness," and the knees of all but the
good and brave, waxed feeble. But never have
we known a season of such universal consternation and anxiety among people of all ranks
and ages, in these colonies, as was occasioned
by that parliamentary procedure, which threat-
ned us and our posterity with perpetual bondage and slavery. For *They*, as we generally
suppose, are really slaves to all intents and purposes, who are obliged to labor and toil only
for the benefit of others ; or, which comes to
the same thing, the fruit of whose labour and
industry may be *lawfully* taken from them without their consent, and they justly punished if
they refuse to surrender it on demand, or apply it to other purposes than those, which their
masters, of their mere grace and pleasure, see
fit to allow. Nor are there many *American*
understandings accute enough to distinguish
any material difference between this being
done by a *single* person, under the title of an
absolute Monarch, and done by a far-distant
legislature consisting of *many* persons, in which
they

they are not reprefented ; and the members whereof, inftead of feeling, and fharing equally with them in the burden thus impofed, are eafed of their own in proportion to the greatnefs and weight of it. It may be queftioned, whether the ancient Greeks or Romans, or any other nation in which flavery was allowed, carried their idea of it much further than this. So that our late apprehenfions, and univerfal confternation, on account of ourfelves and pofterity, were far, very far indeed, from being groundlefs. For what is there in this world more wretched, than for thofe who were born free, and have a right to continue fo, to be made flaves themfelves, and to think of leaving a race of flaves behind them ; even though it be to mafters, confeffedly the moft humane and generous in the world ? Or what wonder is it, if after groaning with a low voice for a while, to no purpofe, we at length groaned fo loudly, as to be heard more than three thoufand miles ; and to be pitied throughout Europe, wherever it is not hazardous to mention even the name of liberty, unlefs it be to reproach it, as only another name for fedition, faction or rebellion?

On the other hand, never did the tide of joy fwell fo high, or roll fo rapidly thro' the bofoms and veins of the people in general, on any public occafion, as on the news of THE REPEAL. " Then was our mouth filled with " laughter, and our tongue with finging," *when the Lord turned our captivity* ; this was received as an *emancipation* indeed, from *unmerited flavery.*

Nor

Nor were there ever before so great external demonstrations of joy among the people of America ; not even when all Canada was reduced, or when it was secured to the crown of England by treaty, and our apprehensions of coming under the yoke of France were vanished away. And some there are, who suppose, that France would not have hesitated at allowing such a number of flourishing colonies the exclusive right of taxing themselves, for the sake of a free trade with them, could they have been prevailed on, by violating their allegiance, to put themselves under her protection ; as I am fully persuaded these colonies would not do, for all thatFrance has to give. In my poor opinion, we never had so much real occasion for joy, on any temporal account, as when we were thus *emancipated*, and our soul escaped as a bird from the dreadful *snare*. And I am perswaded it would rejoice the generous and royal heart of his Majesty, if he knew that by a single turn of the scepter, when he assented to THE REPEAL, he had given more pleasure to three million good subjects, than ever he and his royal Grandfather gave them by all the triumphs of their arms, from Lake Superior Eastward to theIsles of Manilla ; tho' so numerous, so great, so illustrious ; and though WE partook so largely in the national joy on those occasions. A PEPPER-CORN * *a year added to his Majesty's exchequer*, would not surely------! But I forbear.

* See a certain ever-memorable Speech in an august assembly.

If

If you pleafe, we will now defcend to fome farther *particulars*, relative to our late unhappy and prefent joyful circumftances, in order to excite our thankfulnefs to God, for fo memorable a deliverance.

This continent, from Canada to Florida, and the Weft-India Iflands, moft of them at leaft, have exhibited a difmal mixed fcene of murmuring, defpondence, tumult and outrage ; courts of juftice fhut up, with cuftom-houfes and ports ; private jealoufies and animofities, evil furmifings, whifperings and back-bitings, mutual reproaches, open railing, and many other evils, fince the time in which the grievous act aforefaid was to have taken place. Almoft every Britifh American, as was before obferved, confidered it as an infraction of their rights, or their dearly purchafed privileges, call them which you will; and the fad earneft of fuch a galling yoke to be laid on our necks, already fomewhat fore by preceding grievances, as neither we nor our Fathers were able to bear ; or rather, as being itfelf fuch a yoke, and likely to grow heavier by length of time, without any increafe, either of ability or patience to endure it. The uneafinefs was, therefore, juftly great and univerfal, except, perhaps, among a few individuals, who either did not attend to confequences, or who expected to find their private account in the public calamity, by exercifing the gainful, tho' invidious, and not very reputable office of *tafk-mafters* over their groaning countrymen and brethren ;

thren. Even our bought *Negro slaves* apparently
shared in the common distress : For which one
cannot easily account, except by supposing that
even some of them saw, that if *the act* took place,
their masters might soon be too poor to provide
them suitable food and raiment ; and thought it
would be more ignominious and wretched to be
the *servants of servants*, than of free-men.

But to return, The general discontent ope-
rated very differently upon the minds of different
people, according to the diversity of their natural tempers and constitutions, their education,
religious principles, or the prudential maxims
which they had espoused. Some at once grew
melancholy, sitting down in a kind of lethargic,
dull desparation of relief, by any means whatever. Others were thrown into a sort of consternation, not unlike to a phrenzy occasioned
by a raging fever ; being ready to do any thing
or every thing, to obtain relief; but yet, unhap-
pily, not knowing what, when, where, how ; nor
having any two rational and consistent ideas a-
bout the matter ; scarce more than a person in a
delirium has of the nature of, or proper method
of curing the fever, which is the cause of his
madness. Some few were, I believe, upon the
principles of Sibthorp, Manwaring, Filmer, and
that goodly tribe, determined to go no farther in
order to obtain redress, than in the way of petition and remonstrance ; and this, even tho' they
had been sure of success in some hardy enter-
prize. Others, who had no religious scruples of
this kind, yet thought it extremely imprudent

D
and

and hazardous to oppose a superior power in such a manner as might, perhaps, draw the whole weight of its resentment on the colonies, to their destruction. But the greater part, as I conceive, tho' I may be mistaken in this, were firmly united in a consistent, however imprudent or desperate a plan, to run all risques, to tempt all hazards, to go all lengths, if things were driven to extremity, rather than to submit; preferring death itself to what they esteemed so wretched and inglorious a servitude. And even " of de- " vout women not a few" were, I imagine, so far metamorphosed into men on this sad occasion, that they would have declined hardly any kind of manly exertions, rather than live to propagate a race of slaves, or to be so themselves. In short, such was the danger, and in their opinion, so great and glorious the cause, that the spirit of the Roman matrons in the time of the commonwealth, seemed to be now equalled by the fairer daughters of America. The uneasiness of some persons was much encreased by an imagination, that the money to be raised by the duty on stamps, would partly be applied to pay certain civil officers salaries; whereby they would become more entirely and absolutely dependent on the crown, less on the people, and consequently, as was supposed, more arbitrary and insolent. Others were anxious, because they imagined, with how much, or how little reason you will best judge, that the money was to be chiefly applied towards maintaining a standing army in America; not so much to defend and secure the

colonies

colonies from enemies, of whom they had none, except the aforesaid *fowlers*, as to awe the colonies themselves into an implicit obedience to ministerial measures, however unjust or execrable in their nature. There is no end, you know, to peoples *fears* and *jealousies*, when once they are thoroughly alarmed. And so some suspected, that this money was partly intended to maintain a standing army of bishops, and other ecclesiastics, to *propagate* the importance of certain rites and ceremonies, to which they had an aversion ; the divine right of diocesan episcopacy and tythes, with many *et cætara*'s of the like sacred and *interesting* importance. These *strange* notions and fears prevailed very much among certain odd people, who liked their old religion, and were not able to see the reasonableness of their paying for the support of any other. I am not accountable for other people's *whimsical* apprehensions : I am here only representing the perplexity, into which peoples minds were thrown by the novel taxation, according to their different views of it ; a taxation, which was probably never thought of till a few years ago, when it was proposed to a great and good Secretary of State, who was far too friendly to the colonies, as well as too wise, *to burn* HIS *fingers with an American* STAMP-ACT.

This diversity of humours, sentiments and opinions among the colonists, of which I have been speaking, naturally occasioned great animosities, mutual censures and reproaches : Insomuch that it was hardly safe for any man to speak his thoughts on the times, unless he could patiently

bear

bear to lie under the imputation of being a
coward, an incendiary, rebel, or enemy to his
country ; or to have some other odium cast upon him. In the mean time moſt of the courts
were ſhut up, and almoſt all buſineſs brought to
a ſtand ; and, in ſome colonies, wide breaches
were made between their ſeveral Governors and
Houſes of Aſſembly ; thoſe governors thinking
it their duty to puſh the execution of the ſtamp-
act ; and ſome of them trying to prevent the aſ-
ſemblies petitioning, in the joint manner propoſed.
In this ſtate of general diſorder, approaching ſo
near to anarchy, ſome profligate people, in different parts of the continent, took an opportunity to gratify their private reſentments, and to
get money in an eaſier and more expeditious
way than that of labor ; committing abomina-
ble exceſſes and outrages on the perſons or property of others.

What a dreadful ſcene was this ! Who can
take a curſory review of it even now, without
horror, unleſs he is loſt to all ſenſe of religion,
virtue and good order ? Theſe were ſome of the
bitter, and in a good meaſure, the natural fruits
of that unhappy meaſure which preceeded them.
Nor were we wholly unapprehenſive of ſomething ſtill worſe ; of having a more dreadful
ſcene, even a ſcene of blood and ſlaughter opened !
I will not be particular here ; but aſk you what
you think of Britiſh ſubjects making war upon
Britiſh ſubjects on this continent ! What might
this have terminated in ? Perhaps in nothing leſs
than the ruin of the colonies, and the downfall

of

of a certain great kingdom, which has long been
the fupport of other ftates, the terror of her
enemies, and the envy and glory of Europe!—
If I had myfelf, once, fome apprehenfions of this
kind, as I confefs I had, I was very far from being fingular therein. One of the beft judges of
fuch matters, that any nation or age ever afforded, as well as one of the beft men, and moft ac-
complifhed orators, fpeaking on this point in a
certain auguft affembly, is reported to have expreffed himfelf thus. " On a good, on a found
" bottom, the force of this country can crufh
" America to atoms. I know the valor of your
" troops; I know the fkill of your officers.—
" But on this ground, on the STAMP-ACT,
" when fo many here will think it a crying in-
" juftice, I am one that will lift up my hand
" againft it. In *fuch a caufe* your fuccefs may
" be hazardous. AMERICA, if SHE fell, would
" fall like a ftrong man, would embrace the pil-
" lars of ftate, and *pull down the conftitution*
" *along with her.*" Thus the great patron of
America. †Even the remoteft apprehenfions of this
kind, muft give a very fenfible pain to any American, who at once fincerely loves his own country, and wifhes that the happy *civil* conftitution,
the ftrength and glory of Great Britain may be

as

† TheRight Hon, WILLIAM PITT, Efq;--But the author thinks
it a piece of juftice due to fo great and refpectable a name, to
acknowledge that he has no better authority for mentioning it
on this particular occafion, than that of the public prints, lately fpread over America; giving an account of fome debates in
the honorable Houfe of Commons. He alfo acknowledges,
that this is all the authority he has for citing fome other
paffages afterwards, as from the fame illuftrious patriot.

as lasting as the world, and still increasing; as God is my witness, I both wish and pray. If Britain, which has long been the principal support of liberty in Europe, and is, at least *was*, the chief bulwark against that most execrable of all tyrannies, *Popery*, should in destroying her colonies destroy herself; (Heaven forbid it!) what would become of those few states which are now free? what, of the protestant religion? The former might, not improbably, fall before the *Grand Monarch* on this side the Alps; the latter before the *Successor* of the apostle Judas, and *Grand Vicar* of Satan, beyond them; and so, at length, one universal despotism swallow up all! Some of us had, lately, painful apprehensions of this kind, when there was talk of a great military force coming to *stamp* America into a particular kind of subjection, to which most people here have an *invincible* aversion.

It would, doubtless, have been a noble effort of genius and humanity in the —— what shall I call them? *fowlers* or *financiers?*—to extort a little money from the poor colonies by force of arms, at the risque of so much mischief to America, to Britain, to Europe, to the world. And the golden temptation, it is said, took with too many, for while. A Pandora's box, or Trojan horse, indeed!

——O miseri, quæ tanta infania, cives!
Creditis avectos *hostes?* aut ulla putatis
Dona carere *dolis* Danaûm? sic notus——? †

But not to digress. I have now briefly reminded you of our late sad, perplexed, alarming circumstances;

circumſtances; not for the ſake of reproaching
thoſe who brought us into them, but to excite
your gratitude to God, for our deliverance out
of them, and for our preſent happy condition.

The REPEAL, the REPEAL has at once, in a
good meaſure, reſtored things to order, and com-
poſed our minds, by removing the chief ground
of our fears. The courſe of juſtice between man
and man is no longer obſtructed; commerce lifts
up her head, adorned with golden treſſes, pearls
and precious ſtones. All things that went on
right before, are returning gradually to their former courſe; thoſe that did not, we have reaſon
to hope, will go on better now; almoſt every
perſon you meet, wears the ſmiles of content-
ment and joy; and even our ſlaves rejoice, as
tho' they had received their manumiſſion. Indeed,
all the lovers of liberty in Europe, in the world,
have reaſon to rejoice; the cauſe is in ſome meaſure common to them and us. Bleſſed revolution!
glorious change! How great are our obligations
for it to the ſupreme Governor of the world?
He hath given us *beauty for aſhes*, and the *oil of
gladneſs for the* ſpirit *of heavineſs*: He hath
turned our groans into ſongs, *our mourning into
dancing*: He hath *put off our ſackcloth, and gird-
ed us with gladneſs*, to the end that our tongues,
our glory may ſing praiſes to him. Let us all
then rejoice in the Lord, and give honor to him;
not forgetting to add the obedience of our lives,
as the beſt ſacrifice that we can offer to Heaven!
and which, if neglected, will prove all our other
ſacrifices have been but oſtentation and hypo-
criſy, which are an abomination to the Lord.

The

The apoſtle Peter makes a natural tranſition from *fearing God* to *honoring the King.* Let me, accordingly, in the next place, exhort you, my friends and brethren, to a reſpectful, loyal and dutiful manner of ſpeech and conduct, reſpecting his Majeſty and his government; thereby making a ſuitable return to him for the redreſs of our late grievances. I am, indeed, well appriſed of the firm attachment of theſe colonies in general, and of our own province in particular, to the King's perſon, and to the proteſtant ſucceſſion in his illuſtrious Houſe; for the preſervation of which, there is hardly a native of New-England, who would not, upon conſtitutional principles, which are thoſe of liberty, chearfully hazard his life; or even more lives than one, if he had them to lay down in ſo good a cauſe. I have not the leaſt ſuſpicion of any diſaffection in you to his Majeſty: But yet the duty of ſubjects to Kings, and to all that are in authority, is frequently to be inculcated by the miniſters of the goſpel, if they will follow the example of the apoſtles in this reſpect. And the preſent occaſion ſeems particularly proper to remind you of that important duty; ſince we have now before us a recent and memorable proof of his Majeſty's moderation, his attention to the welfare of his people, and readineſs, ſo far as in him lies according to the conſtitution, to redreſs their grievances, on reaſonable and humble complaint. If any perſons among us have taken it unkindly, that his Majeſty ſhould have given his royal aſſent to an act, which they think was an infrac-

tion

tion of thofe liberties and privileges, to which
they were juftly intitled ; and if the ufual tide
and fervor of their loyal affection is in any
degree abated on that account ; yet, furely,
the readinefs which his Majefty has fhewn to
hear and redrefs his people's wrongs, ought to
give a new fpring, an additional vigor to their
loyalty and obedience. Natural parents, thro'
human frailty, and miftakes about facts and
circumftances,fometimes *provoke their children to
wrath*, tho' they tenderly love them,and fincerely defire their good. But what affectionate and
dutiful child ever harboured refentment on any
fuch account, if the grievance was removed,
on a dutiful reprefentation of it ? Hardly any
thing operates fo ftrongly on ingenuous minds,
tho' perhaps of quick refentment, as the mild
condefcenfion of a fuperior to the force of reafon
and right on the part of the inferior. I fhall
make no application of this, any farther than
to remind you, that Britifh kings are the political FATHERS of their people, and the people their CHILDREN ; the former are not
tyrants, or even *mafters* ; the latter are not
flaves, or even *fervants*.

Let me farther exhort you to pay due refpect in all things to the Britifh Parliament ; the
Lords and Commons being two branches of
the fupreme legiflative over all his Majefty's
dominions. The right of parliament to fuper-
intend the general affairs of the colonies, to
direct, check or controul them, feems to be
fuppofed in their charters ; all which, I think,

E   while

while they grant the power of legiſlation, limit
the exerciſe of it to the enacting ſuch laws as
are *not contrary* to the laws of England, or
Great-Britain; ſo that our ſeveral legiſlatures
are ſubordinate to that of the mother-country,
which extends to and over all the King's dominions : At leaſt, ſo far as to prevent any
parts of them from doing what would be either
deſtructive to each other, or manifeſtly to the
ruin of Britain. It might be of the moſt dangerous conſequence to the mother-country, to
relinquiſh this ſuppoſed authority or right,
which, certainly, has all along been recognized
by the colonies ; or to leave them dependent
on the crown *only*, ſince, probably, within a
century, the ſubjects in them will be more than
thrice as numerous as thoſe of Great-Britain
and Ireland. And, indeed, if the colonies are
properly parts of the Britiſh empire, as it is
both their intereſt and honor to be, it ſeems
abſurd to deny, that they are ſubject to the
higheſt authority therein, or not bound to yield
obedience to it. I hope there are very few
people, if any, in the colonies, who have the
leaſt inclination to renounce the general juriſ-
diction of Parliament over them, whatever we
may think of the particular right of taxation.
If, in any particular caſes, we ſhould think our
ſelves hardly treated, laid under needleſs and
unreaſonable reſtrictions, or curtailed of any
liberties or privileges, which other our fellow
ſubjects in common enjoy ; we have an un-
doubted right to complain, and, by humble and
reſpectful,

respectful, tho' not abject and servile petitions, to seek the redress of such supposed grievances. The colonists are men, and need not be afraid to assert the natural rights of men ; they are British subjects, and may justly claim the common rights, and all the privileges of such, with plainness and freedom. And from what has lately occurred, there is reason to hope, that the Parliament will ever hereafter be willing to hear and grant our just requests ; especially if any grievances should take place, so great, so general and alarming, as to unite all the colonies in petitioning for redress, as with one voice. The humble united prayers of three or four million loyal subjects, so connected with Great Britain, will not be thought unworthy of a serious attention ; especially when seconded by such spirited resolutions and conduct of the A-merican Merchants, as they have lately given an example of. Humble petitions, *so enforced*, always carry great weight with them ; and, if just and reasonable, will doubtless meet with a suitable return, as in the late instance ; since Great Britain can scarce subsist without the trade of her colonies, which will be still increasing. And an equitable, kind treatment of them, on her part, will firmly bind them to her by the *threefold cord* of duty, interest and filial affection ; such an an one as the wise man says, is *not easily broken :* This would do more, far more to retain the colonies in due subjection, than all the fleets or troops she would *think proper* to send for that purpose.

But to return; we ought, in honor to ourfelves, as well as duty to the King and parliament, to fruſtrate the malicious prophecies, if
not the hopes of ſome perſons in Britain, who
have predicted the moſt ungrateful and indecent
returns from us to our mother-country, for deliverance from the late grievances. It has been
foretold that, in conſequence thereof, the colonies would grow inſolent and aſſuming ; that
they would affect a kind of triumph over the
authority of parliament ; that they would little
or nothing regard it hereafter, in other caſes ;
that they would give ſome broad intimations
of their opinion, that it was not for want of
inclination, but of power, that the late grievous
act was not enforced ; that they would treat
their brethren in Britain in an unworthy, diſ-
reſpectful manner ; and the like. Such things
as theſe have been predicted, and, probably, by
thoſe very *fowlers* who contrived the *ſnare*, from
which, to their great mortification, our ſoul is
now eſcaped as a bird. Let us, my brethren,
(for it is in our power, and it is our duty) make
ſuch men falſe prophets, by a contrary behaviour ; " prophets of the deceit of *their own*
" hearts." This might, probably, vex them
ſorely ; ſince it is likely, their chief aim is, to
bring about a fixed, confirmed diſaffection on
our part, and a ſevere reſentment on the other,
while the jealous enemies of the growing power of Britain, wagg their ever-plotting and en-
terpriſing heads, ſaying, " Aha ! ſo we would
" have it. " Let us highly reverence the ſupreme

preme authority of the British empire, which
to us is the higheft, under that of heaven.——
Let us, as much as in us lies, cultivate harmony and brotherly love between our fellow
fubjects in Britain and ourfelves. We fhall
doubtlefs find our account in this at laft,
much more than in a contrary way of proceeding. There are no other people on earth,
that fo " naturally care for us." We are connected with them by the ftrongeft ties; in fome
meafure by *blood*; for look but a century or
two back, and you will find their anceftors and
ours, in a great meafure the fame perfons, tho'
their pofterity is now fo divided. We are
ftrongly connected with them by a great commercial intercourfe, by our common language,
by our common religion as proteftants, and
by being fubjects of the fame King, whom
God long preferve and profper, while his e-
nemies are cloathed with fhame.

If we confider things properly, it is indeed
our great felicity, our beft fecurity, and higheft glory in this world, to ftand in fuch a relation as we do, to fo powerful an empire;
one which rules the ocean, and wherein the
principles of liberty are in general predomi-
nant. It would be our mifery, if not our ruin,
to be caft off by Great-Britain, as unworthy
her farther regards. What then would it be,
in any fuppofeable way, to draw upon ourfelves
the whole weight of her juft refentment!
What are *we* in the hands of that nation, which
fo lately triumphed over the united powers of
France and Spain? Though it muft, indeed,
be

be acknowledged, that she did this, in a great
meafure, by means of her commercial intercourfe with, and aids from the colonies :
Without which she muft probably have
made a more inglorious figure at the end,
than she did at the beginning of the laft war ;
even tho' Mr. PITT himfelf had had the
fole direction of it under his Majefty. ——
Confider how many millions of people there
are in other countries, groaning in vain
under the iron fceptre of mercilefs defpotifm,
who, if they were but imperfectly apprifed of
the happinefs we enjoy, would moft ardently
defire to be in our fituation, and to ftand in the
like relation to Great Britain. Let us not be
infenfible of our own felicity in this refpect ;
let us not entertain a thought of novelties or
innovations, or be " given to change." Let us
not indulge to any groundlefs jealoufies of ill
intentions towards us in our mother-country,
whatever there may be in fome defigning individuals, who do the devil's work, by fowing
difcord. It is for the intereft of Britain, *as she
well knows*, to retain the affection of thefe growing colonies, and to treat them kindly to that
end : And this bond of intereft on her part, is
the ftrongeft fecurity to us, which we can
have in any political relation whatever. We
are bound, in honor to the King and Parliament, to fuppofe, that it was not for want of
ability to enforce a late act, and to crufh us,
that it was repealed ; but from a conviction of
the inexpediency, the *dangerous confequences*, and

many

many inconveniencies of continuing it. And
the like reasons will probably operate forever
against any act of the same nature, and grow
stronger and stronger.

It can answer no valuable end, for us to
harbour grudges or secret resentment on account of redressed and past grievances ; no
good end wantonly and grossly to insult, and
thereby to incense any particular powerful
persons on the other side of the water, as the
supposed enemies of the colonies. To me
this seems impolitic at least ; as it may perhaps make such persons our enemies, if they
were not so before ; or, if they were, fix their
enmity ; and make them more industrious than
ever in seeking opportunities to do us 'mischief.
Much less can it answer any good end, to affect to triumph over the power of Parliament:
This would, in short, appear equally insolent,
disloyal and ridiculous, in the eyes of all sober,
unprejudiced men. May God give us the wisdom to behave ourselves with humility and
moderation, on the happy success of our late
remonstrances and struggles !---We are bound
in honor so to behave, not only that we may
frustrate the malignant predictions before referred to, but that we may answer the just
expectation of our friends in Britain, who
so nobly espoused our cause, and, as it were,
pawned their own honor, (how great and
sacred a pledge !) for our good conduct, if
our grievances were removed. By such an
engagement they did us honor, as it manifested
their candid and kind sentiments concerning
us,

us. This lays us under an additional obligation, in point of gratitude, to that good behaviour, which would have been our duty without it. I cannot but here remind you particularly of the words of that immortal patriot
in Parliament, who has now a second time,
been the principal means of saving Britain and
her colonies from impending ruin.† " Say,"
said he, " the Americans have not in all things
" acted with prudence and temper : They
" have been wrong'd ; they have been driven
" to madness by injuftice. Will you now pu-
" nifh them for the madness you have occafio-
" ned ? Rather let prudence and temper come
" firft from this fide ; I WILL UNDERTAKE
" FOR AMERICA that fhe will follow the ex-
" ample." What SON, either of AMERICA or of
LIBERTY is there, that has the leaft fpark of
ingenuity, who can help being touched and
penetrated to the inmoft receffes of the heart,
by fuch magnanimous and generous expreffi-
ons in behalf of the colonies ? Who is there,
that would not almoft as willingly die, as that
THAT illuftrious Patron of America fhould
ever have occafion to be afhamed of efpoufing
its caufe, and making himfelf anfwerable for
us ? We had other advocates of diftinguifhed
eminence and worth, who generoufly came
under fimilar engagements for us. God forbid, my brethren, that any one of them fhould
ever have the leaft reafon to blufh for his ill
placed confidence in us ; as all of them will,
if we fhew any unworthy behaviour towards
the

† The Rt. Hon. Mr. PITT.

the King, the Parliament or our Mother-country, after this proof of their moderation, and regard for us. And if *They*, our friends, should have cause to blush for us in this respect, what must we do for ourselves! Where shall we find caverns far enough removed from the light of day, in which to hide our heads! Or what reason shall we have to expect friends, advocates and sponsors again, how much soever we may need them, if we have no more regard for the honor of those who appeared for us at the late alarming crisis; when it was accounted almost criminal to say any thing in our behalf?

Let me subjoin, that as the good people of this province had the honor to lead in a spirited, tho' decent and respectful application for the redress of our late grievances; methinks they should now be ambitious to have the honor of leading in a prudent, temperate, wise behaviour, in consequence of the success; and, if need be, as I hope there is not, ambitious of setting an example of moderation and discretion to other colonies. This honor would be equal to the first mentioned; and would probably recommend us greatly to those, whom it will always be our interest and duty to please; so long, at least, as we can do it without renouncing our birth-right. It will contribute to remove any impressions that may have been made of late, to our disadvantage. It will at once gratify our best friends, and falsify the slanders of our enemies, who delight in representing us as a seditious, factious and turbulent sort of people, who cannot endure the

F   wholsome

wholefome and neceffary reftraints of government. May God rebuke them for, and forgive
them this wrong !

Let none fufpect that, becaufe I thus urge the
duty of cultivating a clofe harmony with our
mother-country, and a dutiful fubmiffion to the
King and Parliament, our chief grievances being
redreffed, I mean to diffwade people from having
a juft concern for their own rights, or legal, conftitutional privileges. Hiftory, one may prefume
to fay, affords no example of any nation, country or people long free, who did not take fome
care of themfelves; and endeavour to guard and
fecure their own liberties. Power is of a grafp-
ing, encroaching nature, in all beings, except in
HIM, to whom it emphatically " belongeth";
and who is the only King that, in a religious or
moral fenfe, "can do no wrong." Power aims at
extending itfelf, and operating according to mere
will, where-ever it meets with no ballance, check,
controul or oppofition of any kind. For which
reafon it will always be neceffary, as was faid
before, for thofe who would preferve and perpetuate their liberties, to guard them with a
wakeful attention; and in all righteous, juft and
prudent ways, to oppofe the firft encroachments
on them. " Obfta principiis." After a while it
will be too late. For in the ftates and kingdoms
of this world, it happens as it does in the field
or church, according to the well-known parable,
to this purpofe; That while men *fleep, then the
enemy cometh and foweth tares*, which cannot be
rooted out again till the *end of the world*, without rooting out the *wheat* with them.   If

If I may be indulged here in saying a few words more, respecting my notions of liberty in general, such as they are, it shall be as follows.

Having been initiated, in youth, in the doctrines of civil liberty, as they were taught by such men as Plato, Demosthenes, Cicero and other renowned persons among the ancients; and such as Sidney and Milton, Locke and Hoadley, among the moderns; I liked them; they seemed rational. Having, earlier still learnt from the holy scriptures, that wise, brave and vertuous men were always friends to liberty; that God gave the Israelites a King [or absolute Monarch] in his anger, because they had not sense and virtue enough to like a free common-wealth, and to have himself for their King; that the Son of God came down from heaven, to make us " free indeed"; and that " where the Spirit of the Lord is, there is liberty"; this made me conclude, that freedom was a great blessing. Having, also, from my childhood up, by the kind providence of my God, and the tender care of a good parent now at rest with Him, been educated to the love of liberty, tho' not of licentiousness; which chaste and virtuous passion was still increased in me, as I advanced towards, and into, manhood; I would not, I cannot now, tho' past middle age, relinquish the fair object of my youthful affections, LIBERTY; whose charms, instead of decaying with time in my eyes, have daily captivated me more and more. I was, accordingly, penetrated with the most sensible grief, when, about the *first of November last,* that day of dark-

ness

neſs, a day hardly to be numbered with the other days of the year, SHE ſeemed about to take her final departure from America, and to leave that ugly Hag *Slavery*, the deformed child of Satan, in her room. I am now filled with a proportionable degree of joy in God, on occaſion of HER ſpeedy return, with new ſmiles on her face, with augmented beauty and ſplendor.——Once more then, Hail! celeſtial Maid, the daughter of God, and, excepting his Son, the firſt-born of heaven; Welcome to theſe ſhores again ; welcome to every expanding heart! Long mayeſt thou reſide among us, the delight of the wiſe, good and brave ; the proteÆreſs of innocence from wrongs and oppreſſion, the patroneſs of learning, arts, eloquence, virtue, rational loyalty, religion ! And if any miſerable people on the continent or iſles of Europe, after being weakened by luxury, debauchery, venality, inteſtine quarrels, or other vices, ſhould in the rude colliſions, or now-uncertain revolutions of kingdoms, be driven, in their extremity, to ſeek a ſafe retreat from ſlavery in ſome far-diſtant climate ; let them find, O let them find one in America under thy brooding, ſacred wings ; where *our* oppreſſed fathers once found it, and we now enjoy it, by the favor of Him, whoſe ſervice is the moſt glorious freedom ! Never, O never may He permit thee to forſake us for our unworthineſs to enjoy thy enlivening preſenee ! By His high permiſſion, attend us thro' life AND DEATH to the regions of the bleſſed, thy original abode, there

to

to enjoy forever the " glorious liberty of the
" fons of God !"——But I forget myfelf ; whither have I been hurried by this enthufiafm, or
whatever elfe you will pleafe to call it ? I hope
your candor will forgive this odd excurfion, for
which I hardly know how to account myfelf.
——There were two or three things more which
I intended to fay relative to this joyful occafion.

To go on then, thefe colonies are better than
ever apprifed of their own weight and confequence, when united in a *legal* oppofition to
any unconftitutional, hard and grievous treatment; which may be an advatntage to them.
God often bringeth good out of evil ; or what
is intended for evil by men, is by him meant for
good. So it was particularly in the memorable
cafe of Jofeph, whom his hard-hearted, envious
brethren fold as a *flave* into Egypt. There he
became great, and his Father and brethren were
at length obliged to have recourfe to him, to
keep them and their's from perifhing.—— And
thus, not improbably, may good come out of
our late troubles, as well as out of thofe oppref-
fions, which occafioned the flight of our fore-
fathers into the defarts of America. The great
fhock which was lately given to our liberties,
may end in the confirmation and enlargement
of them : As it is faid the ftately oaks of the
foreft take the deeper root, extend their arms
the farther, and exalt their venerable heads the
higher for being agitated by ftorms and tempefts,
provided they are not actually torn up, rent in
pieces, or quite blafted by the lightning of heaven.

ven. And who knows, our liberties being thus established, but that on some future occasion, when the kingdoms of the earth are moved, and roughly dashed one against another, by Him that " taketh up the *isles* as a very little thing," we, or our posterity may even have the great felicity and honor to " save much people alive," and keep Britain herself from ruin. I hope she will never put it out of our power, by destroying us ; or out of the inclination of any, by attempting it.

It is to be hoped, the colonies will never abuse or misapply any influence which they may have, when united as aforesaid ; or discover a spirit of murmuring, discontent or impatience under the government of Great Britain, so long as they are justly and kindly treated. On the other hand, it is to be hoped, they will never lose a just sense of liberty, or what they may reasonably expect from the mother-country. These things they will keep in mind, if they are wise ;, and culti-vate a firm friendship and union with each other upon equal terms, as far as distance and other circumstances will allow. And if ever there should be occasion, as I sincerely hope and pray there may not, their late experience and success will teach them how to act, in order to obtain the redress of grievances; I mean, by joint, man-ly and spirited, but yet respectful and loyal peti-tioning. Setting aside some excesses and out-rages, which all sober men join in condemning, I believe history affords few examples of a more general, generous and just sense of liberty in any country, than has appeared in America within the

the year paſt : In which time the mercantile
part in particular have done themſelves much
honor, and had a great ſhare in preſerving the
liberties of the plantations, when in the moſt
imminent danger : Tho' this is not ſaid with the
leaſt thought of reflecting on any other body or
order of men, as wanting in their endeavours to
the ſame noble end. Had we patiently received
the yoke, no one can tell when, or whether ever
it would have been taken off. And if there be
ſome animals, adapted by nature to bear heavy
burdens ſubmiſſively, one of which, however, is
ſaid, on a certain occaſion, to have had the gift of
ſpeech, and expoſtulated with his maſter for unjuſtly ſmiting him ; I hope the Americans will
never be reckoned as belonging to that ſpiritleſs,
ſlaviſh kind, tho' their " powers of ſpeech"†
ſhould not, in the opinion of ſome nameleſs,
heroic pamphleteer-ſcoffers in Britain, exceed
thoſe of the other. However defective they
may be in point of " eloqence,"† I thank God
they can at leaſt *feel*, and complain ſo as to be
tolerably *underſtood*.

If your patience will hold out, I will add a
few words further, by way of advice, and ſo
conclude. While we endeavour to cultivate
harmony and union with our mother-country
and our ſiſter-colonies, in all generous and man-
ly ways, we ſhould not, ſurely, neglect to cultivate the ſame among ourſelves.

There have, I am ſorry to ſay it, but really
there have lately been many unwarrantable jea-
louſies,

† An abuſive, ſuperficial pamphlet in favor of the meaſures of
the late miniſtry.

jouſies, and bitter mutual reproaches among
the people of this town and province, occa-
ſioned by that unhappy meaſure, which has been
ſo often referred to. Even wiſe and good men,
tho' all equally againſt that meaſure, could not,
however, agree what was to be done, upon
the maxims of prudence, tho' alike concerned
for the public welfare. Accordingly ſome were
blamed as too warm and ſanguine, others as too
phlegmatic and indifferent, in the common and
noble cauſe of liberty. Many were cenſured,
and ſome, I am well aſſured, very unjuſtly, as
being freinds to, and encouragers of, the fatal
meaſure aforeſaid. But how far theſe accuſations
were juſt or unjuſt, on either ſide, I will not take
upon me particularly to determine. Be that as
it may, is it not beſt, my Brethren, to let theſe
contentions ſubſide, now the end is obtained,
and we have ſo fair a proſpect before us? Are
there any valuable ends to be anſwered by per-
petuating theſe diſputes? I cannot readily conceive any: Perhaps it is, becauſe I have leſs penetration than moſt others. Be it as it will, I
know One, and One whom we all profeſs to
reverence, who hath ſaid, "Bleſſed are the *peace-*
"*makers*, for they ſhall be called the children
" of God." And, "Let us ſtudy the things that
" make for peace," ſaid he that was not behind the
chief of the apoſtles, " and the things wherewith
" one may edify another." Theſe ſayings may
apologize for me, if I am wrong in " preaching
peace" at this time. And if none will be offended with me for ſpeaking plainly as to this matter,

To

To me it really seems moſt prudent, moſt chriſtian, to bury in oblivion what is paſt ; to begin our civil, political life anew as it were, from
this joyful and glorious æra of reſtored and confirmed liberty ; to be at union among ourſelves ;
to abſtain from all party names and national reflections, reſpecting any of our fellow ſubjects ;
and to exert ourſelves, in our ſeveral ſtations,
to promote the common good, " by love ſer-
" ving one another." Let us make allowances
mutually for human frailty, for our different
views and conceptions of things, which may
be in a great meaſure unavoidable ; for difference
of natural conſtitution, an unequal flow of animal ſpirits, or ſtrength of nerves : Let no one
cenſure another more hardly, if at all, than the
neceſſity of the caſe plainly requires. I hope
theſe counſels of peace will not be diſreliſhed
by any " Son of peace," or any wiſe and good
man, that does me the honor to be my auditor
on this occaſion ; for I mean not to give offence, but only to do good. Such counſels as
they are, I humbly commend them to the God
of love and peace, to whoſe holy will I believe
them agreeable, for his bleſſing ; that they may
have their juſt influence on all that hear them.
And you will not forget, that we muſt all one
day give an account to Him ; ſo that it nearly
concerns us to have our ways, motives, and all
our doings approved by him. In fine,
Let us all apply ourſelves with diligence, and
in the fear of God, to the duties of our reſpec-

G   tive

tive ftations. There has been a general diffipa-
tion among us for a long time; a great negledt
and ftagnation of bufinefs. Even the poor,
and labouring part of the community, whom
I am very far from defpifing, have had fo much
to fay about government and politics, in the
late times of danger, tumult and confufion,
that many of them feemed to forget, they had
any thing to *do*. Methinks, it would now be
expedient for *them*, and perhaps for moft of
us, to do fomething more, and talk fomething
lefs; every one " ftudying to be quiet, and to
do his own bufinefs;" letting things return peaceably into their old channels, and natural courfes,
after fo long an interruption. My immediate
aim in what I now fay, being only to recommend induftry, good order and harmony,
I will not meddle with the thorny queftion,
whether, or how far, it may be juftifiable for
private men, at certain extraordinary conjunc-
tures, to take the adminiftration of government
in fome refpedts into their own hands. Self-
prefervation being a great and primary law of
nature, and to be confidered as antecedent to
all civil laws and inftitutions, which are fubordinate and fubfervient to the other; the right
of fo doing, in fome circumftances, cannot well
be denied. But certainly, there is no plaufible
pretence for fuch a condudt among us *now*.
That which may be excufeable, and perhaps
laudable, on fome very fingular emergencies,
would at other times be pragmatical, feditious,

and

and high-handed presumption. Let all therefore now join with heart and hand in supporting the lawful, constitutional government over us in its just dignity and vigor; in supporting his Majesty's Representative, the civil magistrates, and all persons in authority, in the lawful exercise of their several offices. No true friend of liberty can reasonably object against this; and if any persons should, it would shew that, while they speak great swelling words of vanity, making liberty the pretext, they themselves are the servants of corruption, the ignoble slaves of sin. Without this due regard to government and laws, we shall still be miserable, my friends, notwithstanding all that God and the King have done to make us happy. If one had wings like a dove, it were better to fly far away, and remain alone in the wilderness, where he might be at rest, than to live in a society where there is no order, no subordination; but anarchy and confusion reign. Of these we have surely had enough already; tho' at the same time I bless God, that there has not been much more, considering the great danger in which we have been with the general alarm and consternation, by reason of that which is said to make " even a wise man mad," and much more the rash and indiscrete, of whom there is a great proportion in all communities; considering also the absolute necessity there was, or at least seemed to be, of some very uncommon struggles and exertions, in order to break the *snare*, and the

natural

natural impetuosity of many people's tempers.
So important a change in the situation of public affairs, so great a deliverance, has, perhaps,
seldom been brought about in any country,
with so little criminal excess, unless it were
done by God alone, without the instrumenta-
lity or agency of men, by nature liable to so
many errors and infirmities. But whatever
there has been of this kind, ought to be, and I
hope is, lamented by all good men. May that
God, in whom our help has been, continue to
protect us, our rights and privileges ! May he
direct our paths thro' this uncertain life, and
all the changes of it ; and, of his infinite mercy in Jesus Christ, finally bring us all to those
peaceful and glorious regions, where no evil
spirits, no wicked *fowlers* will come ; where
no *snares* will be spread for us ; no *proud waters
to go over our soul !* And if we hope for admis-
sion into those eternal mansions of joy, let every one of us, as the apostle Peter exhorts, " ho-
" nor all men, love the brotherhood, fear GOD,
" honor the KING."

A M E N !